ON TEACHER NEUTRALITY

ON TEACHER NEUTRALITY

Politics, Praxis, and Performativity

EDITED BY
DANIEL P. RICHARDS

UTAH STATE UNIVERSITY PRESS
Logan

© 2020 by University Press of Colorado

Published by Utah State University Press
An imprint of University Press of Colorado
245 Century Circle, Suite 202
Louisville, Colorado 80027

 ASSOCIATION of UNIVERSITY PRESSES The University Press of Colorado is a proud member of the Association of University Presses.

The University Press of Colorado is a cooperative publishing enterprise supported, in part, by Adams State University, Colorado State University, Fort Lewis College, Metropolitan State University of Denver, Regis University, University of Colorado, University of Northern Colorado, University of Wyoming, Utah State University, and Western Colorado University.

∞ This paper meets the requirements of the ANSI/NISO Z39.48–1992 (Permanence of Paper)

ISBN: 978-1-60732-998-5 (paperback)
ISBN: 978-1-60732-999-2 (ebook)
https://doi.org/10.7330/9781607329992

Library of Congress Cataloging-in-Publication Data

Names: Richards, Daniel P., editor.
Title: On teacher neutrality : politics, praxis, and performativity / Daniel P. Richards, editor.
Description: Logan : Utah State University Press, [2020] | Includes bibliographical references and index.
Identifiers: LCCN 2020008775 (print) | LCCN 2020008776 (ebook) | ISBN 9781607329985 (paperback) | ISBN 9781607329992 (ebook)
Subjects: LCSH: College teachers—Attitudes. | Prejudices.
Classification: LCC LB1778 .O74 2020 (print) | LCC LB1778 (ebook) | DDC 378.1/2—dc23
LC record available at https://lccn.loc.gov/2020008775
LC ebook record available at https://lccn.loc.gov/2020008776

*To my teaching inspirations and mentors over the years
and the internal commotions their diverse philosophies
will forever produce within me.*

CONTENTS

SECTION III: PERFORMATIVITY

FOREWORD

Patricia Roberts-Miller

Calling for being critical of "teacher neutrality" can seem like a call to be critical of appropriate use of turn signals, saying please and thank you, or being nice to children. It can appear such an unequivocal good. And to call for thinking about it critically can also seem like a call to be *not* neutral—which would seem to be calling for teachers to be openly biased toward some students.

It's difficult to talk about teacher neutrality for all the reasons pursued in this book: we mean different things by it, it means different things in different circumstances, and apparently violating norms of neutrality has different consequences for different teachers. Hence the importance of this book. It isn't a univocal manifesto calling for one definition of teacher neutrality, nor only one stance toward it. Instead, there are a variety of scholars working with different definitions, from different perspectives, and with different stances toward the various issues.

As is appropriate for the topic of teacher neutrality, or neutrality generally.

The topic is vexed because the most common way of thinking about neutrality is simultaneously straightforward, attractive, and wrong: that "neutral" is the default position for most people on most issues, and it is the one from which we deviate when we become biased. The "neutral" position is, in the words of some theorists, the position of the "impartial observer"—the person looking on, understanding the issues, but with no particular investment in the outcome. "Neutral" means a lack of feeling about the issue, a lack of passion. Being neutral in that sense is supposed to mean that one can reason better on the issue.

Yet, as many contributors argue, that model of neutral—not caring and therefore being more reasonable—is incoherent. To be neutral on the question of genocide is to support it. To be impartial in the face of injustice is unjust. There are no bystanders in politics.

And to be completely neutral means to be uninformed. Jason Stanley (2016) describes the goals of a Chinese policy requiring that professors avoid discussing: "universal values, free press, civil society, historical mistakes of the Chinese Communist Party, crony capitalism, and

DOI: 10.7330/9781607329992.c000a

independence of the judiciary."[1] As Stanley says, the goal of not allowing those topics to be covered in courses "is a clear attempt to ensure that students lack crucial political concepts, precisely the ones possession of which would enable them to critique Chinese government policy" (203). The government wants university students to remain entirely neutral on those topics.

The Texas Education Agency specifies[2] in its "Essential Knowledge and Skills" that students should learn about the "benefits" of the "Free Enterprise System," as well as personal financial values (such as having a good personal credit score, avoiding credit card debt, living within a budget, and saving). Many universities have a mission statement that includes the inculcation of certain values in students, and universities require that faculty take action when students sexually harass others, plagiarize work, or damage university equipment. No one really wants teachers to be neutral.

But, what do we want?

This book considers that question, and the others that follow from it—what are better and worse ways of thinking about teacher neutrality? If we stop talking about teacher neutrality, what are more useful models or metaphors? Is teacher neutrality assessed by epistemological, discursive, affective, or behavioral criteria? Is it aspirational? Should we have different standards or pedagogies of neutrality for teachers who are more vulnerable (such as graduate-student instructors, adjuncts, assistant professors)? Is the "neutrality" of a teacher determined simply by whether what she says is unremarkable because it confirms the consensus? And, if so, is it a consensus of the discipline-specific experts (in which case, taking climate change as a fact is the neutral position) or local political community (in which case, the neutrality of a teacher's position on climate change would be subject to political pressure)?

We want a world in which teachers and students *care*—how do we create that world?

NOTES

1.   Jason Stanley, *How Propaganda Works* (Princeton, NJ: Princeton University Press, 2016).
2.   Texas Education Agency. "Chapter 118: Texas Essential Knowledge and Skills for Economics with Emphasis on the Free Enterprise System and Its Benefits. Subchapter C. High School," in Texas Administrative Code Part II. Available at https://tea.texas.gov/sites/default/files/Economics.pdf.

ACKNOWLEDGMENTS

Daniel P. Richards

I have had visions of just such a book for quite a while now, so the circle of people to acknowledge includes teachers, students, classmates, and colleagues across national and state lines over a decade's time. For my tightly knit classmates and mentors at the University of Windsor, where I first learned what it meant to be a teacher of writing—I am thankful. For the intellectually generative classmates, mentors, and students at the University of South Florida, where I then unlearned what it meant to be a teacher of writing—I am thankful. And for the supportive community of colleagues and students I now have at Old Dominion University, where I now continually relearn what it means to be a teacher of writing—I am thankful.

Underlying my ability to even go through these intellectual endeavors is the unwavering support of my wife, Jessica, who has patiently endured the ups and downs of my teaching experiences and unwittingly served as the initial reviewer of the ideas presented in this book.

I would also like to thank the contributors to this collection, whose collective voices are the real essence of this project. I am privileged to have the opportunity to organize and amplify such diverse philosophies and their classroom embodiments.

ON TEACHER NEUTRALITY

Introduction

THE POLITICS, PRAXIS, AND PERFORMATIVITY OF TEACHER NEUTRALITY

Daniel P. Richards

Now let us turn to the terms of repulsion.
— Richard M. Weaver, *The Ethics of Rhetoric*

THE SPECTER OF NEUTRALITY

Before beginning in earnest, let's clear the air: I agree that the phrase "teacher neutrality" is quite terrible—in so many ways.

And so does the American Association of University Professors (AAUP), as evidenced in their 2007 report "Freedom in the Classroom" (Finkin et al. 2007). The public-facing report begins with the following preamble:

> The 1940 *Statement of Principles on Academic Freedom and Tenure* affirms that "teachers are entitled to freedom in the classroom in discussing their subject." This affirmation was meant to codify understandings of academic freedom commonly accepted in 1940. In recent years these understandings have become controversial. Private groups have sought to regulate classroom instruction, advocating the adoption of statutes that would prohibit teachers from challenging deeply held student beliefs or that would require professors to maintain "diversity" or "balance" in their teaching. (54)[1]

Not much has changed since 2007. If anything, the outside efforts to regulate have increased exponentially and in more fervent and well-funded ways. As a response to these outside forces trying to regulate the "rights" held by the professoriate, the writers of the report accumulate, distill, and address four contemporary criticisms levied at the professoriate pertaining to how academic freedom is allegedly being abused in the classroom: first, instructors indoctrinate rather than educate; second, instructors unfairly present or don't present conflicting views;

DOI: 10.7330/9781607329992.c000b

third, instructors are hostile to particular social or religious views; and fourth, instructors interject irrelevant material in courses not related to the subject. On the second criticism, which has to do with exhibiting a proper amount of "balance," the writers of the report have the following words:

> To urge that instruction be "balanced" is to urge that an instructor's discretion about what to teach be restricted. But the nature of this proposed restriction, when carefully considered, is fatally ambiguous. Stated most abstractly, the charge of lack of balance evokes a seeming ideal of neutrality. The notion appears to be that an instructor should impartially engage all potentially relevant points of view. But this ideal is chimerical. No coherent principle of neutrality would require an instructor in a class on constitutional democracy to offer equal time to "competing" visions of communist totalitarianism or Nazi fascism. There is always a potentially infinite number of competing perspectives that can arguably be deemed relevant to an instructor's subject or perspective, whatever that subject or perspective might be. It follows that the very idea of balance and neutrality, stated in the abstract, is close to incoherent. (Finkin et al. 2007, 56–57)

So, perhaps I spoke too soon: the AAUP *doesn't* agree with my assessment that teacher neutrality is a "terrible" phrase. No, it's more damning than that: its ideals are "chimerical," its conceptualizations nearly "incoherent."

And yet, despite our efforts to support academic freedom, that which is apparently chimerical and incoherent continues to gain steam, gaining favor among students and lobbyists alike. How is it that within the same classroom the individual behind the lectern dismisses neutrality as an impossible feat and a student not ten feet away expects it? Perhaps neutrality as a principle or practice or concept is not so chimerical or incoherent, as the rhetorical framing by conservative media outlets seems to make its supposed lack very real and very clear and very urgent. Is it possible, despite our probable aversion to the "principle of neutrality," that we—collectively, in the humanities, as the professoriate valuing academic freedom—could do a better job at articulating our principles of non-neutrality? Might we—more narrowly, those in rhetoric and composition—make our own stances less chimerical and incoherent? Might we need to explore in more depth and with more nuance the assumptions we make about the nature and purpose of higher education and our role within it when we dismiss the increasingly pervasive and popular tropes of teacher neutrality?

It might be that teacher neutrality as a phrase or concept is terrible and chimerical and incoherent. But it also might be the case that we need a book on this very idea.

A LACK OF RHETORICAL STASIS

Historically, *neutral* as an adjective emerged as a descriptor for those who were not taking sides in an agonistic political conflict or war[2]—and in large part, this remains the case today. "Neutrality," as a state of being, has strong connotations with indifference and apathy[3] as well as a history of being a concept abused by those in power to establish dominant ideological frameworks as natural, innocent, or apolitical (Anderson 1997; Sullivan and Porter 1997). It seems that, on the surface, a term—*neutrality*—that denotes, intentionally or unwittingly, a position of passivity or disinterest or dispassion or aloofness or even naïveté ought to have no place in a profession—university teaching—that claims to overcome these very things. And yet, there the phrase is. *Here* it is, explicitly and implicitly in our spaces of learning and in the public discourse on higher education.

So, what do people really mean when they say they expect teachers or the institutions of higher education that house them to be "neutral"? Are those that use this language part of one of the dominant classes seeking to maintain order, the status quo? And if so, is it intentional? Or do they have a narrower scope of politics, one that focuses on the personal and performative inflections of partisanship—our buttons, our bumper stickers, our cynical intonations—and excludes the larger sociopolitical apparatus of higher education that maintains a certain, unique neoliberal ethic built on the ever-fading palimpsest of liberal humanism? Or even still are they recalling a mythic archetype of the Western intellectual tradition that is eternally and absent-mindedly committed to the scientific method above all else, particularly the *ad hominem* vitriol of electoral discourse? Or, finally, are they individuals who just want the skills to succeed in life and want all the agents of education around them to impart these skills without consistently bringing up every Tuesday and Thursday morning the very news stories these individuals intentionally blind themselves to? To these wordy questions, we might respond with a resounding *yes*, most likely to all of the above. To paraphrase Patricia Roberts-Miller (2004, 142) in her work on argument and conflict in the composition classroom, when it comes to conversations about politics in the writing classroom, not everyone means the same thing when they use the term *neutrality*.

And that's really the problem, isn't it? The decided lack of rhetorical stasis on this topic, this phrase, particularly between humanities professors who handily dismiss the very notion of neutrality as an epistemic impossibility and seemingly everyone else—parents, incoming students, politicians, media, and our colleagues in the sciences—who insists that it does exist, or at least ought to? While it is tempting to use this contrast as an opportunity to incorporate the work of Thomas Kuhn and Sarah Ahmed and Randall Collins and use their collective positions on the impossibility of science, self, and sociology, respectively, to be anything but the material exertion of relational power as a springboard into a rigorous epistemological discussion, what I am more interested in pursuing at this point and time is how we as teachers and scholars in rhetoric and composition can bring about and help facilitate some semblance of rhetorical stasis with the concept and usage of teacher neutrality.

For, while we may scoff and confidently throw theory texts at such a suggestion, the fact of the matter is that teacher neutrality is very much a real, felt thing that shapes the way our students, our administrators, our judges,[4] the media,[5] and politicians[6] understand higher education. Circulated widely on social media are popular articles titled, "The Teacher's Great Challenge: Staying Neutral with Students during a Contentious Election" (Strauss 2012), "When Do Teachers Stay Neutral?" (Anti-Defamation League 2017), and "Teaching Trump" (Miller 2016). Our insistent belief in the impossibility of neutrality does not preclude our colleagues in other departments or the public from believing otherwise, and doubling down might not be very helpful. To what extent has overwhelming consensus on the impossibility of neutrality in our field stifled conversations with these bodies and entities? How can stepping back and unpacking for others why we believe what we believe, and what our assumptions about higher education are in relation to these positions (and why), open up pathways for conversations with others with a stake in higher education and potentially put us in positions to serve as public intellectuals?[7] We, the contributors in this collection, argue—albeit to varying degrees—that in order to address any and all of these questions, we must first pursue a more nuanced level of understanding of what we in the field of rhetoric and composition mean ourselves when we use, prop up, or critique some variation of the phrase "teacher neutrality," and, just as important, the assumptions and implied arguments we make about the purpose and nature of institutions of higher education in the United States (Aronowitz and Giroux 1985; Berlin 1996); the role of the teacher in this mission (Bizzell 2001; Freire 1973; Shor 1992; Shor and Freire 1987); and the degree and type of agency students have in this process when we use this language (Cushman 1996, 1999). In seeking a more nuanced level of understanding in our language of "neutrality," we might be better able to understand and build dialogic connections with the various stakeholders of higher education in the United States, including, of course, our students, and particularly build bridges with what *they mean* when they use the phrase *teacher neutrality* or even the term *neutrality* generally in reference to educational bodies and their missions.

Unpacking what we in the field understand *neutrality* to mean or not mean in a teaching context is a tall task, to be sure, considering its connections and implications to much larger, evergreen conversations in our field, namely student resistance (Anderson 1997; Atwood 1994; Boyd 1999; Phelps 1991; Trimbur 2001; Welsh 2001), institutional critique (Olson and Gale 1991; Sullivan and Porter 1997), disclosure of identity (Baillif 1997; Elliot 1996; Patterson 2016), bodily and discursive performativity (Butler 2000; Kopelson 2003), social justice and civic action (Bizzell 1992; Delpit 1988; Fishman and Parkinson 1996), political theory (Jones 1996), writing assessment (Inoue 2015), epistemologies of writing (Bazerman 1988; Levy 2005), and curriculum design (Lindquist 2004; Welch 1987). We must also consider our own political diversity on an individual level as well as the vastly different contexts, institutions, regions, and student populations we find ourselves working in and with. As such we might find that the problem of rhetorical stasis extends far beyond just the term *neutrality* (although that is front and center in this collection) to include even more foundational differences in just what we mean when we utter innocuous descriptors like "political" or "skills" or charged academic nomenclature like "ideological."

THE THREE ARMS OF TEACHER NEUTRALITY

To illustrate, the field of rhetoric and composition, whether in a strain of critical pedagogy (Freire 1970; Giroux 1988), pragmatism (Seitz 2002), or somewhere in between (Durst 1999), ubiquitously acknowledges that all teaching is ideological regardless of its political bent; one cannot simply stand outside of ideology and politics, especially in facilitating educational processes. As James Berlin (1988) arranges it, "a way of teaching is never innocent. Every pedagogy is imbricated with ideology, and a set of tacit assumptions about what is real, what is good, what is possible, and how power ought to be distributed" (490). From the teacher-student power dynamic, to the "subtle creep" of course texts (Welch 1987), to the assessment metrics, to the facilitation of discussion: where there is language, power, and choice, there is rhetoric, and where there is rhetoric, ideology. And if ideology is everywhere, then neutrality is nowhere—for, the two, in these constructions, cannot mutually coexist. From these standpoints teacher neutrality as a phrase, concept, or epistemic position is impossible because it stems from "false" assumptions about how politics work—and what politics means—and how educational institutions operate as power structures.

Perhaps the most common and direct indictment on the notion of educational neutrality at the institutional level comes from the work of Paulo Freire. Richard Shaull, writing in the preface[8] of Paulo Freire's *Pedagogy of the Oppressed* (1970), states confidently—in echoing the Brazilian progenitor of critical pedagogy himself—that

> there is no such thing as a *neutral* educational process. Education either functions as an instrument which is used to facilitate the integration of the younger generation into the logic of the present system and bring about conformity to it, *or* it becomes "the practice of freedom," the means by which men and women deal critically and creatively with reality and discover how to participate in the transformation of their world. (Shaull 1970, 15)

Shaull's either-or characterization not-so-subtly belies the notion—and uses a radical educator to do so—that there simply is no such thing as a *neutral* "process of schooling" (Giroux 1981). Demanding uncritical conformity into the status quo or providing critical power tools to enact social change are similar tasks; they just serve different rulers. So, whether a pedagogy focuses on cultivating student-centered skills, facilitating critical thinking, developing habits of mind, or enacting democratic participation, underlying each and every teaching praxis is a way of understanding the world and, in Shaull's Freirean framework, either functions institutionally to maintain the status quo—most likely behind some coy guise of "neutrality"—or actively change in the system. Such sentiments, I argue, have reached truism status in the field of rhetoric and composition, very much leading to a contemptuous status of the very term *neutrality*, with many of us likely seeing the striving for neutrality in teaching as a futile endeavor at best, and oppressive at worst, as it can never be achieved. This is because neutrality, from rhetorical standpoints, particularly the ones emerging out of first-wave critical pedagogy frameworks, is coded to mean "apolitical," and not in the way of being apathetic about the outcomes of elections or maintaining a disinterest in the daily news, but in the way of having no motive or agenda. A neutral educational process is impossible because no physical body or speech act or curriculum exists outside of political ecologies and the motives and agendas that power their circulation. Claiming to have no agenda does not preclude one from unwittingly participating in education processes as mechanisms for social control—this was crux of Freire's arguments and the driving force behind his liberatory project. So, and rightfully so, healthy amounts of skepticism are directed towards those claiming their educational goals to be "apolitical." In this way, neutrality, pertaining to educational processes or institutions, has become somewhat of a "devil term,"[9] to use the phraseology of Richard M. Weaver from his book *The Ethics of Rhetoric* (1953): a term so connoted with naïveté and myth that it is inescapably, unquestionably negative, suspect, and even repulsive in both usage and application.

Now, while Shaull was concerned with highlighting the practical value and potential overlaps of Freire's work for the late-twentieth-century American educator, even for those who find themselves teaching predominantly young middle-class students, Freire was more careful, writing, mere pages later, that *Pedagogy of the Oppressed* "will probably arouse negative reactions in a number of readers . . . Accordingly, this admittedly tentative work is for radicals" (21). Freire was right about negative reactions. But, in one of the most widely read critiques of radical cultural leftism in the scholarship on the teaching of writing, much of which found kinship with Freirean thinking and first-wave critical pedagogy, we see Maxine Hairston take issue not with the notion that education is inherently non-neutral but with the *degree* to which we engage with, focus on, or disclose these ideologies to others—who were, most importantly for Hairston, our students as well as those outside our profession gauging our legitimacy and growth. Hairston's 1992 article, "Diversity, Ideology, and Teaching Writing," contains a contention that writing courses "should not be *for* anything or *about* anything other than writing itself, and how one uses it to learn and think and communicate" (79), for to do otherwise would be to undermine the growth of our field and operate outside of our subject-matter expertise. The article can be—and was—read as advocating some semblance of skills-based neutrality as a guiding conceptual model of teaching praxis and was critiqued accordingly.[10] The "new model" of composition Hairston was critiquing, mainly from what she calls the radical cultural left, "puts dogma before diversity, politics before craft, ideology before critical thinking, and the social goals of the teacher before the educational needs of the student [and] envisions required writing courses as vehicles for social reform rather than as student-centered workshops designed to build students' confidence and competence" (80). Hairston was not advocating the idea or premise of apolitical teaching, but was merely concerned with the fact that our priorities—the very ones that helped establish rhetoric and composition as a distinct discipline—were being reordered by radicals. Hairston sought to get overt political instruction out of the classroom lest the field be overtaken by radical leftists, for the sake of our own discipline, yes, but also and moreover because she thought that a liberal ethic of listening and attentiveness to the diversity of lived experience came through the acts of writing and reading and sharing themselves. Her critique was therefore not against liberalism, for as she writes, "as educators of good will, we shouldn't even have to mention our anger about racism and sexism in society—that's a given, as is our commitment to work to overcome it" (88), and she was not so naïve as to think that the writing-based writing classroom itself was not an ideological decision. So, while the article left room for critique based on the notion that even those who claim to just "teach writing skills" are still extolling the virtues embedded within writing (Duffy 2017), the critique would have been misguided since it was precisely the politics of writing instruction—writing, sharing, listening, reading, connecting, understanding, empathizing—that were sufficient enough for what we do. Hairston was not claiming that our institutions were or ought to be neutral in the face of oppression, nor was she claiming that her ideas were not ineluctability political; she was concerned with the direction things were headed in our course goals and curricular designs and wanted to ensure that attending to the inescapable political power of the mere act of writing was not set aside to cater to radical leftist ideologues, and, also, that the way we look through the eyes of others outside the discipline remains positive and in good faith.

Hairston's essay helped—albeit in an overlooked way, in my estimation—drive a wedge between the reality of non-neutrality in educational institutions and the decisions we as teachers make in how we structure our classrooms and curricula. When she writes that "those who want to bring their ideology into the classroom argue that since any classroom is necessarily political, the teacher might as well make it openly political and ideological" (88), we see an attempt to pour salt on a slippery slope with the arguments we make about our own curricula stemming from our belief in the impossibility of institutional neutrality. Circling back to our trope of rhetorical stasis, we can see a case made for a clearer separation between what people might mean when they hint at *institutional* versus *curricular* neutrality, indeed between what we think about an institution and how we choose to dwell within it.

While we as a field may have reached consensus in the inescapably political nature of higher education, not everyone has, or at least not in the same way. What we tend to see is the *inverse* or *opposite* of ourselves. The inverse is the students who come expecting teachers to be beacons of neutrality. Now, our students are not dumb—they know we have politics, they know we have preferences on who wins presidential elections. One brief glance at our social media postings or the back bumpers of our Hyundai Elantras will indicate as much. So, *neutrality* isn't really the right word in this context so much as it might be *fairness* (or *unbiased* or *impartial*) but the expectation is undergirded by some attempt on the part of the individual professor towards neutrality. Our students, many of them coming directly from a public educational setting more restricted[11] in terms of teacher disclosure, might think it inappropriate or unfair to show clear favor towards a candidate or for a policy.

But we also see the opposite: students who perceive, as we do, institutions of higher education as inescapably non-neutral, but under the premise that the institutions were constructed and continue to operate as potentially oppressive sites of liberal indoctrination and political recruitment. These students—and parents—might empathize with the more vocal conservative advocacy groups (like Turning Point USA) and online publications focused on covering campus politics (like *Campus Reform*), finding community and a means of relating to others about what it can feel like to be a conservative, fiscal or cultural, on American university campuses. The outward disclosure of a liberal professor's politics—certainly not an uncommon happenstance—is alienating and happens enough times for conservative students to begin to paint a mental landscape of the campus as a place not designed or run by those who think or act like them. This can lead to a distinct, often adversarial or personal form of student resistance, where students are not protesting the biased coverage of trickle-down economics but the bodies and choices of the professors themselves—publicly displaying our faces for spectacle.

In addition to the institutional and the curricular, then, there is a third arm of neutrality: it is us. Our bodies. Our words. Our dress. Our disclosures. Our intonations. We all generate student resistance in some way (and, if we're being honest, probably more so than other disciplines, because is there a course more resisted in and of itself than first-year writing?), but it would be unethical to state that we all experience resistance equally or for the same reasons (Condit 1996; Elliot 1996; Karamcheti 1995). This was the challenge Karen Kopelson was facing when she wrote her 2003 article, "Rhetoric on the Edge of Cunning; Or, the Performance of Neutrality (Re)Considered as a Composition Pedagogy for Student Resistance": that her mere presence, her mere appearance gets coded politically and sounds off an alarm in the minds of those surveilling political behavior. Before even facilitating a discussion or turning a page, the "critical" pedagogical objectives are rendered ineffective, even counterproductive (118). To assuage such resistance, Kopelson sought to co-opt neutrality, the very cornerstone of elitist and exclusionary practices of institutional oppression (Ng 1997), in a performative way to serve her own "cunning" purposes to play with the expectations of students:

> For the marginalized teacher . . . the performance of the very neutral-ity that students expect from their (composition) instructors, and from education more generally, can become a rhetorically savvy, politically responsive and respon*sible* pedagogical tactic that actually enhances stu-dents' engagement with difference and that minimizes their resistance to difference in the process. (Kopelson 2003, 118)

Whereas Hairston merely hinted at performing some sense of political deprioritization, Kopelson argues that those teaching along the margins, ironically, cunningly, try to perform the exact ideology that marginalizes for the "greater good" of student engagement with diversity. The perfor-mance of neutrality for Kopelson offered a productive, pragmatic dis-connect between an individual's beliefs and their outward perceptions, for, as Kopelson also affirms, neutrality "is never a stance that believes in or celebrates its own legitimacy but, rather, feigns itself, *perverts* itself, in the service of other—disturbing and disruptive—goals" (123).[12] Stated differently: neutrality is an exercise in the "rhetoric of cunning," which, drawing from Kenneth Burke, "feigns one purpose in the pursuit of an eventual and seemingly opposed goal" (131); it is, in exemplifying the Greek rhetorical concept of *mêtis*, in which one refuses to fight an oppo-nent head-on, an art of redirection; it is, finally, not an epistemic state-ment about the viability of neutrality but a performative, metaphorical framework for behavior.

THE AIMS OF THE BOOK

Alright. So, now what? Is it enough to just dismiss the phrase *teacher neu-trality* and move on? What do we *do* with these institutional, curricular, and performative frameworks of neutrality? Are they sufficient enough to help us respond to our contemporary moment? Are they dynamic enough to respond to the challenges of our current campus climates? Are they adaptive enough to bring others into conversation? Are they nuanced enough to help us reach outward to public stakeholders, to account for the vast array of difference in our daily experiences as edu-cators of all types of students at all types of institutions? How do our collective and individual beliefs about neutrality color our day-to-day work as teachers and reveal the assumptions and ideologies to which we are so beholden? And are those assumptions shared with those around us? The field's attunements to authority, power, and resistance have accomplished the task of revealing that neutrality is an epistemic impossibility and a problematic holdover from a modernist past that perhaps we never had. But does Freire's oft-cited framing on the inherent non-neutrality of educational processes and Shaull's insistence that it translates to American educational milieux help us in our current contexts and conversations? Our current political climates, where we might hear partisan conversations in our campus Starbucks about just who are the "oppressed," the "dispossessed" subjects maintained through a "culture of silence" on campus? Are we willing, as Patricia Bizzell was in *Academic Discourse and Critical Consciousness* (1992), to part ways with Freirean tenets, specifically ones that oversimplify or offer a reductive vision of our practice? I'm drawn particularly to the tickling imagery that ends one of Ann George's (2001) chapters on critical pedagogy:

> In an interview with Gary Olson, Freire notes the complicated position of the radical writing instructor who stands with one foot in the system, the present, today's reality, and the other foot outside the system, in the future, in utopia: "This is why it is so difficult . . . for us to walk: we have to walk like this. [With playful smile, Freire begins to waddle across the room.] Life is like this. This is reality and history." (109)

I am deeply enamored with the visual of Freire "waddling" across a room. I think it is because it humanizes him and colors him with eccentric charm. I think it is also, more seriously, because it adds a necessarily physical and mental vision of struggle and complexity to the lives of teachers cognizant of the double bind between having power and undermining it, or more pertinently: of disbelieving in neutrality (left foot) while performing a job where the public expects it of you (right foot). It is not the intention of this collection to critique Freire and his work—the limits of critical pedagogy have been explored at length (Seitz 2002, 2004; Thelin 2005). Nor is it the intention of this collection to explore further the realm of the left foot planted in the utopic future envisioned by critical pedagogy proponents. Rather, in repositioning or redirecting Freire's waddle slightly, this collection admonishes teachers of writing to explore further and more fully and honestly the ramifications of a ubiquitous position of non-neutrality—and the authors and texts we use to justify such a position—against a larger social scene that still believes in and expects neutrality in education.

For just as terrible though a term *neutrality* is, so too is *non-neutrality*. Until accompanied with a public-facing vision and articulation of how it connects to the public understanding of education in relation to the larger, and often misunderstood, nature of academic freedom, how useful is the statement of non-neutrality? Have we done a good enough job in connecting our theoretical beliefs to the educational situation as envisioned and experienced by the student? While we as a field might have consensus in the belief that there simply is no teaching without ideology, indeed that ideology is inherently inescapable, there is ample room for conversation about the *degrees to which* we make our commitments and political affiliations apparent and what role these various approaches play in the larger conversation of public perception of higher education and, more urgently, the changing nature and forms of student resistance in our current sociopolitical moment. The problematic neutral versus non-neutral paradigm fails because it does not account for the situational inflections that vary across spaces and populations and might not be refined enough to help facilitate meaningful conversations with those who would genuinely like to have them.

In light of this exigence, this collection aims to provide scholars, teachers, and students in the field of rhetoric and composition with the first edited collection that focuses exclusively on the problematic, contentious, and (always) timely concept of "teacher neutrality." The volume maintains specific emphasis on the practical (im)possibilities of neutrality in the teaching of writing and rhetoric, the deployment of "neutrality" as a political motif in the public discourse shaping policy in higher education, and the performativity of individual instructors in a variety of different institutional contexts. In doing so, this collection provides readers with:

- More *clarity* on the contours around defining *neutrality*.
- More *depth* in understanding how neutrality operates differently in various institutional settings (e.g., two-year-college [TYC] writing instruction versus R1 schools' teacher-training, and graduate-student versus tenure-track positionality).
- More *nuance* in the levels and degrees of neutrality in teaching (i.e., the implications of abiding by neoliberal assessment practices versus the implications of supporting a specific candidate with a button on a lapel).

Rather than act as a polemic for teacher neutrality, or an admonishment against it, this collection consists of sixteen chapters and an interview that make wide-ranging arguments about *neutrality* as a concept or praxis that hinders or helps aspects of the teaching of writing and rhetoric. Given Irvin Peckham's assertion that college composition is "fundamentally a middle-class enterprise" (2010), the strength of the collection resides in the much-needed diversity of ranks (tenure-track, GTAs, lecturers), institutional contexts (R1, TYC, religious), and subject positions (class, race, gender, age) covered in the text. Neutrality, or its inverse, is inextricably connected to privilege, so to have those in tenured positions at R1 schools have sole possession of a conversation that permeates, often in threatening ways, all of our lives would be inappropriate.

The collection insists that while the field of rhetoric and composition by and large rejects the very concept of teaching writing and rhetoric "neutrally"—indeed, Berlin's (1988) insistence that rhetoric *itself* is ideological is widely heeded—there is still more work that needs to be done, specifically as it pertains to more public work. This work includes thinking more about the implications of non-neutrality in our contemporary postsecondary educational and political moment, better communicating our non-neutral pedagogical theories to public stakeholders, better understanding our students' expectations of our neutral positionality, and better understanding of contexts in which neutrality—performed or not—is desired and effective. Ultimately, our field's theoretical allegiance to non-neutrality is being (and I argue, *should* be) tested in real, practical ways. To quote Ann George (2001) again, we might have strong theoretical pedagogical beliefs and allegiances but when class starts, "things get real" (94). This collection explores just such "real" situations as they pertain to neutrality in the institutional, curricular, and lived aspects of our work—framed, in turn, as the *politics, praxis,* and *performativity* of neutrality.

THE CONTENTS OF THE COLLECTION

The organizational strategy of division into three sections is not meant to be reductive. As you'll read, each chapter considers to varying extents the political, the practical, and the performative, and the unique ways in which they inevitably interweave and overlap through lived experience. The decision to place each chapter into one of the three sections was based largely on what I saw as the primary driver of the arguments presented, and the decision to even have three sections in the first place reflects my argument posited above that we need more-refined distinctions about what it is we are talking about when we advocate for or disregard neutrality.

The first section of the collection—*Politics*—by sheer institutional representation alone (graduate students, TYC, religious schools, and contingent faculty) constructs an argument that theories and approaches to transparency, disclosure, and neutrality have been dominated by tenure-track or tenured teacher-scholars at four-year institutions—a more than slight irony when thinking about the contexts out of which Paulo Freire was writing. All chapters in this section direct our attention to institutional differences, governance structures, and labor conditions as invariably determining both what we mean and what we can do about neutrality. Meaghan Brewer (chapter 1) begins this section by providing a research-based exploration of the implications of enacting a pedagogy of neutrality for new graduate instructors tasked with teaching a politically charged composition curriculum that they did not design. Jason Evans continues the section in chapter 2 with an exploration of the recent "translingual turn" in composition and how enacting this ideology at the TYC level places instructors at the "nexus of contradictions." Building off this spirit of contradictions, Jessica Clements in chapter 3 then provides insight by way of a unique application of Kopelson's framing of *métis* in a Christian higher-education setting, suggesting that it might be, rather paradoxically, the best way to get students in these contexts to achieve the academically rigorous critical consciousness these very institutions seek. Building off of Clements's direct attention to governance structures, Robert Samuels (chapter 4) brings our attention to how the current political climate affects vulnerable—read: non-tenured, "contingent"—teachers, arguing that although we should pay attention to how *all* faculty are being threatened, non-tenured faculty are in an especially exposed position because they often lack any type of academic freedom or shared governance rights and thus require a fundamentally different disposition towards the impossible, but in this case, necessary ideals of neutrality. My own interview with John Trimbur ends this section, in chapter 5. The interview covers a lot of ground—from disciplinarity to why he no longer attends CCCC to his relationship to Maxine Hairston to surveillance to why it might not be the best idea to wear a "Fuck Trump" shirt on campus—and as such, in the words of Trimbur near the end of the interview, resembles the "complexity that emerges when you start to talk about neutrality, and to both see what it screens and hides and what it authorizes."

The second section of the collection—*Praxis*—directs the reader's attention away from institutional and governance structures and towards the actual courses, curricula, and projects we develop and deliver. This section begins with Kelly Blewett (chapter 6), taking a cue from Arlie Russell Hochschild's book *Strangers in Their Own Land*. She shares how a participant-researcher relationship provided an opportunity for a conservative, Republican-identified, returning-veteran student (Tyler S.) at a Midwestern university campus to talk openly with Blewett, a liberal, Democrat-identified, doctoral candidate in rhetoric and composition. Christopher Michael Brown then keeps us in this space of the student experience in chapter 7 by offering a reframing of how written narratives get taught. In a close reading of three "conversion" narratives, Brown shows how students submit their deeply held beliefs to careful scrutiny, uncovering and articulating the assumptions that made their "conversions" possible, ultimately suggesting that conversion narratives avoid the pitfalls of assignments that require a critical orientation toward one's beliefs. Continuing with Blewett's and Brown's themes of openness and honesty, Lauren F. Lichty and Karen Rosenberg begin their chapter 8 with *clear* questions: How can a praxis of transparency work in the writing classroom and how can it help students share power in productive ways? How can we work with ideologically charged material without being derailed by unproductive student resistance? Lichty and Rosenberg explore these questions through their experience co-teaching a first-year, themed composition course titled "Gender Under Construction," and argue that enacting a "slow start" method to teaching complex topics helps with student engagement. Heather Fester, also sharing a course design, uses chapter 9 to create space for critical readings of teacher and student narratives around ideological transparency collected during a course on activist writing and research. Fester uses the tool of "interruptive teacher narratives," created by Chris Gallagher, Peter Gray, and Shari Stenberg, to render her own ideological assumptions as an interpreter of cultural practices in the class more transparent and to explore student perceptions of ideological bias as they shape the classroom experience. Chapter 10, by Mara Holt, takes us from projects and course designs to the administrative level, asking: When do teachers have the right to surface their ideology, their social justice concerns? When is it effective, and when and how is it appropriate to integrate it into the first-year curriculum? Holt explores the apparent contradictions in her own stances over the years, arguing that abstract beliefs about the virtue or vice of neutrality or transparency are less useful than an emerging understanding of pertinent material and historical conditions.

Continuing to move up the administrative ladder, chapter 11, written by Tristan Abbott, focuses on assessment and operates from the observation that there exists a split between how writing assessment is understood within administrative and political circles and how it is understood among specialists in rhetoric and composition. In reviewing a number of assessment tools produced within the last decade, Abbott explains how they can help compositionists realize the political goals of the field while still producing institutionally viable, *neutral-seeming* assessment. The final chapter of this section on *praxis* is more in line with the genre of a program profile and takes us all the way up to a global perspective—literally.

In it, we see Adam Pacton (chapter 12) exploring a teaching space undertheorized in terms of teacher neutrality: Massive Open Online Courses (MOOCs). Pacton argues that dislocating college composition from a purely American phenomenon provides a moment of disciplinary *kairos* that troubles performances of ideological neutrality in the composition classroom and that globalizing college composition through the unique MOOC modality reveals a paradox wherein compositionists must neutralize ideological commitments (given the extremely heterogeneous global student population) but are disciplinarily unable to do so.

The third and final section—*Performativity*—builds off institutional and curricular discussions of neutrality to theorize a site often implicated in just such discussions: our selves. As Romeo García and Yndalecio Isaac Hinojosa write in chapter 13 to begin this section, the body can be seen as "the preeminent material upon which inscription of culture and its particular discourses become embedded," influencing "the ways we think and live our social relations" (Shapiro 77). García and Hinojosa offer their lived experiences and academic journies as testament to how our pedagogical and theoretical commitments are grounded in experiences and memories. In light of this call for authenticity, Erika Johnson and Tawny LeBouef Tullia (chapter 14) continue this section by arguing that, rather than falling back into performances of neutrality, composition instructors should take heed of the benefits of authentic engagement for students from a diversity of backgrounds. Johnson and LeBouef Tullia define *authenticity* to be less a rhetorical representation of "truth" or "honesty" than it is a practice of critical and crucial engagement and use the work of Susan Jarratt to position the negotiation of conflict to become the dialogue that explores contradictions present in our classrooms. This may cause tensions; but Jarratt (2003) notes that those who avoid conflict minimize unforeseen possibilities for using argument to reconstruct knowledge. David Stubblefield and Chad Chisholm (chapter 15) connect these notions of authenticity and conflict to power by asking the following questions: How do we address the diverse needs of the discourse communities within our classes, within our various institutional settings, all while guiding them towards a common discourse? In other words, how do we both enact a democratic classroom while simultaneously transmitting authoritative norms? In addressing these questions, Stubblefield and Chisholm broach the pedagogical double-bind, as articulated by Gerald Graff (1995), where teachers need to acknowledge the power they wield while trying to challenge it.

Jennifer Thomas and Allison Rowland (chapter 16) end part three because their work provides the clearest call to action for us moving forward. Their chapter explores how higher education in the United States has witnessed a cluster of activity around the term *transparency*, but also how different stakeholders use the term towards different ends. On one hand, transparency can refer to explicit conversation about beneficial learning practices between instructors and students. This type of transparency, which Thomas and Rowland identify as "learner-centered transparency," assists students in understanding, for example, the learning goals of a particular assignment. By comparison, they identify "consumer-centered transparency" as the appropriation of the rhetoric of transparency in an attempt to foster distrust in institutions of higher education. Consumer-centered transparency can be particularly sly, because it often comes packaged in pro-student rhetoric, such as Turning Point USA's *Professor Watchlist*. To mitigate defensiveness, Thomas and Rowland advance what they call a "translucent pedagogical practice." In other words, Thomas and Rowland argue for the occasional and strategic withholding of learning goals for some classroom activities, especially in courses that critically approach gender, race, sexuality, socioeconomic status, and ability. They close their critical analysis of the transparency imperative with a case study from their team-taught first-year course on sexuality. In doing so, the chapter provides both conceptual and practical resources for navigating the emerging imperative of transparency in higher education in the United States.

Ultimately, and as these chapters reveal, addressing the specter of neutrality requires much more than what is currently being done. It requires considering and incorporating research from other fields. It requires a more holistic perspective on disciplinarity. It requires more critical attention to public discussions of academic freedom. It requires more nuanced understandings of neutrality and all its rhetorical usages—whether it is framed as the paramount value of higher education, a political dog whistle, a naïve assertion, or anything else. It requires classroom research on the observable effects of our decision to engage in self-disclosure. It requires rhetorical-centric longitudinal research on how and why students experience intellectual and emotional change in college. It requires more articulation on our parts about our own assumptions of the purpose of higher education and what our presumed authority is within it.

The collection ends with a conclusion (chapter 17), titled "Full Disclosure / Now What?," which outlines—in full, honest consideration of all the chapters prior to it and a poignant experience I had teaching presidential rhetorics in the fall 2016 semester—a call for us as scholars, as teachers, as public agents of change, as mouthpieces, as representatives of a network of institutions of higher education currently embattled with partisanship to bring some semblance of stasis on teacher neutrality and bring our students along for the ride. For the phrase is terrible, but, alas, there it is. Here it is.

NOTES

1.   The AAUP notes that Missouri House Bill No. 213 (introduced January 3, 2007) "would have done both."

2.   The *Oxford English Dictionary* traces *neutral* as both a noun and an adjective back to the fifteenth century, primarily in warlike contexts. As a noun, the primary definition is "a person or state remaining neutral in a controversy, dispute, war, etc.," with relevant textual examples coming largely from agonistic contexts: e.g., 1601 Ld. Mountjoy *Let.* in F. Moryson *Itinerary* (1617) ii. 173, "The whole Province either is joyned with them, or stand neutrals." In its adjectival usage, *neutral* as a descriptor pertaining to people (as opposed to chemicals) is related to "senses of partiality, determinacy, etc.," namely "not taking sides in a controversy, dispute, disagreement, etc.; not inclining toward any party, view, etc.; impartial, unbiased," with relevant textual examples coming from political contexts: e.g., (1)1876 J. B. Mozley *Serm. preached Univ. of Oxf.* x. 237, "They discard a middle and neutral relation as lukewarm"; and (2) 1987 D. Rowe *Beyond Fear* viii. 317 "Dorothy has . . . no axe to grind. She's completely neutral."

3.   According to its primary definition in the OED, *neutrality* as a noun emphasizes the *ontological* and the *emotional*: "an intermediate state or condition, not clearly one thing or another; a neutral position, middle ground." A secondary definition is given as "the state or condition of not being on any side; absence of decided views, feeling, or expression; indifference; impartiality, dispassionateness."

4.   For a useful overview of the pertinent Supreme Court decisions and state policies relating to advocacy and free speech in the elementary, middle, and high school classrooms, see Underwood (2013).

5.   See *This American Life* podcast, episode 614 ("My Effing First Amendment"), for a journalistic account of conservative student advocacy on state university campuses.

6.   State legislatures such as those in Wisconsin are voting on policy related to free expression in and by state university systems. For example, Assembly Bill 299 requires that "institutions must remain neutral on public policy controversies" (Wisconsin State Legislature 2017), with the intended effect of penalizing those who protest the presence of controversial guest speakers on campus (most recently, Ann Coulter and Milo Yiannopoulos).

7.   See John Duffy's guest spot on NPR's *All Things Considered* from 2016, titled "Professors Take A Different Approach In Responding To 'Leftist Propaganda' Claims" (NPR 2016), about how he and others dealt with the surging popularity of Turning Point USA's *Professor Watchlist* professor-tracking website (npr.org/2016/12 /10/505109280/professors-take-a-different-approach-in-responding-to-leftist -propaganda-claims).

8.   I chose this edition with the foreword by Shaull because of the rhetorical work he does framing the first English translation for an American audience in terms of application:

> If, however, we take a closer look, we may discover that [Freire's] methodology as well as his educational philosophy are as important for us as for

the dispossessed in Latin America. Their struggle to become free Subjects and to participate in the transformation of their society is similar, in many ways, to the struggle not only of blacks and Mexican-Americans but also of middle-class young people in [America]. And the sharpness and intensity of that struggle in the developing world may well provide us with new insight, new models, and a new hope as we face our own situation. For this reason, I consider the publication of *Pedagogy of the Oppressed* in an English edition to be something of an event. (Shaull 1970, 10)

9. *God terms* are those powerful words that seem to be beyond critique and immediately infuse a phrase with unquestionably positive meaning, stemming from the "inherent potency" of the term itself. Inversely, *devil terms* are what you would expect after learning what god terms are. For Weaver (1953) and his historical moment in the 1950s, *progress* and *freedom* were god terms; *Communist* and *un-American* were devil terms. Weaver's argument was that rhetoricians ought to apply an ethical rhetoric to such vague and potentially propagandist terms and "hold a dialectic"—yes, in the Platonic sense of it—with oneself to gain deeper understanding of the intention behind the usage of the term. It is a fair reading to conceive of this very book as doing this sort of dialectical work on the term *neutrality*. Of further note, it could also be considered that *neutrality* is a god term in that it could be used by ideologues to forward whatever they think it means to suit their purposes. I'm thinking of how Turning Point USA and their *Professor Watchlist* might hold up teacher neutrality as an abstracted ideal against which to judge and publicly blacklist those who, wittingly or unwittingly, don't follow suit.

10. See *College Composition and Communication* 43, no. 2 (1992): 179–193, and subsequent responses in the following issue, namely John Trimbur's (1993) response. Trimbur, included in this collection by way of interview, reflects on his experience writing the piece and his relationship with Hairston later in this collection.

11. Consider that in 2008 the New York City School District enacted a policy (based on *Weingarten v. Board of Education* [680 F.Supp. 2d 595 (S.D.N.Y. 2010) at 597]) on the visual aspect of partisanship: "While on duty or in contact with students, all school personnel shall maintain a posture of complete neutrality with respect to all candidates. Accordingly, while on duty or in contact with students, school personnel may not wear buttons, pins, articles of clothing, or any other items advocating a candidate, candidates, slate of candidates, or political organization/committee" (https://casetext.com/case/weingarten-v-bd-of-educ-of-city-school-dist). The New York City School Chancellor rationalized the policy by stating that when "teachers wear political paraphernalia in schools, they may improperly influence children and impinge on the rights of students to learn in an environment free of partisan political influence" (quoted in Underwood 2013, 30). The phrasing in these excerpts—of teachers being "on duty" and maintaining a "posture of complete neutrality"—seem to hint at an ideology, much like the French vision of higher education, that teachers are first and foremost public servants and, like other types of public servants, must posture, or perform, neutrality in school settings.

12. See Kopelson (2020) for her reconsideration of her approach to cunning and neutrality.

REFERENCES
Anderson, Virginia. 1997. "Confrontational Teaching and Rhetorical Practice." *College Composition and Communication* 48 (2): 197–214.

Anti-Defamation League (ADL). 2017. "When Do Teachers Stay Neutral?" *ADL.org*, www .adl.org/education/resources/tools-and-strategies/classroom-conversations/when-do -teachers-stay-neutral. Accessed 20 May 2017.

Aronowitz, Stanley, and Henry Giroux. 1985. *Education under Siege: The Conservative, Liberal, and Radical Debate over Schooling*. South Hadley, MA: Bergin and Garvey.

Atwood, Johanna. 1994. "Good Intentions, Dangerous Territory: Student Resistance in Feminist Writing Classes." *Journal of Teaching Writing* 12: 125–143.

Baillif, Michelle. 1997. "Seducing Composition: A Challenge to Identity-Disclosing Peda- gogies." *Rhetoric Review* 16 (1): 76–91.

Bazerman, Charles. 1988. *Shaping Written Knowledge: The Genre and Activity of the Experimental Article in Science*. Madison: University of Wisconsin Press.

Berlin, James. 1988. "Rhetoric and Ideology in the Writing Class." *College English* 50 (5): 477–494.

Berlin, James. 1996. *Rhetorics, Poetics, and Cultures: Refiguring College English Studies*. West Lafayette, IN: Parlor Press.

Bizzell, Patricia. 1992. *Academic Discourse and Critical Consciousness*. Pittsburgh, PA: Univer- sity of Pittsburgh Press.

Bizzell, Patricia. 2001. "Power, Authority, and Critical Pedagogy." *Journal of Basic Writing* 10 (2): 54–70.

Boyd, Richard. 1999. "Reading Student Resistance: The Case of the Missing Other." *JAC* 19 (4): 589–605.

Butler, Judith. 2000. "Changing the Subject: Judith Butler's Politics of Radical Resignifica- tion." Interview with Gary Olson and Lynn Worsham. *JAC* 20 (4): 727–765.

Condit, Celeste M. 1996. "Theory, Practice, and the Battered (Woman) Teacher." In *Teaching What You're Not: Identity Politics in Higher Education*, ed. Katherine J. Mayberry, 155–174. New York: New York University Press.

Cushman, Ellen. 1996. "The Rhetorician as an Agent of Social Change." *College Composition and Communication 47 (1): 7–28.*

Cushman, Ellen. 1999. "The Public Intellectual, Service Learning, and Activist Research." *College English 61 (3): 328–336.*

Delpit, Lisa. 1988. "The Silenced Dialogue: Power and Pedagogy in Educating Other People's Children." *Harvard Educational Review* 58 (3): 280–298.

Duffy, John. 2017. "The Good Writer: Virtue Ethics and the Teaching of Writing." *College English* 79 (3): 229–250.

Durst, Russel K. 1999. *Collision Course: Conflict, Negotiation, and Learning in College Composi- tion*. Urbana, IL: NCTE.

Elliot, Mary. 1996. "Coming Out in the Classroom: A Return to the Hard Place." *College English* 58 (6): 693–708.

Finkin, Matthew W., Robert C. Post, Cary Nelson, Ernst Benjamin, and Eric Combest. 2007. "Report: Freedom in the Classroom." *Academe* (September–October): 54–61.

Fishman, Stephen M., and Lucille Parkinson McCarthy. 1996. "Teaching for Student Change: A Deweyan Alternative to Radical Pedagogy." *College Composition and Commu- nication* 47 (3): 342–366.

Freire, Paulo. 1970. *Pedagogy of the Oppressed*. New York: Seabury Press.

Freire, Paulo. 1973. *Education for Critical Consciousness*. New York: Seabury Press.

George, Ann. 2001. "Critical Pedagogy: Dreaming of Democracy." In *A Guide to Composition Pedagogies*, ed. Gary Tate, Amy Rupper, and Kurt Schick, 92–112. New York: Oxford University Press.

Giroux, Henry A. 1981. *Ideology, Culture, and the Process of Schooling*. Philadelphia, PA: Temple University Press.

Giroux, Henry A. 1988. "Postmodernism and the Discourse of Educational Criticism." *Journal of Education* 170 (3): 5–30.

Graff, Gerald. 1995. "The Dilemma of Oppositional Pedagogy: A Response." In *Left Margins: Cultural Studies and Composition Pedagogy*, ed. Karen Fitts and Alan W. France, 325–329. Albany: State University of New York Press.

Hairston, Maxine. 1992. "Diversity, Ideology, and Teaching Writing." *College Composition and Communication* 43 (2): 79–93.

Inoue, Asao B. 2015. *Antiracist Writing Assessment Ecologies: Teaching and Assessing Writing for a Socially Just Future*. Fort Collins, CO: WAC Clearinghouse and Parlor Press.

Jarratt, Susan C. 2003. "Feminism and Composition: The Case for Conflict." In *Feminism and Composition: A Critical Sourcebook*, ed. Gesa E. Kirsch, Faye Spencer Maor, Lance Massey, Lee Nickoson-Massey, and Mary P. Sherdan-Rabideau, 263–280. Boston, MA: Bedford/St. Martin's.

Jones, Donald. 1996. "Beyond the Postmodern Impasse of Agency: The Resounding Relevance of John Dewey's Tacit Tradition." *JAC* 16 (1): 81–102.

Karamcheti, Indira. 1995. "Caliban in the Classroom." In *Pedagogy: The Question of Impersonation*, ed. Jane Gallop, 138–146. Bloomington: Indiana University Press.

Kopelson, Karen. 2003. "Rhetoric on the Edge of Cunning; or, The Performance of Neutrality (Re)Considered as a Composition Pedagogy for Student Resistance." *College Composition and Communication* 55 (1): 115–146.

Kopelson, Karen. 2020. "Rhetoric on the Edge of Cunning Revisited: Of Truth and Lies in an Extra Urgent Sense." *Pedagogy* 20 (1): 13–20.

Levy, Matthew A. 2005. "Cynicism, Social Epistemic, and the Institutional Context of College Composition." *JAC* 25 (2): 347–370.

Lindquist, Julie. 2004. "Class Affects, Classroom Affectations: Working through the Paradoxes of Strategic Empathy." *College English* 67 (2): 187–209.

Miller, Sam. May 2, 2016. "Teaching Trump." *Jacobin*. Retrieved from www.jacobinmag.org /2016/05/donald-trump-school-teachers-students-children/.

Ng, Roxana. 1997. "A Woman Out of Control: Deconstructing Sexism and Racism in the University." In *Racial In(ter)ventions: Identity, Politics, and Difference/s in Educational Praxis*, ed. Suzanne De Castell and Mary Bryson, 39–57. New York: State University of New York Press.

NPR (National Public Radio). 2016. "Professors Take a Different Approach in Responding to Leftist Propaganda Claims." *All Things Considered*. 10 December 2016. Accessed 26 April 2018. https://www.npr.org/2016/12/10/505109280/professors-take-a-different -approach-in-responding-to-leftist-propaganda-claims.

Olson, Gary A., and Irene Gale, eds. 1991. *(Inter)views: Cross-disciplinary Perspectives on Rhetoric and Literacy*. Carbondale: Southern Illinois University Press.

Patterson, G. 2016. "The Unbearable Weight of Neutrality: Religion and LGBTQ issues in the English Studies Classroom." In *Sexual Rhetorics: Methods, Identities, Publics*, ed. Jonathan Alexander and Jacqueline Rhodes, 134–146. New York and London: Routledge.

Peckham, Irvin. 2010. *Going North Thinking West: The Intersections of Social Class, Critical Thinking, and Politicized Writing Instruction*. Logan, UT: Utah State University Press.

Phelps, Louise Wetherbee. 1991. *Composition as a Human Science: Contributions to the Self-Understanding of a Discipline*. New York: Oxford University Press.

Roberts-Miller, Patricia. 2004. *Deliberate Conflict: Argument, Political Theory, and Composition Classes*. Carbondale, IL: Southern Illinois University Press.

Seitz, David. 2002. "Hard Lessons Learned since the First Generation of Critical Pedagogy." *College English* 64 (4): 503–512.

Seitz, David. 2004. *Who Can Afford Critical Consciousness? Practicing a Pedagogy of Humility*. New York: Hampton Press.

Shapiro, Sherry B. 1999. *Pedagogy and The Politics of the Body: A Critical Praxis*. New York: Garland Publishing, Inc.

Shaull, Richard. 1970. "Preface." In *Pedagogy of the Oppressed*, Paulo Freire. New York: The Seabury Press.

Shor, Ira. 1992. *Empowering Education: Critical Teaching for Social Change.* Chicago, IL: University of Chicago Press.

Shor, Ira, and Paulo Freire. 1987. *A Pedagogy for Liberation: Dialogues on Transformative Education.* Westport, CT: Greenwood, Bergin-Garvey.

Strauss, Larry. 2012. "The Teacher's Great Challenge: Staying Neutral with Students during a Contentious Election." *Huffington Post* November 12, 2012. Retrieved from www .huffingtonpost.com/larry-strauss/teaching-election_b_1877104.html.

Sullivan, Patricia, and James E. Porter. 1997. *Opening Spaces: Writing Technologies and Critical Research Practices.* Greenwich, CT: Ablex.

Thelin, William H. 2005. "Understanding Problems in Critical Classrooms." *College Composition and Communication* 57 (1): 114–141.

Trimbur, John. 1993. "Counterstatement: Responses to Maxine Hairston, 'Diversity, Ideology, and Teaching Writing.'" *College Composition and Communication* 44 (2): 248–256.

Trimbur, John. 2001. "Student Resistance as a Tragic Trope." In *Insurrections: Approaches to Resistance in Composition Studies,* ed. Andrea Greenbaum. Albany, NY: SUNY Press.

Underwood, Julie. 2013. "Do You Have the Right to Be an Advocate?" *The Phi Delta Kappan* 95 (1): 26–31.

Weaver, Richard. (1953) 1985. *The Ethics of Rhetoric.* Davis, CA: Hermagoras Press.

Welch, Kathleen. 1987. "Ideology and Freshman Textbook Production: The Place of Theory in Writing Pedagogy." *College Composition and Communication* 38 (3): 269–282.

Welsh, Susan. 2001. "Resistance Theory and Illegitimate Reproduction." *College Composition and Communication* 52 (4): 553–73.

Wisconsin State Legislature. 2017. "Assembly Bill 299." Retrieved from www.docs.legis. wisconsin.gov/2017/proposals/ab299.

SECTION I

Politics

1

THE LIMITS OF NEUTRALITY
How New Graduate Instructors Negotiate Politics, Race, and Ideology in the Composition Classroom

Meaghan Brewer

In his often-cited "Rhetoric and Ideology in the Writing Class," James Berlin (1988) contends that there is no such thing as a politics- (or ideology-) free classroom. As framed in the introduction to this collection, scholars working in rhetoric and composition have long argued, albeit from various standpoints, that because language and literacy are political and ideological, such ideology inevitably enters the writing classroom. Critical pedagogy maintains that because schooling is "an instrument of domination," even educators who profess to leave politics out of the classroom are political in that they are reproducing dominant ideology and maintaining acceptance of inequality, a stance recently affirmed by the National Council of Teachers of English (George 2014, 78; NCTE 2017).

However, public conceptions of teaching and classrooms undoubtedly portray a much different picture. The idea of the teacher as politically neutral appears to be a cultural commonplace, documented in work by scholars like Linda Brodkey (1996). Stanley Fish (2008), who often speaks against the politicization of the classroom in public forums, charges that "the present state of composition studies is the clearest example of the surrender of academic imperatives to the imperatives of politics," admonishing academics to "do their jobs" instead of taking up politics in the classroom (49). Conservatives also repeatedly argue for instructors' political neutrality by invoking the image of leftist, radical instructors indoctrinating their students.[1]

This chapter draws on data collected from a two-semester study of new graduate instructors at a large public university to discuss how they negotiated the political and identity-based nature of the pedagogy presented in their teaching-methods course (hereafter "the Practicum"), including a required syllabus for the composition classes they were

DOI: 10.7330/9781607329992.c001

teaching that assigned a number of readings with underlying socialist premises. The graduate instructors expressed concerns about teaching this material during the week of their teaching orientation, a three-day introduction to composition pedagogy the week before the semester started. They wondered how to teach readings by Mohandas Gandhi for the first unit on nonviolent protest, while, in the words of one graduate instructor, "avoiding his political agenda" (Brewer field notes, 25 Aug.). Some graduate instructors, in other words, seemed to have assimilated the cultural idea of the teacher as politically neutral.

To be clear, many of the graduate instructors understood and acknowledged that classrooms were necessarily political spaces and that they would have to acknowledge political and sociocultural realities in their teaching. Some even bemoaned undergraduates' lack of political and cultural awareness. However, they thought they (as teachers) should not impose their own views on students or do too much of what one graduate instructor called "ideological leading," even when the views being expressed by students were problematic (Brewer field notes, 22 Oct.).

The graduate instructors had good reason to be wary of teaching visibly political content. Russel K. Durst (1999) describes the "collision" that occurs when students, expecting straightforward, practical instruction in writing skills, encounter instructors educated in critical literacy whose goals are to complicate, rather than simplify, their conceptions of writing (59). This chapter chronicles a collision that happens even before the one Durst describes, in which *graduate instructors'* concerns about teaching the political as marginalized teacher-subjects come into conflict with curricula they did not create and which require them to teach content aimed at making undergraduates more "reflective [and] politically aware" (6). As Durst contends, the hesitation graduate instructors might feel in teaching political content is justified, as many undergraduates in the United States are conservative and "resistant to questioning established views" (130–131). Graduate instructors, consequently, might feel that it is both uncomfortable and dangerous to engage in political critique, even as they recognize the value of challenging students' assumptions.[2]

I begin this chapter by exploring the marginalized, liminal positions of graduate instructors. I then discuss the graduate instructors' attitudes toward teaching "politically." The data I collected included interviews, field notes from the Practicum, two drafts of a literacy autobiography, and observations of the classes they were teaching.

I identify two strategies graduate instructors used to perform neutrality in the classroom: (1) teaching the text and (2) positioning themselves to their students as "open" to any readings of the texts, as long as their students could justify them. Both strategies were potentially problematic in that they forwarded views of pedagogy and literacy that would violate compositionists' view that language is ideological and political. Moreover, performing neutrality can also have psychic costs and may challenge graduate instructors' sense of selves. Nevertheless, I also point to ways graduate instructors might be taught to use these strategies with more awareness of them *as strategies*, adopting a kind of wily, sophistic approach to teaching. In other words, I argue that neutrality in the classroom is only ever a performance and that the training of new graduate instructors should incorporate assignments and readings that help them recognize the embodied, performative nature of teaching. This chapter thus builds on Karen Kopelson's (2003) argument for performing neutrality as a useful strategy for marginalized teacher-subjects by focusing on the experiences of graduate instructors, using their voices and experiences to develop a deeper, more nuanced approach to neutrality as a strategy that is *both* problematic and potentially useful.

GRADUATE INSTRUCTORS AS ACADEMIC "OTHER"

Kopelson (2003) calls attention to how a teacher's identity in the classroom can be marginalizing, particularly when students identify teachers as having "some sort of axe to grind" (129). While many of the graduate instructors in the present study did not have the same sort óf irrepressible markers of difference Kopelson describes, as Ann George (2014) argues, "difference and oppression come in many forms, not all of which are visible" (88). Indeed, graduate instructors' marginalization has long been recognized in the literature on graduate teacher training (Rankin 1992; Taylor and Holberg 1999; Durst 1999).

One of the main fears described by graduate instructors is "the rejection of their very authority to teach" (Kopelson 2003, 119). Jessica Restaino (2012) points to graduate instructors' desire simply to be perceived as "legitimate" instructors of composition (24). The graduate instructors' feelings of marginalization in the present study were exacerbated by age and gender. Lily and Max (who were 26 and 23, respectively) mentioned their age as something that affected their teaching. However, whereas Max presented his age in positive terms, a common ground he shared with his students, for Lily, it was a challenge to be managed, suggesting that maleness seemed to compensate, at least partially, for graduate students' marginalized status.

The interaction between gender and authority was evident during a discussion of how gender affected graduate instructors' classroom ethos.

Blake, a first-year student in the literature PhD program, proclaimed that even though he was "only 140 pounds" his students seemed naturally to "defer" to him (19 Nov.). However, he realized that the women in his group had to think more consciously about how they were able to claim this authority. "Anthony [another male graduate student] and I both have difficulty not dominating the classroom," Blake continued. "There's something going on there that I have to resist" (Blake interview, 19 Nov.). Karen, a first-year PhD student in composition concurred, saying, "Yeah, in our group, Daniel [one of the graduate student mentors] said that he never had to think about the fact that he had authority in the classroom. I had to think a lot about it" (Karen interview, 19 Nov.) Karen's observation was surprising in that she was older than the other graduate instructors (at 41) and brought with her ten years of experience teaching high school. Even age and experience couldn't counter having to wrestle with how students might perceive her as a woman and graduate student.

In recognition of graduate instructors' marginalized status, Restaino (2012) theorizes a "middle space" for graduate students, which she sees as existing in the borderlands between public and private. Given their student and novice-teacher status, this middle space acts as "a supportive atmosphere" in which graduate instructors can "experiment safely" and "figure things out" (16, 95). Invoking Hannah Arendt, Restaino warns against models of training that force graduate students "into political actors before they are ready" (56). Yet she also acknowledges that Arendt's warning is a reference to children, asking, "Just how protected should graduate students be, as they are, after all, 'grown ups,' though certainly students nonetheless?" (57). Though the idea that writing program administrations need to "protect" graduate instructors is certainly apt, these graduate instructors would have to "appear before others," and this appearance, in the act of teaching, appears to be increasingly public and political (57).

In contrast to Restaino's concept of a protective middle space, other scholars have called for graduate-instructor training to be disruptive. This scholarship points out that graduate instructors often have tacit, abstracted senses of their teaching selves, their relationships to their students, and the reading and writing conventions they are expected to teach (Dryer 2012; Micciche, Rule, and Stratman 2012). However, the multimodal projects described by Laura Micciche, Hannah J. Rule, and Liv Stratman (2012) point to the possibility of the graduate practicum as both protective and, as Dylan B. Dryer (2012) argues, disruptive, so that graduate instructors can experiment and question preexisting views without feeling that they need to stake out a political or pedagogical identity before they're ready.

Following Micchiche, Rule, and Stratman (2012), I suggest a performative approach to teaching that can both protect graduate instructors by showing them ways of performing neutrality and create the productive dissonance that is necessary for them to learn as teachers. For new graduate instructors, viewing neutrality *as* performance can also reveal how ideologically determined other aspects of their teacher identities are, enabling a greater awareness of their preexisting views as they develop as teachers.

THE GRADUATE PRACTICUM AT PUBLIC UNIVERSITY

The Practicum was a semester-long course designed to introduce graduate instructors to composition pedagogy and support them during their first semester of teaching. The week before the start of the semester, graduate instructors took a three-day crash course in composition pedagogy, where they received a required, standard syllabus with a detailed schedule of readings and assignments.

Although the curriculum for the composition courses the graduate instructors were teaching had readings based in Marxist philosophy and tackled issues like race and immigration, the Practicum did not explicitly focus on critical pedagogy or forward an overtly political or activist agenda. However, the question of how to address politics in the classroom came up frequently. David, the Practicum instructor, encouraged students to talk about politics and identity in their classes, reminding them that "You can't make it [politics] go away" (Brewer field notes, 10 Sept.). He also created opportunities for the graduate instructors to be co-constructers of the Practicum; for example, he invited one of the graduate instructors who identified as queer and non-binary to give a presentation on language and transgender identities. Thus, although the Practicum did not forward an explicitly critical pedagogy, it provided a fertile ground for discussing issues related to identity, social justice, and composition's role in language gatekeeping.

"YOU HAVE TO KEEP IT TEXT BASED"

In order to mitigate the dangers of talking about issues related to identity, social justice, and politics, the graduate instructors used strategies to help them appear neutral on these topics. However, many of them appeared to use these strategies without awareness of them *as* strategies.

The graduate instructors' teaching strategies were also influenced by interactions with past professors and other literacy sponsors, as well as cultural prototypes for the "ideal professor." The quotation that heads this section comes from a Practicum meeting early in the semester, in response to two graduate instructors (both women) who were wondering how to talk about politics and religion in the classroom. Some of the graduate instructors saw the text as a potentially neutralizing medium. If you can keep it "text based," to use the words of the male graduate instructor who responded, you can talk about almost anything (Brewer field notes, 10 Sept.).

These attitudes reflect New Critical assumptions about texts and language, namely that we can study texts apart from their historical and sociopolitical contexts. Although New Criticism is no longer considered a valid set of critical assumptions, because of its influence on pedagogy, graduate instructors, particularly those with literature backgrounds, may unknowingly believe in many of its assumptions. In Brodkey's (1996) terms, the "scenes of writing" they had been exposed to could have signaled to them that texts are arenas where they can safely "manage" conflict, difference, and politics (66). For the graduate instructors, grounding discussion in close readings of texts protects them from revealing their own subjectivity.

Consider, for example, Blake's description during our first interview of a paper he had written as an undergraduate. He states: "This is basically New Criticism, and undergrads mostly write New Criticism from what I can tell. So it is . . . a more contained body of evidence. . . . I wonder if that's a difference between disciplines where, in English, if we can restrict ourselves to the body of evidence of one text, we can let students be a little more free" (Blake interview, 1 Nov.). Here, I read an interesting back and forth between "restriction" and "freedom." Blake believes, paradoxically, that restricting students to the "evidence of one text" can actually give them more freedom. That is, he sees the text as a safe space; it is "contained" from the messiness that other, presumably more political, subjects might accrue.

Blake continued to position the text as a neutralizing medium. In the following statement, he conveys his frustration with students using their papers to forward political views: "I'm just having trouble getting them to couch their opinions in terms of the close reading. . . . I might just need to change the prompts more dramatically, so that . . . they can't miss the requirement that they *use* the text, rather than that they discuss a text and then forward a particular political agenda" (Blake interview, 22 Nov.). While Blake's statement reflects a concern many compositionists would share, that his students need instruction in how to use evidence to support their positions, I also see an opposition between using textual evidence and "forward[ing] a . . . political agenda" that I would break down. For example, couldn't students use texts *in order to* forward their politics? Why are texts and politics opposed? To put it simply, Blake appears to accept the New Critical position that the relationship between texts and social and political reality needs to be made indirect in order for students to gain the critical distance to produce the coolly rational, disinterested writing that instructors would like to see.

Although I initially considered Blake's views problematic, a more rhetorical reading of his stance might provide an opportunity for him to recognize texts as political while also using commonplaces about texts as distanced from politics to his advantage. Blake wasn't the only graduate instructor to describe texts as a safe space, something to hold on to during an uncertain first semester of teaching. To return to Restaino's (2012) concept of middle space, I wonder if this might present an opportunity to engage in these understandings of texts while also problematizing them. For example, Blake could encourage his students to establish connections between their readings and current political events but then challenge them to produce evidence for their views when a discussion becomes too contentious, reflecting that, as Samuels (chapter 4, this volume) contends, while students are "entitled to their own opinions . . . they are not entitled to their own facts" (73).

Max, an MFA student in creative writing, is an example of someone who was beginning to grasp the performative nature of teaching. As with some of the instructors described by Kopelson (2003), who performed neutrality with an eye to transforming students' views by not being too outward with their own political views, Max often resorted to "cunning" (Kopelson 2003, 130). For example, during one Practicum meeting, he described a strategy he had found himself using in the classroom, saying, "one thing I do is pose questions that are leading, where I know the answer, but pretend I don't" (Brewer, field notes, 19 Nov.). Max uses a technique similar to one described by Susan Talburt, in which a teacher "performs herself as a tabula rasa," presenting seemingly "open-ended" questions that really lead toward her desired conclusions (quoted in Kopelson 2003, 129). Talburt's participant performs neutrality so that students believe any conclusions they come to are theirs and not the participant's, who identifies as a lesbian. While Max was not similarly marked, identifying as White, male, and straight, he had identified a way to neutralize his marginalized status as a graduate student.

"OPEN TO ANY READINGS": REJECTING THE MOTHER-TEACHER

Although the graduate instructors voiced concerns about revealing their ideological commitments in the classroom throughout the semester, one Practicum class in particular foregrounded these issues. The reading assigned was Susan Jarratt's (2003) "Feminism and Composition: The Case for Conflict," in which Jarratt challenges composition instructors whose desire to validate and create a supportive environment for students leads them to minimize conflict. For Jarratt, this nonconflictual stance "leaves those who adopt it insufficiently prepared to negotiate the oppressive discourses of racism, sexism, and classism surfacing in the composition classroom" (264). She thus argues that neutrality or "openness" in itself can be marginalizing because it leaves instructors and students alike open to oppressive discourse without equipping them to correct it.

Jarratt's article had immediate usefulness in that it presented an opportunity for the graduate instructors to work through the problematic dichotomy of either teaching politically or viewing themselves as "vessels" whose role it was to channel a variety of messages in the classroom (266). However, many of the graduate instructors challenged Jarratt's argument. During a small-group activity, two male graduate students dominated the conversation, accusing Jarratt of "essentialism," setting up other feminists as "straw men," and "poisoning the well" (Brewer field notes, 19 Nov.). Because of this initial resistance to Jarratt's ideas, many graduate instructors left the classroom unsure about how to manage students whose speech crossed the line.

The initial conversation about Jarratt's article occurred in groups of four. The group I observed consisted of two men, Anthony and Blake, and two women, Karen and Grace. Anthony talked first, and he launched into a diatribe, telling the rest of the group that even though Jarratt's article engages with the work of bell hooks, she would have "take[n] this woman [Jarratt] to the cleaners" for her "essentialism" (19 Nov.). Both he and Blake stated that as men they felt silenced by Jarratt's views.

Ironically, for two men who were feeling silenced, they did most of the talking in the group. Grace barely spoke, but when she did, she expressed appreciation for Jarratt's explanation of the special challenges women might face in the classroom. Towards the beginning of the exchange, Karen also appeared to agree with Jarratt, telling Anthony and Blake, "I actually kind of liked it" and bringing up situations when she, as a woman, felt that she was caught in a double bind between non-argument and appearing either "bitchy" or "emotional" (19 Nov.). However, as the conversation continued, Karen began to assent more and more to Anthony and Blake's views, stating eventually that Jarratt's argument, "does seem a bit contrived, like it's making something out of nothing" (19 Nov.). I was, again, struck by the irony of what was happening; Karen and Grace were being silenced, the very thing Jarratt warns will happen when classrooms position women as having to be "open" to others' views.

I had scheduled time to talk to Karen after class that day, giving me the opportunity to ask her what she thought was happening during that small-group discussion. However, Karen initially did not support my view that she was being silenced. When I asked her about the article, she responded, "To be honest . . . I found certain things that were interesting to me . . . but I felt that she was a bit too extreme" (19 Nov.). As we continued to talk, Karen revealed that she found Jarratt's (2003) references to having to "swallow" others' views as a kind of "rape" particularly off-putting (268). However, much of her resistance also resulted from her misunderstanding of the text. Karen thought, wrongly, that Jarratt was contending that because argument is "violent" it is "unsuitable for women," when in fact, these were views Jarratt was ventriloquizing but arguing against (Brewer field notes, 19 Nov.) As Karen and I revisited the article, it became clear that she actually agreed, at least partly, with Jarratt.

Another potential reason for Karen's disagreement with Jarratt's argument was that she did not initially find the image of the nurturing mother-teacher, which Jarratt addresses in her article, to be problematic. Indeed, elsewhere in her interview and literacy narratives, she invoked the idea of the mother-teacher (whom she contrasted with the male, authoritarian teacher), to describe the teacher identity she wanted to inhabit. Karen often sounded like an expressivist, a view of literacy that has been critiqued for its lack of political engagement and that Jarratt explicitly criticizes in her article.

Karen then described a conflict she had had with a White male student in her composition class. In his earlier papers, the student had difficulty formulating arguments, and Karen had pushed him to take a position. In his last paper, which he had just turned in, Karen was shocked to find that he appeared to be "justifying slavery" (19 Nov.). Karen hadn't read the entire paper and thus couldn't provide specifics, but the paper, which analyzed Octavia Butler's *Kindred*, appeared to channel a kind of Magnolia Myth view, which Karen found reprehensible and which, as someone married to an African American man, she took personally. Karen stated, "I won't say you can write anything you want. You can't say slavery is great" (19 Nov.) Here, Karen draws the proverbial line in the sand. Although she had said earlier that "I do not think it is effective to say, that's wrong and you can't do that," she acknowledged that in some situations, it was more important to correct students than to validate them (19 Nov.).

I was still surprised, however, at how accommodating Karen described herself as being to the student who was presenting racist and historically inaccurate views of slavery. Karen stated,

> I think I'll get him and say, I think you want to be original here, and your impulse to do that is wonderful . . . but the thing that you have to be careful of is, who is your audience here, and are you going to offend them? And if so, are you going to achieve what you want to achieve? . . . so that he's considering other things beyond himself. The audience's reception. . . . The kind of ethos he wants to present as an author. (19 Nov.)

As I listened to Karen's plan to confront this student, it seemed evident that she needed to present his statements as more than just "offensive" to "some" audiences. His argument, if he is indeed justifying slavery, is both objectively offensive and false.

I am reminded here of an interview conducted by *BBC Newsnight*'s Emily Maitlis of the Nigerian novelist, Chimamanda Ngozi Adichie, and the editor-in-chief of the conservative *American Spectator*, R. Emmett Tyrrell, shortly after Donald Trump's election as president. During the interview, Adichie responds to Tyrrell's assertion that Trump is not racist, saying, "You don't get to sit there and say that he hasn't been racist when objectively he has." Adichie is troubled by the creation of what she calls an alternate reality, which she, and others, have called attention to as in need of immediate correction. As educators, it would seem that such correction is part of our jobs, even if we are not outwardly positioning ourselves as educating for social justice.

On the other hand, Adichie and Karen are occupying two very different roles with regards to this correction. While Adichie is a woman of color and Karen is not, Adichie also has more resources at her disposal for correcting Tyrrell's assertion than Karen has in correcting her student. Viewing their roles rhetorically, Adichie has more ethos and greater available means for persuasion than Karen. While Adichie is expected to provide a strong counterposition and act as a corrective to Tyrrell's White misogyny, Karen is expected, culturally, to enact a more neutral role. Karen's experience also demonstrates how different institutional settings demand different degrees of neutrality: as a former high school teacher, Karen was accustomed to presenting herself as even more neutral than she did as a graduate instructor at an R1 university.

Karen is, of course, in an impossible position here, and it is one that calls attention to the problems inherent to a system that places graduate instructors in classrooms in their first semester, with only a three-day orientation under their belts. And while part of me wants to push graduate instructors like Karen to confront their students in less-couched terms, to do so is to force someone in a marginalized position to enact a role she is not yet comfortable with and does not yet have the expertise to occupy. Certainly, Karen's student needs correction, and Karen does plan to confront him. She even goes a step further, stating, "I think that that's your job as a teacher, to help mold them. Because they're not thinking about those things" (Brewer field notes, 19 Nov.). Especially given how instructors' overt attempts to "correct" students' views can backfire, maybe Karen's more tactful approach could, in this situation, be more effective.

Karen's situation also reveals that teacher neutrality really doesn't exist; instead, as Kopelson (2003) argues, there are only *performances* of neutrality. In her own performance, Karen is caught in another double bind. On the one hand, her impulse is to nurture her student, as her ten years of experience as a high school teacher tell her to do. On the other, she knows she has to call out racism and that not doing so is yet another affront to herself, both personally and as a teacher who believes she should be "molding" her students. This double bind might be even more difficult if Karen were a woman of color. As Carmen Kynard (2015) argues, "many of us do not have the luxury of overlooking such violence because we are its targets" (3). Moreover, the results of a recent Reuters/Ipsos poll call into question whether people can ever be neutral when it comes to issues like racism and White supremacy. According to the poll, individuals who reported being neutral about assertions like the idea that White Americans are "under attack" (a central tenet of White supremacy) were more likely to lean "toward intolerance than away from it" (quoted in Branigin 2017). The knowledge that she is *performing* neutrality is not totally absent from Karen's statements; she talks about her plans to "approach" this student strategically. However, I am unsure, if I were to ask her directly, whether Karen would consider what she is doing a performance.

Jarratt (2003) addresses the performances we call on teachers and students in marginalized positions to make, stating that while she is "confident that many teachers . . . intuitively negotiate such situations with sensitivity . . . we can't always control the ways discursive power works in our classes" (268). Jarratt contends that because we "can't force female students to speak out against men, or students of color to speak out against whites," instructors need to be willing to correct racism, misogyny, ableism, homophobia, elitism, and so on. Yet, with new graduate instructors, we also need to consider their positioning as students and not "force" them to speak out either. Restaino (2012) states that "there is a kind of betrayal . . . in asking students to stake out a public, political identity before they are ready" and, further, that pushing them to do so "'can have the ill-effect of . . . freezing the development of someone 'who is in the process of becoming but not yet complete'" (57). Restaino's words call attention to the tenuous position of being a graduate instructor and to the responsibility of mentors and WPAs to help them develop strategies for confronting discourses of oppression, while still allowing them to fall back on the support of the institution when such confrontations endanger them.

CONCLUSION: MULTIMODAL PROJECTS AS
A WAY TO CRITIQUE NEUTRALITY

The experiences of the graduate instructors described here demonstrate that neutrality can be at times vexing, useful, impossible, and even meaningless. Karen's experiences, in particular, reveal the psychic costs of a new graduate instructor positioning herself as "open" to her students' interpretations. However, neutrality also functioned, for Karen and Blake, as a first step to protect against complex forces too heavy for early-career writing instructors. To conclude, I draw on the work of Micciche, Rule, and Stratman (2012) to discuss how WPAs can both leverage and problematize neutrality as a concept, creating scenarios that allow graduate instructors to critique neutrality as a viable position while also exploiting it as a way to come to more performative understandings of their teaching roles and identities. Jarratt (2003) explicitly calls on teacher training to do more in terms of preparing new instructors to deal with the kinds of scenarios that Karen is confronting with her student (269). And because this training involves shifting graduate instructors' ideology away from concepts like "authenticity" and "neutrality" and toward more performative, contingent versions of their role in the classroom, it will undoubtedly take longer than a three-day orientation or even a semester-long course. However, as Micciche, Rule, and Stratman (2012) argue, WPAs can *begin* this work in graduate instructors' first years by engaging them in multimodal projects.

The self we present in the classroom is never a completely "authentic" self; teaching is rhetorical work, and we perform the identities that work best for us to accomplish the goals we set forth. While the concept of teaching rhetorically is not new to compositionists, it most likely will be for new graduate instructors, many of whom tacitly subscribe to cultural commonplaces elevating authenticity or being "true to yourself." However, graduate training programs and practica can create productive dissonance between students' senses of self and the selves they perform in the classroom.

Micciche, Rule, and Stratman (2012) argue that multimodal teacher research projects can create awareness in graduate instructors of themselves as "performing subjects." Beginning with the premise of teaching as inherently embodied, relational, and performative, they describe projects that enable graduate instructors to move past naturalized states of being that have "congeal[e]d over time" (Butler, quoted in Micciche, Rule, and Stratman 2012). For example, Rule describes video recording herself leading students in discussion and realizing that she spoke more than she thought she had, an observation that conflicted with her sense of her teaching self as more of a "guide on the side." Such projects made the graduate instructors more conscious of the differences between their abstracted senses of their teacherly selves and what was actually happening in the classroom.

Similar multimodal projects might make other new graduate instructors more comfortable with the idea of performing neutrality when it comes to political and contentious subjects. For example, graduate instructors could record videos of themselves teaching class sessions in which the subject matter might be particularly contentious or controversial. They may find that their memory of how they handled and responded to students' positions is much different from how it is depicted in the video. Seeing their actual performances in these videos, and contrasting them with their imagined sense of themselves both within the classroom and outside of it, can prompt new graduate instructors to recognize the strategic ways in which they can play with their identities in the classroom.

Graduate instructors can also view each other's performances and use them similarly to how I did in this chapter: to create a kind of typology of different approaches to neutrality. As Samuels's chapter in this collection also addresses, within this current political climate especially, creating supportive structures for graduate students and other marginalized faculty is particularly important. As important is training them to operate as teacher-rhetors, recognizing the classroom as a rhetorical space for accomplishing the work of education.

NOTES

1. One recent tactic these accusations have taken is to characterize liberal professors as both suppressing the views of their conservative students and creating (or abetting) overly sensitive students with trigger warnings and policies against microaggressions. See, for example, Vice President Mike Pence's (2017) Notre Dame commencement address.

2. This reality is shared by adjuncts and other contingent instructors as well (see Samuels, chapter 4 in this collection).

REFERENCES

Berlin, James. 1988. "Rhetoric and Ideology in the Writing Class." *College English*, 50 (5): 477–494. doi:10.2307/377477.

Blake. Interview. 1 Nov. 2010.

Blake. Interview. 22 Nov. 2010.

Branigin, Anne. 2017. "New Poll Finds Majority Oppose White Supremacists—Even While Sharing White Supremacist Views." *The Root*. http://www.theroot.com/new-poll-finds -majority-oppose-white-supremacists-even-1809072111.

Brewer, Meaghan. Field notes. 25 Aug. 2010.

Brewer, Meaghan. Field notes. 10 Sept. 2010.

Brewer, Meaghan. Field notes. 22 Oct. 2010.

Brewer, Meaghan. Field notes. 19 Nov. 2010.

Brodkey, Linda. 1996. *Writing Permitted in Designated Areas Only*. Minneapolis, MN: University of Minnesota Press.

Dryer, Dylan B. 2012. "At a Mirror, Darkly: The Imagined Undergraduate Writers of Ten Novice Composition Instructors." *College Composition and Communication*, 63 (3): 420–452.

Durst, Russel K. 1999. *Collision Course: Conflict, Negotiation, and Learning in College Composition*. Urbana, IL: National Council of Teachers of English Press.

Fish, Stanley. 2008. *Save the World on Your Own Time*. Oxford: Oxford University Press.

George, Ann. 2014. "Critical Pedagogies: Dreaming of Democracy." *A Guide to Composition Pedagogies*, 2nd ed., ed. Gary Tate, Amy Rupiper Taggart, Kurt Schick, and H. Brooke Hessler, 77–93. Oxford: Oxford University Press.

Jarratt, Susan C. 2003 [1991]. "Feminism and Composition: The Case for Conflict." *Feminism and Composition: A Critical Sourcebook*, ed. Gesa E. Kirsch, Faye Spencer Maor, Lance Massey, Lee Nickoson-Massey, and Mary P. Sheridan, 263–280. Boston, MA: Bedford/ St. Martin's.

Karen. Interview. 19 Nov. 2010.

Kopelson, Karen. 2003. "Rhetoric on the Edge of Cunning; Or, the Performance of Neutrality (Re)Considered as a Composition Pedagogy for Student Resistance." *College Composition and Communication*, 55 (1): 115–146. doi:10.2307/3594203.

Kynard, Carmen. 2015. "Teaching While Black: Witnessing and Countering Disciplinary Whiteness, Racial Violence, and University Race-Management." *Literacy in Composition Studies*, 3 (1): 1–20. http://licsjournal.org/OJS/index.php/LiCS/article/view/62/84.

Micciche, Laura, Hannah J. Rule, and Liz Stratman. 2012. "Multimodality, Performance, and Teacher Training." *Computers and Composition Online*. http://www2.bgsu.edu/depart ments/english/cconline/cconline_Sp_2012/Multimodality_Rev-2011-12/tdm.html.

NCTE Standing Committee Against Racism and Bias in the Teaching of English. 2017. "There Is No Apolitical Classroom: Resources for Teaching in These Times." http:// blogs.ncte.org/index.php/2017/08/there-is-no-apolitical-classroom-resources-for -teaching-in-these-times/.

Pence, Mike. 2017. "The Future is Yours." Address at the University of Notre Dame, May 21. http://time.com/4787520/mike-pence-university-of-notre-dame-commencement -graduation-2017/.

Rankin, Elizabeth. 1992. "In the Spirit of Wyoming: Using Local Action Research to Create a Context for Change." *WPA: Writing Program Administration*, 16 (1–2): 62–70. http://wpacouncil.org/archives/16n1-2/16n1-2rankin.pdf.

Restaino, Jessica. 2012. *First Semester: Graduate Students, Teaching Writing, and the Challenge of Middle Ground*. Carbondale, IL: Southern Illinois University Press.

Taylor, Marcy, and Jennifer L. Holberg. 1999. "'Tales of Neglect and Sadism': Disciplinarity and the Figuring of the Graduate Student in Composition." *College Composition and Communication* 50 (4): 607–25. doi:10.2307/358483.

2

LIVING IN CONTRADICTION
Translingual Writing Pedagogies and the Two-Year College

Jason C. Evans

What are we doing, really? For English teachers at community colleges, the answers are as contradictory as they ever have been. We are preparing students for definite post-college careers; we are preparing students for a dynamic, learn-as-you-go series of careers; we are advancing the liberal arts; we are transmitting the dominant culture; we are resisting the dominant culture; we are reinforcing America's social class and racial divisions; we are breaking down America's social class and racial divisions. The experienced two-year-college (TYC) teacher knows that all of these may be true at the same time, that there is no neutral ground from which we might observe our work, but rather many grounds; and we know that a teacher can occupy more than one political position even in the same class with the same students.

Such is the case with English teachers in the two-year college (TYC), but perhaps also with any teacher who works in a capitalist economy in a democratic society in an institution with roots in medieval European culture. Contradictions abound! But English teachers at two-year-colleges are especially under scrutiny here—first, because I am one, and second, because we work with the, numerically speaking, largest population of college students in the United States but in institutions that occupy a low rung on the ladder of prestige. As English teachers, we are in a funky position vis-à-vis social class and race and language. Charged with introducing students, many of whom are "first generation" college students, into "academic discourse," and with maintaining standards of communication and rigor of thinking at the institution, we are both the student retention problem and the solution, the gateway and the barrier.

This isn't a lament. Rather, I think it is helpful to situate the TYC English teacher in a nexus of contradictions in order to explore how some of composition's dominant attitudes about language position us in relation to our students.

DOI: 10.7330/9781607329992.c002

LANGUAGE GAMES

Language has long been a special focus in composition studies. Decades ago, many in our field began to reckon with the ways that language is integral to privilege, and to explore policies and practices that could make our classrooms more inclusive: Students' Right to Their Own Language, code-switching, and code-meshing, for example. Recently, composition scholars have re-theorized the relationships between students' home and school languages by adapting a concept from adjacent fields: translingualism. This reimagining grew out of the work of Suresh A. Canagarajah and came to our field's attention more broadly in a 2011 issue of *College English* by Bruce Horner, Min-Zhan Lu, Jacqueline Jones Royster, and John Trimbur (Horner et al. 2011). Translingual writing pedagogies offer promising insights to TYC English teachers, but these teachers can in return offer insights for others considering translingual writing pedagogies.

The translingual approach, as Horner et al. describe it, "sees difference in language not as a barrier to overcome or a problem to manage, but as a resource for producing meaning in writing, speaking, reading and listening" (2011, 303). They contrast this translingual view of language difference with "traditional" or monolingual approaches to language difference, which allegedly "take as the norm a linguistically homogeneous situation: one where writers, speakers, and readers are expected to use Standard English or Edited American English—imagined ideally as uniform—to the exclusion of other languages and language variations" (303). In their account, writing teachers who take this traditional, monolingualist approach are trying to homogenize students' language by reducing "interference" from supposed non-Standard language varieties. And they argue that a translingual approach offers new linguistic resources by legitimating previously forbidden linguistic habits and by encouraging instructors to read with greater patience and generosity. To demonstrate that their translingual approach had solid support within the field, Horner et al. list at the end of their 2011 piece fifty scholars who endorse the project they outline, and in a selected bibliography they name another hundred or more books and articles. Since then there have been at least a half dozen or more books, many journal articles, and a proliferation of sessions at the Conference on College Composition and Communication all focused on exploring the translingual turn. Indeed, in recent edited collections about translingual writing pedagogies, such as *Crossing Divides* (Horner and Tetreault 2017), chapters may begin with a reference to the growing number of articles and conference sessions devoted to translingualism or translanguaging. Clearly, translingualism has arrived.

But as I read and listen to this discussion, I sometimes feel a tingle of alienation: perhaps much of this work on translingual pedagogies is not for me. It's not that I disagree about the substance; I agree with these accounts of how language works and the call to respect "differences" in students' language. As an admiring reader of Pierre Bourdieu, I am convinced that schools and universities use language difference to reproduce unequal class relations and to regulate who gets in and who does well there (Bourdieu and Passeron 1977). And as an admiring reader of Geneva Smitherman, I am convinced that our culture's and our institutions' attitudes towards many "non-Standard" Englishes is a form of racism, pure and simple, and that, for instance, "to deny the legitimacy of Africanized English is to deny the legitimacy of black culture and the black experience" (Smitherman 1977, 175). In other words, I don't see myself as some staunch monolingualist, bent on reproducing reified "proper" English.

I think my feeling of alienation comes from my experiences trying to live out some of these underlying principles about language in my own classrooms. For more than fifteen years, I've taught composition and basic writing at a predominantly Black community college. For many of those years, I've talked with first-year composition (FYC) students about monolingualism and code-meshing, about translanguaging, about their right to their own language. Together, we've read Smitherman, Vershawn Young, Scott Lyons, David Kirkland, James Baldwin, Lisa Delpit, and various linguists and educators writing about language diversity and especially African American English (AAE). At times I tried, like Mara Holt (chapter 10 in this collection), to leave it up to these authors "to teach the students how to engage in difficult conversations about race and difference." But ultimately I found that it is more helpful if I eventually state my own views about race and language directly, to make clear that I agree with, say, Smitherman. Even so, I almost always remain alone in my agreement.

In our discussions, inevitably a student raises a question about whether writers in my class can "write like that" in their papers. That is, can they intentionally incorporate elements of AAE into a college paper? When I ask "Why not?" students almost always react with some blend of interest and politely decline—"This openness is all well and good, Jason, but please still teach us to write, well, 'professionally.'" On the occasions when I have tried to convince Black students that AAE should be welcome in school and professional settings, and is worth celebrating, almost every one of them has effectively said, "Yes, I agree, AAE should be welcome but, No, thanks, I'll stick with code-switching, one language for school and work and another for home." Not all of my Black students use AAE nor are all of my students who use AAE Black. But in every class and from almost every student I encounter resistance to the idea that monolingualism is suspect. Rather, they say, "Teach us to write in the dominant discourse." Was I doing it wrong, or was this advice about translingual approaches to language difference meant for other people's students?

For it seemed to me as if, based especially on the early moments of the translingual turn, I should keep trying to convince my students not to be such linguistic retrogrades. According to my read of the early discussion, it's not enough that teachers should be more enlightened, but that writing classes themselves should conduct a kind of linguistic subversion of the dominant ideologies—if code-switching is segregation, as Young argues (2009), I should fight it, right? But this version of the politics of linguistic progressivism starts with an inequality: When I try to enlighten my students about the value of their own language, I am the person who knows the Truth, and the students are unenlightened; I am the person who explains things, the students are to understand; I am the keen-eyed intellectual vanguard, my students are blind, hopeless proles. Even if I approach my students with respect and dignity, I'm still explicating something to them, and so we're not in a relationship of equality. As Jacques Rancière puts it: "To explain something to someone is first of all to show him that he cannot understand it by himself" (1991, 6). I like the aims of the translingual approach, in which I imagine myself fighting racism by spreading linguistic ideologies that are more just, but in carrying out my translingual mission I am put in the awkward position of convincing my students of what they should really want. My position is also fraught because of my own identities: a straight, White, middle-aged, middle-class man. I hear echoes of the invisible man's response to the "progressive" leftist leaders in Ralph Ellison's great novel: "Who are you, anyway, the great white father?" (1995, 473). Who am I, anyway? And what am I doing, really?

Horner and others have more recently addressed the practices and aims of translingual writing pedagogies in ways that point to some problems in my thinking. In his view, translingualism isn't about pushing students to do translanguaging or to accept translingual attitudes about writing, but rather it is an orientation that helps students to see how they already translanguage and to increase their sophistication about the choices they make. In his chapter in the collection *Crossing*

Divides, Horner (2017) illustrates one pedagogical alternative to presenting students with a choice: a translation assignment that encourages students to experience the ambiguities of language without explicitly "present[ing] students with something called a *translingual approach* for them to consider, select, resist, or oppose" (94). After all, "the ideology of monolingualism . . . does not announce itself as a language ideology for students to choose (or not) but, rather, inheres in conventional composition pedagogical practices in the United States (and elsewhere)" (95). So rather than call out monolingualism and rail against it, Horner suggests that teachers and their students patiently examine language practices—doing so reveals the limitations of a monolingual orientation to English. In any case there's no "choice" to be made about translingualism or translanguaging. As Horner has clarified, it's simply how language works, and translingualism aligns writing pedagogies with linguists' understanding of the fluidity of languages. When my students resist my efforts to welcome diverse Englishes in academic writing, it may be monolingualism speaking through them, but it is also, Horner points out, monolingualism speaking through me when I try to "convince" them.

But what do my students hear spoken through me? In my openness to students' writing in Black English in FYC (I never require this nor assume that all students will be fluent in AAE), they may feel that their White teacher is implying that they should "stay in their place," that the language of the academy, the Language of Wider Communication (Smitherman 2006, 142), is not theirs and their use of it will forever be marked. And they may, on some level, challenge what they see as a false essentialism that connects their racial identity to a specific kind of language performance. Royster (1996) outlines some questions about language and authenticity in her foundational *College Composition and Communication* article, "When the First Voice You Hear Is Not Your Own." She cites occasions in which others assume that because Royster is African American, her "natural" voice must not be the "academic language" that she often uses when speaking at university functions. But Royster rejects this way of defining her identity: "I claim all my voices as my own very much authentic voices, even when it's difficult for others to imagine a person like me having the capacity to do that" (37). Likewise, Scott Lyons addresses the apparent dilemma of identity and language when he argues that Standard English is an Indian language (2009, 101). Well-meaning instructors may sally forth to battle racism and White supremacy, only to find that some of their assumptions about language and identity, gleaned, they thought, from the most correct and progressive of our field's sources, aren't shared by many of their students.

So rather than assume that my students' responses reveal an internalized racism, I wonder if they're on to something important that I was missing in the discussions of translingualism, if their approaches to language and identity are more flexible and copious than my own. As a White colleague, Jessica Gravely, put it: "Most students have waaaaaaay more experience adapting their language to different situations than I do, and the stakes are never as high for me." And as Heather Fester puts it (chapter 9 in this collection), I should be open to "the viability of student values and the way their resistance can be seen as a type of authorship" (158). What, then, are these authors saying? My students may also resist some of our profession's attitudes about language because they detect a social-class attitude towards language that is inimical to their own.

CONCEPTUAL MODELS OF LINGUISTIC CAPITAL AND ITS VALUES

It seems that, in the view of many who think about translingualism, monolingualism is the linguistic ideology of capitalism. In an economic world that privileges "native-speakers" and "fluency" and "correctness," those who are perceived to be closer to the norm (read: middle- and upper-class, White, English-speaking Westerners) are advantaged, and those who are "Othered" are disadvantaged. These inequalities result in much suffering: linguistic prejudice and stereotyping, gate-keeping, self-hating, language death and language attrition, and even language murder, and more (Obeng 2002). A vivid example: tongue surgeries are reportedly increasingly popular in China and South Korea so that people can "be freed 'from that tongue-tied feeling'" when speaking English (Lu 2010). FYC in the United States, in this account of capitalism, contributes to the order of things by acting as a gatekeeper and a guardian of monolingualism, training new generations in these codes of power and excluding those unable or unwilling to conform.

What kind of capitalism demands conformity? A capitalism that shuns diversity, that looks out for the cultural, not just the economic, interests of investors, a capitalism that ties itself to the past and to culturally hegemonic ways of being. A capitalism in which there are rules to follow and play by, rules that serve the interests of capital. If you play by The Rules, this capitalism tells you, you are more likely to be rewarded.

So when my student asks me to help her sound more professional, she is showing her belief in a certain kind of capitalism—she wants me to teach her The Rules so that she may be rewarded, too. Hello again, monolingualism. And not by coincidence, the capitalism that my students would seem to prefer would be the stable, patriarchal capitalism of the past—I agree to The Rules, I give you my life and do things your way, and you grant me permanent access to the middle class. (I hope it's obvious that I'm simplifying to make a point here. Still, students often have an underlying faith in The Rules—otherwise they wouldn't be in college.) Students look to the English professor as a privileged person within this world, as a Knower and Promulgator of The Rules.

But there is another specter of capitalism haunting the world today, a capitalism that embraces "disruption," that seeks new economic territory by creating "synergies" across previously unconnected industries and locations and peoples and markets, a capitalism that is agnostic towards culture because it has realized that there is money to be made in openness to diversity. In this capitalism, rules are made up or broken as we go, because the new rule is that ossified rule-bound structures are inflexible and therefore get in the way of capital, which must be free and flexible. The demonic genius of this capitalism is that no one has permanent access to the middle class—one must continually account for oneself and one's value, continually negotiate one's contingent position.

In the past, we've thought that composition serves capitalism's flexibility by producing a kind of uniformity—if all workers have the same-ish language and orientation towards communication, there will be less communicative friction and companies will be ever more free to treat workers as interchangeable and expendable. But there is just as much reason to think that, if all US composition students suddenly engaged openly and adroitly in translanguaging, capital would welcome a slew of new workers whose generous dispositions towards difference in language would open up new markets for products; would eliminate communicative friction not through uniformity but by allowing corporations to hire folks skilled at global, cross-cultural communication; and would generally find ways to turn a profit and accumulate ever greater sums of financial, cultural, and symbolic capital for those at the top. (Read in this way, the title *Crossing Divides* has an entirely different resonance from the one that was likely intended—capital, like people or ideas or words, wants to cross divides.) Translanguaging makes the earth flat.

What's more, if the abstraction we call capitalism suddenly widely celebrated the wisdom of translingual approaches to language difference, our own social class, we college English professors would be well-positioned in the marketplace. We are trained to be exquisitely sensitive readers and have the leisure to do so, we are well-equipped already to navigate cultural differences, we are relatively cosmopolitan and tolerant (or at least we love to tell ourselves that we are all these things!). In short, in addition to bolstering capitalism's market flexibility and helping it to cross divides, translingualism may also bolster the authority, and the use-value, of the English professor. Monolingualism and Fordist capitalism value the English professor for purportedly knowing and transmitting the dominant code; translingualism and late/global/neoliberal capitalism value the English professor for her ability to read, to negotiate meanings, and to model a tolerance of ambiguity.

Consider this: the translingual attitudes toward language that I would want to champion—in Keith Gilyard's words, "that language and language standards are situational, political, arbitrary, and palimpsestic"—also *feel right* according to the prevailing norms of my own social class fraction (2016, 284). Attention to the arbitrary and political aspects of situations—my bread and butter! Palimpsests—there's nothing I love more! And don't even get me started on language sedimentation . . .

So when my students resist an openness to language difference, part of that resistance may be towards what they see as the interests of a class fraction that doesn't really want to welcome them, at least not as they are, with their Rule-seeking social-class sensibilities, and perhaps they see ahead to a version of capitalism characterized by flexibility and disruption in which they and theirs would continue to be chewed up and spit out. I think that's key here: in resisting my more progressive aims, my students may reject not just me but a harsh economic world order that is inimical to their own being. Put another way, my students might recognize that, however well-intentioned I may be, in a certain sense I'm trying to sell them a version of capitalism that's even scarier and more atomizing than the one that came before it. If monolingualism is the language ideology of Fordist capitalism (and of the capitalist formations that preceded it), and translingualism is the language ideology of late/global/neoliberal capitalism, no wonder my students would resist it. For all of its faults, the promise of stable access to the middle class has a strong human appeal and sounds a whole lot better than having to be an entrepreneur of the self (Foucault 2008).

In making a case that translingualism is capitalism, too, I am not trying to suggest that English teachers have yet another reason to feel guilty for doing their jobs. Nor do I suggest that we simply aid and abet whatever ideologies we and our students seem to have been hailed into. But I do believe that if we do not examine our own class interests, we will misrecognize students' resistance. We might adopt the neutral-sounding position that translingualism is just how all language works always and already, that negotiating difference is the norm; we might rehearse moral arguments or political arguments about language diversity; we might reach for the language of rights, as in Students' Right to Their Own Language (SRTOL). But as long as we frame our approach to difference without acknowledging our own class interests, as long as we talk about translingualism without acknowledging that it serves our own interests and also the interests of a powerful version of capitalism, we're leaving out an important part of the picture that might help students understand and accept more generous approaches to language difference. We should, in other words, be clear, at least to ourselves, about the ways in which translingual writing pedagogies are part of our own social-class identities and therefore might make us insensitive to the varieties of threats students feel, leading us to read as cultural or racial a resistance that may also be based in economics.

SOCIAL-CLASS CONFLICTS IN FYC

In our field, race and gender—rightly, I think—tend to be the dominant lenses through which we consider our teaching. But there are some excellent works on social class and FYC that I find helpful as a two-year-college teacher. In one, *Going North Thinking West,* Irvin Peckham draws our attention to the gulf between working-class college students and their middle-class English teachers. In his account, the teacher is an unwitting enforcer of the dominant discourse and a partisan of a class fraction of the dominant classes: think critically, like me, in the way that I deem legible, or you aren't really thinking at all. He points out that "critical teachers . . . may be re-inscribing social class by privileging the ways of thinking, acting, and writing that are characteristic of the higher social groups and antithetical to the working-class habitus" (2010, 89). On the face of it, students might say that they are in college precisely to learn the "ways of thinking, acting, and writing that are characteristic of the higher social groups." As Karen Kopelson puts it, "Many if not most students come to the university in order to gain access to and eventual enfranchisement in 'the establishment,' not to critique and reject its privileges" (2003, 119). Yet I possess an impulse, which stems in part from my own social-class position and is encouraged by our profession's progressive positions about language, to question this privileging. I find myself and my FYC course both reinforcing and trying to undermine social class hierarchies.

Attention to our social class identity positioning would be a helpful extension of Kopelson's discussion of the performance of neutrality in "Rhetoric on the Edge of Cunning." If a teacher's performance of neutrality is important for productive classroom discussions of sexuality, gender, and race, what are students' perceptions of the social class of their instructor? And how does that perception factor into the kinds of resistance I describe above?

Kopelson speaks from the position of "marginalized teacher-subjects," "who stand before our students as the very subjects/objects of their terror every day" (2003, 140). I would submit that the progressive college writing professor's social class status may also provoke in students a kind of terror—not just the "Better watch my grammar!" terror that English teachers seem to stimulate, nor quite the same as the terror of difference that Kopelson discusses, but the terror of economic contingency. Kopelson seems to posit a "majority" student audience, whose beliefs in gender, sexual, and racial hierarchies come under threat by their composition teachers, especially when they read their composition teachers as being personally invested in upending those hierarchies. Likewise, students' beliefs in language hierarchies come under threat from progressive English teachers—we've got little to lose if there are no linguistic hierarchies, since many of us have already (arguably) secured our place in the social order, but how in the world can a student who doesn't already inhabit a privileged social position hope to do so in a world of flux and liquidity? And when the system has been rigged against you and your people for 400 years or more, why would an invitation to negotiate meaning not create apprehension?

Two examples from *Crossing Divides* may help to highlight why students could feel threatened. In Horner's translation assignment, the dispositions of our own class fraction appear in the very first sentence of the assignment he presents, when students are asked to "consider the differences that might result from a change in choice of words, or vocabulary" (Horner 2017, 93). "Consider," "differences," "might," "change," "choice": the language of flux and negotiation, and the stuff of rhetoricians since ancient times. I like it. And it seems to avoid the problem of explication—it's the activity, not the teacher, that's doing the revealing here. But I think our own social-class position could make us underestimate the level of threat that students may feel lurking in even this assignment. That feeling of threat may ultimately be a good thing, a sign of growth or change—after all, it may be the monolingualist in them that thinks there must be a right answer, a single correct translation out there—yet I could imagine students resisting and rejecting the aims of even this well-designed assignment, and I can easily imagine an instructor (like me) wondering what the heck is going on.

In another chapter of *Crossing Divides*, Katie Malcolm introduces a "translingual studio approach" in the remedial writing program at a community college. There's much to admire in the program she describes, especially in the ways a corequisite course, English 100, serves as a "third space" for students taking transfer-level FYC, English 101. Students from several different sections of English 101 enroll in a section of English 100. Rather than speak authoritatively about students' 101 assignments, English 100 instructors "would ask students to explore how *they* were interpreting a 101 assignment's requirements, what the purpose of the assignment might be, how they were being assessed, what particular ways of reading/writing/thinking they hoped to gain practice with as they worked on an assignment, and whether there were any particular requirements they might want to negotiate, why, and how" (2017, 108, emphasis in original). Furthermore, instructors discourage students from focusing narrowly on "correctness" and redirect students to what we used to call "higher-order concerns" about meaning and rhetoric. This approach struck me as particularly sensitive to a community-college student audience—rather than directly challenge the students' conceptions of composition, or set up a class in which cultural critiques are the main focus, the instructors honor students' desires to work on their writing even while helping them to expand their conceptions about what writing is all about.

And yet I wonder about how successfully such a course can shift students' conceptions about writing or themselves. Malcolm concedes that the student work she presents contains "a number of concessions to monolingualist assumptions" (112)—embodying "an alternate academic approach" (2017, 113) to language difference is a tall order, especially in the institutional conditions of a two-year college! While English 100 sounds awesome to take and to teach, Malcolm concedes that not all students at the institution have to enter this third space, only students who have been "Othered" through the placement process. In my experience, the filtering and sorting of the placement process casts a long shadow over remedial courses and continues to influence students' self-understanding as writers and as students, making them feel contingent and out of place. From our perspective as teachers, all students have to negotiate requirements in writing assignments; but asking this one group explicitly to think about why and how to negotiate an assignment's requirements could subtly underscore a feeling of contingency.

LIVING IN CONTRADICTION: A CONCLUSION

It's not just students and English teachers who need better self-understanding in this "new" economy, but higher education more generally is suffering from what seem to me like multiple identity crises and it's easy to tie ourselves into knots trying to work out the contradictions. In his book *Class Dismissed,* John Marsh (2011) argues that we oversell students and ourselves on the idea that college is our best collective route to prosperity. One implication I take away from his argument is that colleges, and college teachers, should be more invested in making the experience of college itself feel like a worthwhile way to spend one's time. If this class, this degree, may not really lead in a straightforward way to a secure economic future, why not make the experience of going to college more pleasurable, more an end in itself?

From the perspective of gaining students' cooperation, and bearing in mind that there is no neutral ground, I would underline the importance of joy, of making the processes of writing and thinking pleasurable. Royster uses the language of pleasure when responding to someone who thinks she should speak less in academic language and instead "be herself": "I do have a range of voices, and I take quite a bit of pleasure actually in being able to use any of them at will" (1996, 37). Like Kopelson, James E. Seitz showed that earnest, explicit attempts to introduce political subjects—for example, through reading and writing about race and gender—can fail. Seitz describes a basic writing course he designed that focused on oppression and that "made many of the students feel oppressed" (1993, 13). Rather than make politics and oppression the explicit subject matter of the course and the examination of oppression the key to the students' putative liberation, Seitz draws on Roland Barthes to suggest that we ought "to invite [students] to play along a spectrum of rhetorical occasions" and "provide opportunities for students to 'reproduce the people they want to be'" (1993, 14). Seitz's larger point is that in order to satisfy our desire to be "political" and fight against the -isms that define and oppress us, we can be "political" through other, more discreet means, maybe even cunningly discreet, as Kopelson suggests. We may perhaps enjoy more "success" in the process, and also just enjoy more.

Given students' instrumental understanding of college and the conflicts inherent in the social climbing they can imagine they're engaged in, contradictions between students' home cultures and school cultures may be inevitable. As an FYC teacher in the two-year college, I appreciate models like Malcolm's that demonstrate sensitivity towards those contradictions and the unexpected threats students may feel when they discover that their teachers do not think as they do about language, culture, or education. Even in the critiques of teachers' positioning in the composition classroom that come from four-year settings, there is a patience and wisdom that I appreciate as a community-college English teacher. Much as I would like to, I won't be able to resolve any of the contradictions facing my students, unburden them or me of the legacies of White supremacy, secure for them stable and meaningful employment, or help them achieve their goal of sounding thoroughly "professional." And though I may be able to be cunning in my teaching strategies, I inhabit too many overlapping positions as a teacher to pretend I'm politically or morally neutral. But the nature of language difference—like racial and social-class difference—and my students' steady desire to move on up and get over means that there will be many more opportunities to explore contradictions in my FYC teaching, and I hope to remember that even exploration itself is non-neutral and contradictory. This is where we live, together.

REFERENCES

Bourdieu, Pierre, and Jean-Claude Passeron. 1977. *Reproduction in Education, Society, and Culture.* Translated by Richard Nice. Thousand Oaks, CA: Sage.

Ellison, Ralph. 1995 [1947]. *Invisible Man.* New York: Random House.

Foucault, Michel. 2008 [1979]. *The Birth of Biopolitics.* New York: Palgrave Macmillan.

Gilyard, Keith. 2016. "The Rhetoric of Translingualism." *College English* 78 (3): 284–289.

Horner, Bruce. 2017. "Teaching Translingual Agency in Iteration: Rewriting Difference." In *Crossing Divides: Exploring Translingual Writing Pedagogies and Programs*, ed. Bruce Horner and Laura Tetreault, 87–97. Logan, UT: Utah State University Press.

Horner, Bruce, Min-Zhan Lu, Jacqueline Jones Royster, and John Trimbur. 2011. "Language Difference in Writing: Toward a Translingual Approach." *College English* 73 (3): 303–321.

Horner, Bruce, and Laura Tetreault, ed. 2017. *Crossing Divides: Exploring Translingual Writing Pedagogies and Programs.* Logan: Utah State University Press.

Kopelson, Karen. 2003. "Rhetoric on the Edge of Cunning: Or, The Performance of Neutrality (Re)Considered as a Composition Pedagogy for Student Resistance." *College Composition and Communication* 55 (1): 115–146.

Lu, Min-Zhan. 2010. "Living English Work." In *Cross-Language Relations in Composition*, ed. Bruce Horner, Min-Zhan Lu, and Paul Kei Matsuda, 42–56. Carbondale, IL: Southern Illinois University Press.

Lyons, Scott. 2009. "The Fine Art of Fencing: Nationalism, Hybridity, and the Search for a Native American Writing Pedagogy." *JAC* 29 (1/2): 77–105.

Malcolm, Katie. 2017. "Disrupting Monolingual Ideologies in a Community College: A Translingual Studio Approach." In *Crossing Divides: Exploring Translingual Writing Pedagogies and Programs*, ed. Bruce Horner and Laura Tetreault, 101–118. Logan, UT: Utah State University Press.

Marsh, John. 2011. *Class Dismissed.* New York: Monthly Review.

Obeng, Samuel Gyasi. "The Politics about Languages." In *Political Independence with Linguistic Servitude: The Politics about Languages in the Developing World*, ed. Samuel Gyasi Obeng and Beverly Hartford, 7–14. Hauppauge, NY: NOVA Science Pub Inc.

Peckham, Irvin. 2010. *Going North Thinking West: The Intersections of Social Class, Critical Thinking, and Politicized Writing Instruction.* Logan, UT: Utah State University Press.

Royster, Jacqueline Jones. 1996. "When the First Voice You Hear Is Not Your Own." *College Composition and Communication* 47 (1): 29:40.

Seitz, James E. 1993. "Eluding Righteous Discourse: A Discreet Politics for New Writing Curricula." *WPA: Journal of the Council of Writing Program Administrators* 16 (3): 7–14.
Smitherman, Geneva. 1977. *Talkin and Testifyin.* Detroit, MI: Wayne State University Press.
Smitherman, Geneva. 2006. *Word from the Mother: Language and African Americans.* New York: Routledge.
Young, Vershawn A. 2009. "Nah, We Straight." *JAC* 29 (1/2): 49–76.

3

WALKING THE NARROW RIDGE
When Performing Neutrality Isn't an Option in the Vocation of the Christian Professor

Jessica Clements

In *Negotiating Religious Faith in the Composition Classroom,* bonnie lenore kyburz (2005) offers the following call to rhetoric and composition scholars investigating religious faith in institutional contexts: "I want to argue that while the authors . . . find notions of linguistic hegemony and community available for analysis, we must also read against such notions" (138). In this chapter, I take up kyburz's call. I offer the perspective of a professor at a liberal arts university in which each faculty member must be a practicing Christian while the student body is not required to prescribe to any faith tradition. This means I am not afforded the opportunity to perform neutrality in the classroom; so, "How might [I] speak, as whom might [I] speak, so that students listen?" (Kopelson 2003, 142). I ultimately argue that *mêtis*—"all 'forms of wily intelligence, of effective, adaptable cunning,' that work through the implementation of 'resourceful plays . . . and stratagems'" (Detienne and Vernant 1978, 3–4, quoted in Kopelson 2003, 130)—looks different in religious contexts but forwards the same pedagogical goal; that is, if the goal of the religiously affiliated university is to help students understand that "intellectual inquiry and deep Christian conviction [are] complementary rather than competing values" (Whitworth University "Goal 1"), then such institutions should be willing to reward their instructors for subversive performance of neutrality as purposeful pedagogical *mêtis* rather than perpetuate the binary thinking that has continually dominated both institutional and disciplinary rhetoric on religion in the composition classroom.

THE CALL

In "Rhetoric on the Edge of Cunning," Karen Kopelson (2003) claims that to teach composition is to encounter resistance and that that resistance

DOI: 10.7330/9781607329992.c003

cannot be narrowed to one form of expression. It would also be erroneous to say that that resistance comes from one specific source. Above
and beyond a not-unexpected distaste for a required English course,
though, students in the twenty-first-century composition classroom
have, according to Kopelson (2003), developed a widespread distaste
for an "inappropriately politicized" learning environment (116–117). If
objective knowledge is the primary instrument of the learned individual,
and the university classroom is where that knowledge is developed,
then the composition classroom, in particular, should involve nothing
other "than impartial instruction in the transferable and neutral skill of
writing 'correctly'" (117). While this student sentiment may extend to
other classes in different disciplines, composition—the course "without
content"—remains a particularly vulnerable target (117).

The idea that writing is a neutral skill transferrable through a course
without content has its roots in eighteenth-century Scottish Common
Sense Realism and concrete expression in the late nineteenth-century
rhetorical texts of Hill, Wendell, and Genung (Berlin 1982, 769). This
current traditional stance dominated the field's pedagogical thinking
(or at least the textbooks it published) well into the 1980s. Current-
traditionalists (see Cohen 1977) believed that truth was discoverable *only*
through induction: "The world readily surrenders its meaning to anyone
who observes it properly, and no operation of the mind . . . is needed
to arrive at truth" (Berlin 1982, 770). Composition was to be exclusively
concerned with developing skills in arrangement and style, practically
facilitated as the correction of error; anything sociopolitical was outside
the scope of the composition instructor's duty. While the field has since
moved into and through more complex and complicated notions of cultural studies and critical approaches to teaching composition, students
seem to expect this nostalgic disinterestedness of their composition
classroom. Why, then, would Kopelson (2003) seemingly advocate an
acquiescence to the student and their desire to return to antiquated
notions of a "neutral" domain for composition instructors?

Kopelson (2003) is *not* advocating that we return to an error-
correction–focused composition classroom. Rather, she deftly reminds
us that we are rhetors who have forgotten foundational rhetorical
principles. Just as blanket policies of exclusive attention to surface-level
errors will not lead to better writing, so too will uniform application
of critical pedagogies sans attention to "differences among classroom rhetorical contexts and among teacher subject positions" also
fail (118). More specifically, Kopelson suggests that the composition
teacher marked by marginalization can perform "the very neutrality

that students expect"—an invocation of authority, objectivity, and neutrality—in order to minimize resistance and open possibilities for critical student engagement with difference. It is often less an issue of student un/willingness to critically engage dominant discourses and more an issue of student un/willingness to respond beyond what the outward markers of their composition instructor might seem to warrant (119); students tend to believe that we teach and grade according to the "story of ourselves in the world" (Karamcheti 1995, 138, quoted in Kopelson 2003, 120).

Writing in 2003, Kopelson implored "composition instructors [. . .] to invent and adjust our praxes—as all rhetors do—based on the audience we face *and* based on how we are read by that audience" (121). The contributors to the present collection are posing the question, Just how much have our audiences and their reading of us changed? Does "the performance of neutrality, or of greater teacher distance . . . [still] help to increase students' critical involvement with difficult issues by decreasing their preoccupation with the teacher's identity position" (Kopelson 2003, 126)? More specifically, I investigate what happens when performing neutrality *isn't* an option.

ON MÊTIS

Kopelson (2003) reminds us we can turn to rhetorical history for the exigence of performing neutrality. *Mêtis*, she argues, is related to *kairos* as "an ability . . . not simply to seize the moment but to seize it with forethought, preparedness, and thus with fore*sight* as to how events should unfold" (Detienne and Vernant 1978, 16, quoted in Kopelson 2003, 130). *Mêtis* is, productively, a pedagogical strategy that attends to short-term contextual variables for long-term pedagogical gains. Performance of neutrality, as *mêtis*, flips power dynamics on their head (Kopelson 2003, 130); it considers how to incorporate the greatest possible breadth of contributors to the composition class for an eventual unfolding of depth in critical consciousness; it is born of "the honest desire and honest effort . . . to keep students open, keep students learning, keep students open *to* learning, so that they may engage with rather than shut out difference" (135). However, it "willingly operates through reversal, deception, and disguise when necessary" (Detienne and Vernant 1978, 3, 21, 44, quoted in Kopelson 2003, 131); "the cunning ploys and stratagems in the performance of neutrality are decidedly impure, sneaky, covert, mired in established and perhaps even coercive power" (Kopelson 2003, 136).

I quote Kopelson's (2003) article at length to place emphasis on what a religiously affiliated institution might find objectionable about such well-intentioned pedagogy as that driven by *mêtis*: "Davis asks us to *refuse* to be ourselves and to revalue and celebrate self-creation and artifice instead" (Davis 2000, 200–201, quoted in Kopelson 2003, 134, emphasis added). Kopelson (2003), speaking through D. Diane Davis, invites us to embrace a pedagogy of *mêtis*, a pedagogy that operates through disingenuousness and trickery as an artful means to productive pedagogical ends; yet nouns like "trickery," "deception," "disguise," and "artifice" and adjectives like "impure," "sneaky," and "covert" speak directly *against* what my small liberal arts, religiously affiliated university asks for in its faculty candidates: "*In a one-page essay (approximately 300 words), describe your personal Christian faith.* This essay about your Christian commitment is intended to be a *personal, authentic* statement in your own words that will help the committee to determine your interest in joining [our] 'community of Christian scholars'" (Whitworth University, "Faculty Faith Essay," emphasis added). That is, to be hired by my institution, faculty candidates must provide convincingly written statements of their "personal, authentic" walk with Christ as part of their employment materials, an authenticity that must be genuinely extended to performance of classroom pedagogy.

THE NARROW RIDGE: A SLIPPERY SLOPE

To be fair, my university's employment search rhetoric is clear in its intention *not* to pigeonhole future faculty into performing a particular type or kind of Christianity: "We do not expect that all faculty will have the same denominational affiliation or theological outlook, but we seek highly qualified academics who embrace the great tradition of historic Christian faith" (Whitworth University, "Faculty Faith Essay"). They are, however, unapologetic about the institution's commitment to hiring faculty who are willing (required) to perform explicit faith-learning integration to achieve tenure and promotion, and their directive is to make one's Christian worldview *authentically* clear. This institutional mandate is often expressed in the rhetoric of "the narrow ridge."

In Theory

The geographical situatedness of my university (a small liberal arts university in the Pacific Northwest) lends credence to the metaphor of the narrow ridge. The "narrow ridge" refers to "the institution being situated on a precarious mountain crest that connects two steep and dangerous slopes" (Taylor 2013). One slope is said to represent "the temptation that Christian universities . . . have faced historically to jettison their Christ-centered missions in favor of things like greater academic reputation or an easier time navigating an increasingly pluralistic society" (Taylor 2013). The other slope is said to represent a temptation to abandon what might feel more familiar to academics outside the Christian university: "the temptation for many Christian universities to abandon their commitments to open and fearless intellectual inquiry and academic freedom" (Taylor 2013).

My university firmly believes in the possibility of avoiding the slopes of temptation and walking the narrow ridge, of wedding "intellectual inquiry and deep Christian conviction as complementary rather than competing values" (Whitworth University, "Goal 1"). On one hand, the university seems to share an interest in the intellectual virtues that are the goals of Kopelson's (2003) referenced critical pedagogies. Rather than operate through a sociopolitical demarcation or lens, however, my university is unabashed in its mission to "engage challenging contemporary issues with intellectual rigor through the lens of Christian faith" (Whitworth University, "Goal 1"), in other words, to institutionally mark its faculty with a religious agenda. On the other hand, then, embracing Kopelson's pedagogical strategy of performing neutrality would be to acquiesce to the temptation to jump off the narrow ridge, to shed one's religious skin in favor of pursuing more traditionally acceptable modes of academic inquiry in the composition classroom, a notion formally addressed in university handbook language.

To be a faculty member at my university, you must be an "articulate Christian" with "a personal commitment and practice of the Christian faith" (Whitworth University 2018b). To obtain tenure, you must write multiple narrative self-assessment essays that evidence your faith in relation to your teaching, service, and scholarly agendas (Whitworth University 2018a). The clear and abiding thematic tie of these essays is the need to provide explicit evidence that one is an authentic Christian in all facets of his or her professorial vocation.

There is, in this case study, no option for the (successfully tenured and promoted) faculty member to be anything but an "authentic Christian" in the classroom. The institution has a clear, prescriptive notion of the larger *ethos* they are building through the faculty they hire: "Through decades of change, this fundamental purpose has remained firmly centered in the person of Jesus Christ. Our understanding of Christ is based on Scripture, the inspired and trustworthy record of God's self-disclosure and our final rule for faith and practice" (Whitworth University, "Faculty Faith Essay").

Perhaps none of this reads as overly problematic; the institutional rhetoric is arguably clear and transparent, a "you knew what you signed up for" employment context, if you will. Yet *students* at my institution *do not* have to subscribe to the Christian faith tradition—or any faith tradition, for that matter. They do not have to sign a Christian code of conduct or attend mandatory chapel. But, students enter under the promise that faculty will "equip and inspire students to cultivate character, seek justice, and proclaim salvation" given that we live in "a world fractured by sin and transformed by Christ's grace and truth." "Students will," the strategic plan argues, "pursue opportunities to lead and participate in national and international initiatives that reflect [the university's] commitment to faith-learning integration" (Whitworth University, "Goal 1"). This raises the question: If students at this university and countless others have proven openly hostile to instructors marked with clear ideological agendas (see this chapter's "Learning from History")—and the university demands an explicit, authentic Christian pedagogy on the part of its faculty—how does a faculty member navigate the potential landslide that is "You know I'm a Christian, I'm not sure where you stand, and the university wants us to walk this narrow ridge together?"

In Practice

The university's answer to how not to fall off the narrow ridge is faculty-development opportunities like the Vocation of the Christian Professor (VCP) Workshop, as the university is aware of the need to support faculty in their understanding and execution of faith-learning integration expectations. The workshop was developed in May of 2005 for that very reason, with a particular focus on providing instruction on practical classroom strategies. During the workshop, faculty participants are introduced to a history of Christian faith-learning integration at church-related universities. It involves intense reflection upon "personal calling" and on "the unique opportunities of serving at a Christian institution" (Whitworth University 2015). More specifically, the workshop asks faculty to create a tangible "project" for implementation in a future class at the university, one that "effectively integrates Christian faith with academic content" (Whitworth University 2015).

I participated in the VCP Workshop in the summer of 2015, crafting a video narrative project for my new media-focused first-year composition course. The assignment asks students to tell a story—a narrative—about

Figure 3.1. Collective concept mapping of the term "Faith."

faith in digital form, combining spoken voice with video clips or timed still images. The assignment also includes a word-based reflection essay in which students evaluate the efficacy of their writing processes and their engagement with the topic of faith.

To invent content for this composition project, we (students and instructor) engage in collective concept mapping. At the center of our classroom whiteboard I draw a bubble around the term "faith" and ask students to add to the board, to physically link that bubble to any and all terms that come to mind when they hear the word "faith." Inevitably, they begin by adding words like "religion," "prayer," and "spirituality"— what they assume I want to see as a Christian-marked teacher.

Students are unsure how to proceed when I add terms like "Santa" or "pacemaker" to our "faith" concept map. Whereas institutional rhetoric might predispose these students to think they must compose a video narrative about the virtues of contemporary Christianity in order to get an A on their video narrative, my subtly performed stratagem of neutrality emboldens them to think critically, to add terms like "loss of faith," "hypocrisy," "challenge," "confusion," "fear," and so on to the board, to reflect the sometimes difficult and always messy discourse that is contemporary faith-based exchange. In not directing my pedagogical contributions in the manner of "if I were to write a narrative about faith, I would have to expound on my growth as a Christian," I seem to belie the institutional mission of authentic Christian pedagogical commitment; yet the covert stratagem of grounding our discussion in terms I don't associate with my personal, religious faith offered critical dividends in the students' reflections.

After collective and individual brainstorming, collaborative research and storyboarding, gathering/creating/splicing A- and B-roll footage, rough-video peer review, and final editing, students showcase their completed video-narrative projects to the class as a whole. We celebrate overcoming the challenges inherent in this vulnerable type of writing and laugh through process stories highlighting how that two-second clip rendered upside down was an engaging accident. Yet, students' individual reflections reveal much deeper learning linked to the pedagogical strategy of performed neutrality.

In a reflective essay titled "More Than Words on a Page," Student 1 wrote, "Having a class brainstorming session where we all talked about what it is that faith can mean really broadened my idea of what faith was and helped make the concept of writing a narrative about faith far less daunting." In this response, Student 1 attests directly to the restrictive power ideologically laden terms such as "faith" can, consciously or unconsciously, impose on a student's thinking and writing. More important, the essay attests to how a pedagogical strategy grounded in performed neutrality (the expansive collective concept map) freed that student to think and write about such a topic in a safe and sophisticated way.

Student 2, in "Project #1 Reflection," wrote of a similar epiphany: "We were targeting students who have had, or are in the middle of, a crisis of faith. If anything, one of our goals was to show the active separation from church and an institution, but that still wanting to hold onto faith is normal—even at Whitworth University. This project really did help me consolidate my thoughts about faith. *It's not limited to religion,* but [my partner] and I found common ground on this topic of disappointment and pain" (emphasis added). Student 2 revealed a growth trajectory that offered concrete evidence that exploration and critical expression of faith were not tied to the instructor's presumed preference; Student 2 found common ground with a disparate discourse partner not at the surface level of Christian faith but through underlying threads of human experience in disappointment and pain.

The engagement of Student 3 with the sensitive and highly charged subject of faith was also "broadened": "This project made me think a lot about faith, and it broadened how I think about it. I used to just think of religion—mainly Christianity came to mind—when the word 'faith' was said. Coming up with different idea possibilities, listening to other's ideas, and exploring the topic, I learned that faith isn't just religion, and it isn't the same for everyone."

If one of the goals of a critical (cultural studies) approach to composition is to afford students open-minded engagement with diverse perspectives on difficult issues, then my work in deflecting students' presumptions of the limited Christian worldview of their instructor succeeded through a small-scale writing-to-learn activity. Students were not only able to navigate the challenge of communicating through the wall of perceived fundamentalist Christian belief but were also able to achieve measurable success both in the outcomes of the writing course and in the university's desire to have rich and varied conversations about faith. In Kelly Blewett's words from this collection (chapter 6), I utilized neutrality to build an empathy bridge to trust: "neutrality—an openness to listening, a making of space for the student to explore their own ideas—can be a natural precursor to trust (102)," a trust that led to faith-based discourse in a much richer "contact zone" of open and fearless intellectual inquiry.

Student 1 also evidenced a fair focus on audience, a foundational goal of any first-year composition course: "Almost immediately, [my partner] and I agreed that we wanted to talk about how college students are prone to losing their faith. This agreement directed us to the audience of college students, which we tried to keep in mind in the production of our project." Further, Student 1 spoke to the research that went into this video-narrative project and to how that audience-focused research had real-world implications for their immediately lived faith experience on a campus comprising Christian faculty but a student body not mandated to practice a particular religion: "Perhaps the most important takeaway from this project for me was the meaning of faith in college. Through some of the research [my partner] and I did to put together our project, I learned that more than 80 percent of high schoolers who went to youth group in high school stop going to church at all by the end of their college careers. We realized that in our own, albeit limited, college experiences, it is easy for faith to get pushed aside behind homework and social activities without being consciously discarded" (Student 1).

Student 2 also spoke to a nuanced understanding of audience: "We had a hard time finding headlines and audio clips other than those crazy extremists (that I'm pretty sure everyone hates . . .). What we were really interested in were small-scale experiences within the church of hypocrisy and lies. It was not easy to convey that, so we went with an 'Other/All' separation from church and the hesitation to be a part of that community." Student 2 may not have felt empowered to tackle the topic of "hypocrisy" and Christianity in a project being graded by a committed

Christian had I not chosen to perform neutrality in the initial brain-storming phases of this project; in the process, the student also might have missed the invaluable lesson of writing to an audience, a lesson likely to inform the students' writing successes and failures throughout their college careers.

Student 3 demonstrated growth in critical thinking and writing skills in suggesting how one goes about finding common ground in faith-based discussion: "The direction that my partner and I went in was really interesting to explore. We thought about the different things that peo-ple put their faith in in their everyday lives. People don't typically think about the simple things like medicine or everything functioning how it is supposed to but when you do think about it you realize that everyone puts their faith in those simple things." If the university is looking for students to connect and discourse with their diverse peers on difficult topics, then it seems that not highlighting my own Christian journey in an assignment about faith is, at least in part, what got them there.

The theme that comes through loud and clear in these reflections is a project that could have easily become a trite exploration of Christian faith, produced for a teacher institutionally marked as a practicing Christian, became something other—something much broader, deeper, and more valuable—from my insistence on performing neutrality in the early stages of the writing process.

A large part of my argument in this chapter explores the necessary tension within contemporary Christian universities that insist on an overt facilitation of faith-learning integration juxtaposed to the poten-tial benefits of dynamic integration of a teacher's performative neu-trality. What I am advocating, then, is a bit of risk-taking on the part of instructors employed by such institutions, that instructors risk implicit, perhaps "inauthentic," integration of faith into their pedagogy in order to open the doors to the desirable "narrow ridge" of wedded Christian and academic rigor—a pedagogy that shows students Christian and critical worldviews are not uncomplementary. The question remains, however, particularly for those instructors: why should I risk promo-tion and tenure? (Why didn't *I* do *more*?). As Robert Samuels in (in chapter 4 in this collection) reminds us, it is non-tenured faculty who are most vulnerable, situated at the crossroads of ideology and peda-gogy; this is a charge that affects the *livelihood* of the Christian teacher. An answer can be found in the twenty-five-year (plus) history of the religious student in composition (Lynch and Miller 2017); indeed, in this regard, the student should be schooling the teacher, or, rather, the institution.

LEARNING FROM HISTORY

In "It's a Question of Faith: Discourses on Fundamentalism and Critical Pedagogy in the Writing Classroom," Amy Goodburn (1998) suggests that, traditionally, "students with fundamentalist assumptions often view teachers as the enemy, secular humanists who attempt to destroy faith by undermining religious authority" (339), that response to student writing in the composition classroom can become a negotiation of "competing assumptions about texts, authority, and knowledge" (346). Goodburn's very important question, though, is whether religious fundamentalism and critical pedagogy really are so far apart as to not be "negotiable."

Goodburn (1998) further remarks that fundamentalist and critical thinking tend to share the following qualities: "oppositional stance to the status quo," "critique of mass culture," "assumption that school curriculum is a site of struggle over values and representation," "questioning of the nature of authority," "examination of sources of knowledge and belief," and "desire to convert the 'other'" (348). There is not just commonality but *significant* commonality, then. That commonality only comes to light, according to Goodburn, when the critical educator is willing to "reread the discourse of critical pedagogy through the mirror of fundamentalist discourse . . . to point out uninterrogated assumptions that limit teachers' understanding of their students' responses" (349). Ultimately, it is about understanding the webbed reality of our beliefs (349).

Lizabeth A. Rand, in her 2001 article "Enacting Faith: Evangelical Discourse and the Discipline of Composition Studies," also details the similarities between Christian discourse and the goals of the composition classroom. There is the common language of "saving": "Our testimonials suggest that we desperately want our students to 'get saved'—to get outside themselves so that life-changing transformation can occur" (360). And there is a common focus on social justice: "in our commitment to defend the oppressed we must 'bear witness' . . . to ongoing struggles for social justice" (360). Evil is seen as a lack of critical consciousness in both cases, and religion "rightfully understood, is a subversive force"; that is, transgressive action is a common goal and a common good (360–361).

Rand argues that we tend to overlook these similarities because "peoples of diverse cultures are welcomed into respectable academic culture, but only on the condition that they leave the religious dimensions of their cultures at the door" (Marsden 1997, 33, quoted in Rand 2001, 351). We, instructors of composition, are invited, implicitly or explicitly, to not talk about religion in the classroom. Our training in postmodern theories of knowledge tends to cement this invitation (Rand 2001, 351) when we butt heads with students who are looking toward a "constrictive . . . God to be at the center of [their] universe" (362). From a disciplinary perspective then, we have tended to couch our call to action as how to "deal with" these disruptive students and their inappropriately narrowed worldviews: "Our professional conversations have implied that older and less postmodern theories often sound too evangelical and, therefore, should be scorned" (354). Time and again we have scholars calling out the field on the "dichotomous relationship we maintain between the 'evangelical' and the work we ourselves do in composition studies" (356).

Writing in 2017, Michael-John DePalma confirms that this binary thinking still exists: "First, there is a tendency among scholars in our field to view religious rhetorics as incommensurate with thoughtful public discourse" (254). DePalma suggests that discussion, intellectual inquiry, and advancement of knowledge are goals of the composition classroom sometimes thought of as incompatible with religious rhetoric, yet he argues that "the study of religious rhetorics need not be restricted to religious students or religious institutions" (254). Religious rhetorics "might serve as vital resources for civic engagement and political action" (254) but (and this is a big *but*) they often don't, because our students do not have the rhetorical resources to discuss religion and spirituality in substantive ways: "Findings from the National Study of Youth and Religion show that students struggle to articulate religious perspectives in meaningful ways because they have not been taught to do so" (255). This stems from a larger "culture of intolerance—a culture of people that are unwilling to listen, consider, or take seriously epistemological, ontological, and ideological positions that differ from their own" (261) but also, and more specifically, from a disciplinary narrative that has situated our religious students' thinking as "synonymous with the breeding of hypocrisy, arrogance, narrow-mindedness, censorship, racism, homophobia, classism, sexism, and so many other well-documented evils that plague humankind" (261).

If we, the scholars and teachers of composition, consciously or unconsciously think of our religious (particularly fundamentalist Christian) students as the purveyors of said evils, it is no wonder that students bring the same credulity to a classroom in which the teacher is marked as "Christian educator." DePalma (2017) suggests that we must "think at length about our positionality and the performance of our identities when teaching such [religious rhetorics]" (270). More practically, DePalma suggests it's about "unpacking reductive notions of religious and spiritual communities, points of overlap and distinctions between religion and spirituality, and convergences and divergences of political and religious identities, too" (270). It can start with the unpacking of a single word or words. DePalma quotes David James Duncan at length in a convincing manner:

> America's spiritual vocabulary—with its huge defining terms such as "God," "soul," "sacrifice," "mysticism," "faith," "salvation," "grace," "redemption"—has been enduring a series of abuses so constricting that the damage may last for centuries . . . The defamation of religious vocabu-lary cannot be undone by turning away: *the harm is undone when we work to reopen each word's true history, nuance, and depth.* Holy words need steward-ship as surely as do gardens, orchards, or ecosystems. (Duncan 2006, 53, quoted in DePalma 2017, 264; emphasis added)

Collectively, Goodburn (1998), Rand (2001), DePalma (2017), and oth-ers are inviting us to implode the binary thinking that has stunted the critical growth of both Christian students and Christian educators in the composition classroom, to explore and elevate the commonalities that link the complex ideological and epistemological webbed beliefs supporting student-instructor discourse. In our disciplinary history, this binary has been too long performed as the fundamentalist Christian stu-dent versus the secular, cultural-studies-interested professor. At my cur-rent institution, this is the Christian professor versus the often skeptical and sometimes spiritual student, who may or may not have a stronghold in any faith.

In my case study, however, I opted to shed the identity of overt and narrowly defined Christian educator and performed neutral-ity through a webbed concept mapping exercise. My students and I *actualized* networked thinking—rather than identity-bound, binary thinking—initiating a video-narrative project on faith that expanded the diverse students' understandings of and possibilities for critical inquiry. To perform neutrality, I argue, is not necessarily to sidestep or reject a Christian worldview. In my case study, it proved a productive means to reopening a conversation about religious rhetoric that has long been fraught with such binary "us" versus "them" frameworks.

The requirement that students explore their relationship with faith through a video-narrative, specifically executed through a performance of neutrality, afforded them a richer learning opportunity than would a stratagem that more neatly embraced institutional rhetoric that demands an authentic facilitation of integration with Christian faith. I earned the students' trust by opening up the loaded term of "faith" and by encouraging them to find their own paths through this exploration rather than accommodating any decidedly Christian take on my part.

What is important here is not that students enjoyed the project, necessarily, or even that they made strides of personal growth. What is important is that *not* forcing my personal Christian faith on my students in an explicit way afforded them much deeper/more meaningful intro-spection of faith of their own accord; they also thought critically about how the words and images they compiled in their video compositions would affect others and *continue the discourse outside the composition class-room*, which seems to be the goal of the Christian-affiliated university, the university that brands itself as contrary to the "impure," "sneaky," and "covert"—inauthentic—"trickery," "deception," "disguise," and "artifice" that is the performance of neutrality as pedagogical *mêtis*.

CONCLUSION

In chapter 2 of this collection, Jason C. Evans argues convincingly that "higher education more generally is suffering from what seems to me like multiple identity crises, and it's easy to tie ourselves into knots trying to work out the contradictions" (52). The "narrow ridge" of the modern-day Christian-affiliated university may well comprise one of these crises. More specifically, I argue that the institution undermines the very outcome of the "narrow ridge" Christian critical consciousness that it seeks by privi-leging overtly enacted (more easily assessable) faith-learning integration measures tied to tenure and promotion; rather, if we seek to support disparate voices with a powerful entryway into today's complicated global discourses, we might more productively perform expressions of faith on a kaleidoscopic continuum of implicitness and explicitness, including what has been deemed the duplicitous "performance of neutrality." This message is both most apropos and most dangerous for the junior faculty member facing tenure and promotion hurdles at Christian-affiliated uni-versities. Consider Meaghan Brewer's emphasis (in chapter 1 of this col-lection) on the vulnerability of graduate instructors negotiating politics, race, and ideology in the classroom for the first time. Newly hired faculty at Christian-affiliated universities, too, often experience the (mandatory) opportunity to overtly integrate faith and learning *for the first time* and "to do so is to force someone in a marginalized position to enact a role she is not yet comfortable with and does not yet have the expertise to occupy" (37). Increased institutional support in targeted professional develop-ment is as essential as increased flexibility in promotion and tenure assessment measures tied to faith-learning integration.

Like DePalma (2017), I suggest that the strategic performance of neutrality as covert methodology to recovering and redressing the power inherent in the complicated and damaged history of religious rhetoric would be beneficial in most all classrooms charged with exploring the subjects of rhetoric and composition. If we continue to forward the lore of the impossibly dualistic Christian fundamentalist student struggling against the progressively challenging instructor, we risk further skewing the alignment between rhetoric and religion; we should not and cannot stand to forward an agenda as seemingly oppressive as the intractable institutional rhetoric that does not inherently make room for the good that comes of performative neutrality.

My call, then, in revisiting Kopelson (2003), is for Christian-affiliated institutions to re-vision their rhetoric. Instead of positioning professors in perceived precarity, in metaphorically suggesting they are part of an unfortunate and vocationally damming landslide if they participate in the performance of neutrality, they should embrace *mêtis* as a rhetorically savvy means to the Christian-focused, academically rigorous critical consciousness they seek.

REFERENCES

Berlin, James A. 1982. "Contemporary Composition: The Major Pedagogical Theories." *College English* 44 (8): 765–777.

Cohen, Murray. 1977. *Sensible Words: Linguistic Practice in England 1640–1785.* Baltimore, MD: Johns Hopkins University Press.

Davis, D. Diane. 2000. *Breaking Up [at] Totality: A Rhetoric of Laughter.* Carbondale: Southern Illinois University Press.

DePalma, Michael-John. 2017. "Reimagining Rhetorical Education: Fostering Writers' Civic Capacities through Engagement with Religious Rhetorics." *College English* 79: 251–275.

Detienne, Marcel, and Jean-Pierre Vernant. 1978. *Cunning Intelligence in Greek Culture and Society.* Trans. Janet Lloyd. Atlantic Highlands, NJ: Humanities Press.

Duncan, David James. 2006. *God Laughs and Plays: Churchless Sermons in Response to the Preachments of the Fundamentalist Right.* Great Barrington, MA: Triad Books.

Goodburn, Amy. 1998. "It's a Question of Faith: Discourse of Fundamentalism and Critical Pedagogy in the Writing Classroom." *JAC* 18 (2): 333–353.

Karamcheti, Indira. 1995. "Caliban in the Classroom." In *Pedagogy: The Question of Impersonation*, ed. Jane Gallop, 138–146. Bloomington: Indiana University Press.

Kopelson, Karen. 2003. "Rhetoric on the Edge of Cunning; Or, The Performance of Neutrality (Re)Considered As a Composition Pedagogy for Student Resistance." *College Composition and Communication* 55 (1): 115–146.

kyburz, bonnie lenore. 2005. "Religious Faith in Context—Institutions, Histories, Identities, Bodies: Introductory Comments." In *Negotiating Religious Faith in the Composition Classroom*, ed. Elizabeth Vader Lei and bonnie lenore kyburz, 137–140. Portsmouth, NH: Boynton/Cook.

Lynch, Paul, and Matthew Miller. 2017. "Twenty-Five Years of Faith in Writing: Religion and Composition, 1992–2017." *Present Tense* 6 (2). http://www.presenttensejournal.org/volume-6/twenty-five-years-of-faith-in-writing-religion-and-composition-1992-2017/. Accessed September 30, 2018.

Marsden, George M. 1997. *The Outrageous Idea of Christian Scholarship*. New York: Oxford University Press.

Rand, Lizabeth A. 2001. "Enacting Faith: Evangelical Discourse and the Discipline of Composition Studies." *College Composition and Communication* 52 (3): 349–367.

Taylor, Beck. 2013. "An Update from Whitworth University President Beck A. Taylor." *Mind and Heart*. http://www.whitworth.edu/administration/presidentsoffice/mind&heart /2013/October13.htm. Accessed November 10, 2017.

Whitworth University. 2015. *VCP*. PDF. Accessed November 10, 2017.

Whitworth University. 2018a. "Faculty Evaluation." *Faculty Handbook 2018*. https:// www.whitworth.edu/cms/media/whitworth/documents/administration/academic -affairs/faculty-handbook/section%207.pdf. Accessed February 22, 2019.

Whitworth University. 2018b. "Faculty Recruiting and Appointment." *Faculty Handbook 2018*. https://www.whitworth.edu/cms/media/whitworth/documents/administration /academic-affairs/faculty-handbook/section%203.pdf. Accessed February 22, 2019.

Whitworth University. "Faculty Faith Essay." *Human Resource Services*. http://www.whitworth .edu/Administration/HumanResources/FacultyFaithEssay/Prompt.htm. Accessed November 10, 2017.

Whitworth University. "Goal 1: Advance Whitworth University's Distinctive Approach to Integrating Christian Faith and Learning." *Whitworth University 2021*. https://www .whitworth.edu/GeneralInformation/Whitworth2021/Goal1.htm. Accessed November 10, 2017.

4

CONTINGENT FACULTY, STUDENT EVALUATION, AND PEDAGOGICAL NEUTRALITY

Robert Samuels

Now that most of the people teaching in higher education in the United States do not have their academic freedom protected by tenure, it is important to look at how all faculty deal with ideology in a polarized culture and the special challenges faced by untenured faculty (Bradley 2004). Not only can many contingent faculty be let go at any time for any reason, but they often are rehired and promoted based solely on student evaluations (Langen 2011). The insecurity of these teachers is therefore coupled with a system of assessment in which students can unknowingly and knowingly harm their teachers if the students feel that they are being taught in an overly political and ideological fashion. In this context, I examine if it is still possible to follow the modern educational values of neutrality, objectivity, and universality in classroom discussions. My central focus is on how a close reading of modern thinkers like Descartes and Freud reveals how neutrality is a key to understanding the scientific method and our democratic institutions; however, neutrality has not been represented as an ethical ideal in culture and society, and so it is often seen as merely an empty gesture. I also argue that this necessary but impossible ideal of neutrality represents the foundations of university discourse and can help to protect all faculty, including the untenured. Of special interest will be how teachers of writing can use neutrality to protect their jobs and create a more open and critical discourse.

DESCARTES AND MODERN NEUTRALITY

My theory of pedagogical neutrality is derived from René Descartes's notion of modern science and Sigmund Freud's conception of analytic neutrality. For Descartes, the first stage of any scientific investigation is for the scientist to remove any prejudice and anticipation so that

DOI: 10.7330/9781607329992.c004

he can approach the subject matter with an open mind (Descartes 1996). Through his use of methodological doubt, Descartes sought to clear a space for a new mode of intellectual discovery that was separate from the premodern focus on belief, faith, and tradition. From this Enlightenment perspective, to be neutral required a conscious effort of introspection and self-effacement: the early modern scientist was supposed to search his mind for any preconceptions that would block him from seeing the world in an honest and truthful way.

If we look at what Descartes actually wrote about science and reason, we see how his establishment of the scientific method relies on effacing self-interest and inherited beliefs: "The first [step] was never to accept anything for true which I did not clearly know to be such; that is to say, carefully to avoid precipitancy and prejudice, and to comprise nothing more in my judgment than what was presented to my mind so clearly and distinctly as to exclude all ground of doubt" (Descartes 1996, 26). Descartes's methodological doubt is not only a clear effort at breaking with the premodern stress on tradition, but it also shows how a scientist has to seek out the certainty of material reality through a process of introspective self-erasure. Here we find one of the origins of the modern conception of neutrality as it relates to reason, education, and scientific discourse. For example, in a writing course, the teacher following these modern ideals will seek to reject his or her own prejudices and preconceptions in order to open the class up to a process of discovering new knowledge. Unlike many other chapters in this collection, I am stressing how teachers need to examine their own prejudices before they are able to take on a neutral position in the classroom. The goal then is not to cater to everyone's different identities, but rather, to push for an impartial perspective.

The conception of modern education that I am presenting here can be understood through Immanuel Kant's notion of the division of higher education between professional schools and general education, where students are supposed to learn the foundations of public reason and democratic discourse (Kant 1992). Unfortunately, this connection among modern science, reason, and education is rarely explicitly addressed. In fact, very little has been written on the topic of how the modern scientific method relates to the way educators should teach (Readings 1996). However, I argue here that we can use the principles of the scientific method to posit that instruction should also be based on the ideals of neutrality, objectivity, empiricism, and universality. In other words, teachers should try to be impartial, objective, open, and honest.

On the most fundamental level, at the heart of modern science is the notion that one must pursue truth wherever it leads, and this entails a conscious effort of eliminating all personal self-interests and cultural bias. In reading Descartes's text, we see how his constant use of self-doubt and introspection helps him to open a space for empirical analysis; in fact, his text is an autobiographical account of his effort to discover certainty through self-doubt. Of course, many people have argued that this goal for objectivity is impossible and hides vested interests, but what is important to stress is that the goals of objectivity, neutrality, and empiricism are impossible but necessary ideals. Moreover, neutrality represents an artificial practice that has to be learned and constantly monitored, and this subjective attitude represents some of the core moral values of the Enlightenment, which have helped to define modern university discourse (Readings 1996: Lacan 2007).

My argument, therefore, is that a fundamental aspect of all higher education is the underlying belief that one should follow truth wherever its leads one, and that in order to pursue this ideal, one has to be self-critical about one's own prejudices and self-interests. From this perspective, neutrality in research and teaching both rely on the combination of self-effacement and the pursuit of empirical evidence. However, with the recent growth of identity politics on the Left and the Right, this notion of neutrality has been challenged. For instance, many scholars and activists on the Left have argued that only privileged wealthy White men can pretend to be neutral and unbiased (Grossberg 1996). Moreover, Elizabeth Wardle and Doug Downs have argued that in the field of composition, neutrality and universality are impossible because there is no such thing as unmotivated writing (Wardle and Downs 2014, 277). Asao B. Inoue adds that the universal and neutral prose that we try to instill in students actually represent the values and ideas of White middle-class culture (2014, 84). Moreover, several of the authors in this present book—see Brewer, chapter 1; Evans, chapter 2; and Lichty and Rosenberg, chapter 8—argue that teachers should stress the specific identities of their students and the instructor. Yet, I am arguing that the principles of neutrality and universality represent a bias against all biases. In other words, the European White males who first promoted the ideas of neutrality and universality undermined their own positions of authority by producing a discourse suspending all privileges.

I stress that I am not endorsing the idea that all opinions or views should be endorsed or tolerated: we should teach students that everyone is entitled to their own opinions, but they are not entitled to their own facts. What we need to pursue in both our teaching and research are facts, and we have to resist injecting opinions into our academic discourse. Once again, this is very hard to do and may be an impossible ideal, but we still need to strive to promote a culture of empirical evidence. By examining our own prejudices and ideological commitments, we can work on suspending them in our scholarly activities.

In terms of teaching, neutrality helps the teacher present material in an unbiased and objective way, and it also prevents the students from simply rejecting knowledge because they do not like the beliefs or the politics of the teacher. Just as it is difficult for the scientist to remain neutral and avoid all prejudices, it takes great effort for a teacher to use introspection to avoid bias. In fact, I have used my training as a psychoanalyst to help me try to attain and maintain neutrality in the classroom, and this turn to psychoanalysis can aid us in our efforts at understanding why neutrality is necessary in teaching.

FREUD, NEUTRALITY, AND FREE ASSOCIATION

It is interesting to note that Freud's conception of the neutrality of the analyst dovetails with many of Descartes's arguments about the scientific method. Freud believed that the analyst should also suspend any preconceptions and develop a free-floating attention so that the patient could be free to express whatever came to his or her mind (Greenberg 1986). The neutrality of the analyst then helped allow for the free associations of the patient, and in this new form of discourse, the analyst attempted to remove himself or herself from the "normal" mode of communication in which the speaker engages in self-censorship and selective memory in order to influence or bond with the listener. In fact, once Freud stopped sitting face-to-face with his patients, he realized that they were better able to speak without trying to impress him or censor their illicit thoughts.

Freud also believed that the analyst should never play the role of the parent or the authority or the savior. In order to allow for the maximum freedom of the patient to express himself or herself, Freud constantly moved away from his early position of being the "one who knows." Freud realized that if interpretations came only from the analyst, not only would the patient become dependent, but the patient would reject the knowledge as being imposed or unconvincing. For instance, Freud discovered that people only really allowed a new perspective to change their behavior if they thought the new idea came from themselves. Freud also affirmed that the true driving force behind science was the affirmation of a lack of knowledge, which can be seen as playing the same role as doubt in Descartes's discourse. In fact, in *Totem and Taboo*, Freud writes "that the scientific view of the universe no longer affords any room for human omnipotence; men have acknowledged their smallness and have submitted resignedly to death and to other necessities of nature" (Freud 1950, 88). Freud is arguing here that in past forms of culture (animism and religion), people believed in the power of their ideas to shape reality, but with modern science, one has to give up the belief in omnipotent knowledge. Thus, in opposition to the current focus on the all-knowing scientist, Freud and Descartes believed that a discourse of discovery must begin with a declaration of non-knowledge.

TEACHING, CONTINGENCY, NEUTRALITY, AND IDEOLOGY

In terms of teaching, I have found that one can help to keep an open discourse by following this psychoanalytic theory of neutrality because students are often quick either to conform to what they think the teacher wants them to think, or to rebel against a teacher with a different ideology or value system. After all, our education system socializes students from a very early age to figure out what the teacher values and desires. Especially in the context of a competitive grading system, students will often conform to the teacher from a position of cynicism (Samuels 2017). In other words, they have been trained that if they want to get good grades, they should tell the teacher what the teacher wants to hear, even if they do not understand what they are learning or they do not believe in the value of the knowledge they are internalizing. According to this logic, if you want to use the classroom to influence students' political beliefs, you may get students to comply with your ideas on a test, but once they walk out of the classroom, they may walk away from those ideas.

When it comes to the vulnerability of non-tenured faculty, not only is it ineffective to try to convince students of political values or ideas, but students will often use evaluations to get revenge on teachers who they think have the wrong ideology or who are seen as being too forceful in their expression of political beliefs. Often, it will be hard to detect that students are responding to their perceptions of the teacher's ideology because the students might simply give a low evaluation grade or make a comment about something else. I have found that there is a psychological tendency in many students that makes them defensive about any political argument leading to a sense of personal guilt, shame, or anxiety. In the age of new media narcissism and political polarization, students may experience any political critique as an attack on their self-esteem and personal identity.

I have also found that many conservative students feel like they are victimized minorities on campus because they believe they are surrounded by people who do not respect or value their political beliefs. Moreover, conservatives have been arguing for forty years that they are the victims of taxes, government regulation, and liberal culture, and so they are sensitive to anything that can be read as a rejection of their politics. For example, I once had a very staunch conservative in my course who told me that he refused to speak in class because he knew that the liberals would only attack him. I have also noticed that many conservative students accuse their teachers of bias, even if those teachers make a conscious effort to repress their own beliefs in the classroom.

From the opposite perspective, I have seen Leftist students attack teachers for not being sufficiently politically correct. For example, in one of my classes, a student responded to almost anything I said about science, objectivity, and empiricism with the argument that my views should be rejected because I am a White male, and by definition, I must be biased. Here we see one of the possible downsides of an extreme form of identity politics; there is no possibility for neutrality since every person is defined by his or her group interests. While I would not deny that people are full of self-interest and hidden prejudices, the idea of modern neutrality is to try to avoid these biases through introspection and self-criticism. However, many students with strong political beliefs have a hard time pursuing neutrality, and they see modern reason as just one strategy belonging to one group (White male Europeans).

In this tense educational environment, the desire of contingent faculty to remain as neutral as possible may not only help to save their jobs but could also allow for a more open discussion with fewer students simply reacting to the perceived politics of the teacher. Although I would not deny that all knowledge is shaped by its historical, cultural, and institutional context, it is still possible to seek to expose these social forces as one directs one's efforts towards developing a more neutral approach.

I am not arguing here that educators should not involve themselves in the political arena outside of the classroom; rather, their teaching and research should always attempt to be objective and neutral because without this effort to follow the necessary but impossible ideals of reason, we will end up devaluing science, education, and rationality. If we want to introduce our students to university thinking, reading, and writing, then it is essential to discuss with them the underlying ethical ideals that shape the modern investment in neutrality, objectivity, and reason.

Moreover, even though many people now argue that modern science is without any moral foundation, I would affirm that the goal of being open, honest, unbiased, rational, and empirical are very important ethical attitudes shaping secular humanism. The problem is that we rarely discuss these ideals with our students in an open and honest way, and so we need to present the modern principles of universality, neutrality, and objectivity as ethical and moral notions.

THE CRITIQUE OF NEUTRALITY

It is important to note that my call for pedagogical neutrality will probably be met with the same type of criticism that has occurred in the context of Freud's original notion of analytic neutrality. Many post-Freudian schools of analysis have argued that Freud neglected intersubjectivity, and his focus on reason, science, and objectivity represented a Western and masculine bias. In particular, female analysts have contended that the Freudian model privileges reason over emotion and individuality over community, and so they have developed theories and practices that focus on the affective relationship between the analyst and the patient (Chodorow 1989). I would argue that the problem with this response to neutrality is that it fails to see that psychoanalysis relies on an artificial environment founded on the necessary but impossible ideals of reason, freedom, neutrality, objectivity, and universality. It is, then, essential to stress that neutrality is not a natural relationship or attitude; rather, it is an artificial practice, which has to be learned and maintained (Kopelson 2003). Furthermore, it is vital to emphasize that the type of neutrality I am discussing here has more to do with the teacher's attitude and method of analysis than the content of the course. In other words, neutrality represents an effort to approach each subject with an open mind, but this can only be done through introspection and radical self-criticism. The idea here is not to deny the importance of discrimination and prejudice; rather, the goal is to seek to reduce their power through self-awareness.

Another criticism against neutrality from within and outside of psychoanalysis is that it represents a Eurocentric bias that discounts other cultural beliefs and values. From this perspective, nothing is really neutral, and the claim of neutrality just serves to hide undisclosed special interests. For instance, it is argued that ideals of neutrality, objectivity, and individual freedom are really based on the self-definition of European Protestant middle-class capitalists who sought to break away from the power of the feudal lord, the monarch, and the Catholic

Church (Pagden 2013). Yet, even if this is true, it is still possible that these biased philosophers and political actors ended up valorizing a set of ideals that transcended their own personal and group interests. In other words, neutrality is an empty universal that worked against the interest and biases of the White European males who promoted it.

Not only then is neutrality a bias that undermines all biases, but we can also consider neutrality to be a key ideal of our democratic institutions. After all, the notions of "one person one vote," due process, and universal human rights rely on the ideal of universal neutrality. Since the legal system is supposed to be neutral and unbiased, one can critique it when it fails to live up to its ideals. One can also criticize our political system when it is undermined by special interests, and one should condemn our education system for creating a system in which most of the faculty do not have the same rights and privileges as tenured professors.

INSTITUTING BIAS

Since the majority of instructors are not able to vote in their faculty senates or departments, we have created a situation in which the values and practices of higher education are being undermined from within. In the context of the overreliance on non-tenured faculty, we have subjected teachers to a system of evaluation that makes it hard for them to teach in an objective and neutral way. Since these vulnerable instructors know that students often like to be entertained by teachers who give high grades without demanding much work, non-tenured faculty have a strong incentive to stay away from challenging subject matters and from engaging with their students in an open and honest way. Neutrality, here, is threatened because the contingent faculty members must please the students, and this often means not pursuing truth for truth's sake.

Of course, a conflict arises when a teacher is discussing a subject with students that has an explicit political content. Here, it appears to be impossible to be neutral because one is engaged in ideas and events that are highly divisive in a polarized world. In this difficult situation, I still believe that it is possible to try to present the materials with a conscious effort to exclude one's own beliefs and biases. Through introspection and self-criticism, one should seek to allow for a discourse that does not place the teacher in the position of the only person who knows the truth. Furthermore, in the field ofrhetoric and composition, it may be much easier to avoid being identified with a particular political ideology, since one can focus on the form and not the content of discourse. In other terms, by stressing grammar, rhetoric, process, organization, genre, transfer, and metacognition, non-tenured composition faculty can stay away from divisive issues as they make sure that writing remains the focus of their courses.

This distinction of form and content will push some to claim that it is impossible to teach the formal aspects of writing without also engaging in some content, and this argument is true, but one can still make sure that students understand the emphasis is placed on how people communicate in specific contexts using particular formats and appropriate rhetorical devices. In this type of instruction, we see how composition plays a key role in presenting the modern ideals of neutrality, objectivity, and method. This approach also fights against the conservative claim that liberal faculty no longer teach the important values of reason, individual freedom, and open-mindedness (D'Souza 1991).

Essential to my notion of neutrality, then, is a dialectical relationship between the modern quest for universality and the postmodern emphasis on cultural and historical differences. The goal here is not to declare the need for a colorblind society or affirm a post-prejudice state; instead, I want to point to how the universal is always being expanded by the inclusion of new protected categories, and this expansion is fueled by postmodern minority-based social movements. Yet, I also want to stress the need to separate what a teacher does in a course and what happens outside of the classroom; although I do not think a teacher should advocate for a particular political position while teaching, we should reconceive service as including public advocacy.

ACADEMIC FREEDOM AND CONTINGENCY

I began to think about this distinction between service and teaching when I was at a conference on academic freedom. The speakers at the main forum were all very secure tenured faculty, and they were all speaking about how they were victimized by outside forces commenting on their scholarship and public pronouncements. Even though none of these faculty members lost their jobs, they stressed how vulnerable they felt. As one of the few non-tenured faculty members in the room, I couldn't help to think about all of the contingent teachers I have known or read about who lost their jobs for what they had said outside of the classroom. In fact, I got involved in union politics because my first review by my chair was based mainly on a letter I wrote to the school newspaper questioning the value of student evaluations. Here, we see how non-tenured faculty are particularly vulnerable because of their lack of academic freedom outside of the classroom in the area that I am now calling service.

Once again, my point is that all faculty should have their academic freedom protected (Bérubé and Ruth 2015), but it is especially important for non-tenure-track faculty who often have no recourse to due process to protect their jobs against unfair accusations. For example, when I asked my chair why she wrote in my review that she was worried that I was using my classroom for political indoctrination, I questioned how she came to this conclusion. After all, politics were not mentioned in the peer review of my teaching or any of the narratives in my student evaluations. She responded that my editorial revealed my politics, and she added that I used the word "postmodernism" in several of my course descriptions, and she knew that this term usually referred to graduate students using the classroom to indoctrinate students into Left-wing ideology. I responded to her by asking her if she had read any of my books and articles on this subject because I clearly articulated how I define postmodernity. She told me that she did not examine my work, and I believe she relied on her own prejudices to interpret my teaching.

Luckily in the University of California system, we have a good contract protecting the rights of non-tenure-track faculty against a lack of due process, but most other untenured faculty do not have any protections, and they now make up the majority of the faculty in American higher education. Moreover, even with our comprehensive contract, every year we run into several cases in which lecturers are dismissed or denied a merit raise because of student evaluations, or for some undisclosed reason. In other words, faculty are not being reviewed in a neutral way.

What is so disheartening is that even though the vast majority of faculty do not have their academic freedom protected by tenure, many tenured professors act as if this problem does not affect these vulnerable faculty members. However, if most people are denied basic rights and protections, how can our institutions of higher education continue to pursue truth for truth's sake? Moreover, in many cases, the decrease of faculty with tenure has resulted in an increase in administrators with a very different set of values and goals. Since most faculty have been denied the right of shared governance, universities and colleges have been forced to rely on business-minded administrators who often focus on reputation management, and these administrators often waste no time letting go of non-tenured faculty who make a controversial tweet or engage in a campus protest.

The few tenured professors who have lost their jobs due to controversial activities have received most of the headlines, but every year, an unknown number of non-tenure-track faculty are let go without any reason or public attention. This failure to protect these vulnerable faculty members against political intimidation has undermined the entire edifice of American higher education. Although many people now see tenure as a purely personal right, it was originally conceived as a collective necessity based on the need to protect faculty against unwarranted dismissals centered on the political bias of powerful administrators. One guiding idea behind tenure was that faculty should be free to pursue truth in their teaching and research without fear of political intimidation, but now that most people do not have tenure, it has often devolved into a marker of privilege and has lost its connection to the values of neutrality, objectivity, and universality.

Of course, the term *university* is itself derived from *universality* because the central idea behind modern education is that all people have the ability to use reason to discover a shared empirical reality. Once again, this ideal can be criticized and shown to be lacking in many instances, but it still is an important goal that is now threatened by the way most faculty are treated. How can we expect teachers to remain neutral and unbiased when their own institutions treat them so badly? These vulnerable teachers experience on a daily basis the effects of a political and economic system centered on perpetuating inequality, and yet, I do not think that it helps these faculty members to discuss their plight in their classrooms, even if students remain completely ignorant about the labor structures shaping their education. What these faculty members should be doing is to fight to change institutional hierarchies through collective action and public advocacy (service). Moreover, faculty should be rewarded and not punished for their political advocacy for higher education outside of the classroom.

I have been therefore arguing for a clear separation between teaching and research on the one side and public advocacy and service on the other side. While neutrality should be the central force in teaching and research, advocacy always requires a particular perspective and position. These differences need to be clearly defined and protected, and we have to see them as necessary but impossible ideals that are worth defending and pursuing. On one level, some conservative critiques are right to challenge political bias in the classroom, but their total lack of concern for the vulnerability of the majority of most faculty shows that they are not really interested in protecting freedom, neutrality, and open discourse. They often want to demonize higher education in order to justify defunding it and to show how even the wealthiest Americans are victims of liberal culture. Instead of defending our right to politicize the classroom, we should promote neutrality in teaching and research, while we defend the right for public advocacy outside of the classroom.

To help protect neutrality in the classroom, administrators and faculty need to work together to reduce the role played by student evaluations in the assessment of contingent instructors. It is also necessary to include all faculty in shared governance and make sure that every teacher has his or her academic freedom protected. On a more fundamental basis, we have to affirm the value of scientific neutrality as the foundation of the modern university, and we also need to clearly communicate this foundational value to our students.

REFERENCES

Bérubé, Michael, and Jennifer Ruth. 2015. *The Humanities, Higher Education, and Academic Freedom: Three Necessary Arguments*. New York: Palgrave Macmillan.

Bradley, Gwendolyn. 2004. "Contingent Faculty and the New Academic Labor System." *Academe* 90 (1): 28–31.

Chodorow, Nancy J. 1989. *Feminism and Psychoanalytic Theory*. New Haven, CT: Yale University Press.

Descartes, René. 1996. *Discourse on the Method, and, Meditations on First Philosophy*. New Haven, CT: Yale University Press.

D'Souza, Dinesh. 1991. *Illiberal Education: The Politics of Race and Sex on Campus*. New York: Simon and Schuster.

Freud, Sigmund. 1950. "Totem and Taboo." Trans. J. Strachey. New York: W. W. Norton.

Greenberg, Jay R. 1986. "Theoretical Models and the Analyst's Neutrality." *Contemporary Psychoanalysis* 22 (1): 87–106.

Grossberg, Lawrence. 1996. "Identity and Cultural Studies: Is That All There Is." In *Questions of Cultural Identity*, ed. Stuart Hall and Paul Du Gay, 87–107. Thousand Oaks, CA: Sage.

Inoue, Asao B. 2014. "A Grade-Less Writing Course That Focuses on Labor and Assessing." In *First-Year Composition: From Theory to Practice*, eds. Deborah Coxwell-Teague and Ronald F. Lunsford, 77–110. Anderson, SC: Parlor Press.

Kant, Immanuel. 1992. *The Conflict of the Faculties (Der Streit der Fakultaten)*. Lincoln, NE: University of Nebraska Press.

Kopelson, Karen. 2003. "Rhetoric on the Edge of Cunning; Or, the Performance of Neutrality (Re)Considered as a Composition Pedagogy for Student Resistance." *College Composition and Communication*, 55 (1): 115–146.

Lacan, Jacques. 2007. *The Other Side of Psychoanalysis*. New York: W. W. Norton.

Langen, Jill M. 2011. "Evaluation of Adjunct Faculty in Higher Education Institutions." *Assessment and Evaluation in Higher Education* 36 (2): 185–196.

Pagden, Anthony. 2013. *The Enlightenment: And Why It Still Matters*. New York: Random House.

Readings, Bill. 1996. *The University in Ruins*. Cambridge, MA: Harvard University Press.

Samuels, Robert. 2017. *Educating Inequality: Beyond the Political Myths of Higher Education and the Job Market*. New York: Routledge.

Wardle, Elizabeth and Doug Downs. 2014. "Looking into Writing-about-Writing Classrooms." In *First-Year Composition: From Theory to Practice*, eds. Deborah Coxwell-Teague and Ronald F. Lunsford, 276–320. Anderson, SC: Parlor Press.

5

THE NON-CONTROVERSY AND CONTROVERSY OF NEUTRALITY
A Conversation with John Trimbur

Daniel P. Richards

Aside from admiring his work for years but only from afar,[1] I wanted to sit down with John Trimbur—well, we actually used FaceTime—to get some perspective on the nature of neutrality from a longstanding member of the field (but not of CCCC—more on that below), specifically one involved in the responses to Maxine Hairston after the publication of her 1992 *CCC* article, "Diversity, Ideology, and Teaching Writing."[2] I wanted to see how and if his thinking had changed and how the conversation between Hairston and others in the pages of a major journal manifests today. As you'll read, John is quick to point out that he and Hairston were friends and the disagreement was less about conservative versus liberal and more about a "beef" between liberals and radicals—what he phrases as "shades of liberalism."

When I asked him what he thought of Paulo Freire's notion that there is no such thing as a neutral educational process, he deemed it a non-controversial statement: "I think, to start, for me, the university is not neutral. It is pro-capitalist. They are non-profits increasingly run as a market model. To then say it is a free marketplace of ideas is to naturalize that." This very much reads as Freirean, taking an institutional vision of the university as an economic force and function in society. That said, John also reveals that he thinks that the primary political activity of a professor goes beyond the classroom. He shares an example of a colleague of his at Emerson who wore a "Fuck Trump" shirt on campus and explains why he thinks it wasn't such a good idea. In keeping with the theme of the present book, there is nuance between the ineluctable non-neutrality of the university as an increasingly capitalist enterprise and campus "manners."

Trimbur also expresses deep concern with how the business-like ideology may have infiltrated such organizations as NCTE and CCCC,

DOI: 10.7330/9781607329992.c005

specifically with the capacity of each organization to make an official statement affirming academic freedom when issues arising from controversies such as the Steven Salaita case come to bear on our field. Trimbur explains that he is no longer a member of CCCC for this and other reasons and thus could not really comment on what he sees as the main areas of public contention in the field now. I'll let him speak more for himself through the transcript below as well as in the chapter for *Unruly Rhetorics* (2018) he references in the interview, which has since been published.[3] This chapter follows along with Trimbur's longstanding concern to write about the implications of politics and political allegiances. This interview has been edited for readability.

DANIEL RICHARDS (DR): I'd like to begin with a book of yours perhaps less read by our rhetoric colleagues: *A Short Guide to Writing about Chemistry*.[4] As it is coauthored with a chemistry faculty member, Herbert Beall, you no doubt received a relative crash-course into the field during the writing process (a joy, I'm sure, given your interest in collaborative learning to start your career). You also coauthored a piece in *College Teaching* with Herbert Beall[5] where you use Erving Goffman's underlife to explore the writing perspectives of chemistry students, which by and large were characterized in terms of resistance. I'm wondering if you could discuss for a bit how you think political conflict manifests differently in various disciplines. In rhetoric and composition, we have long discussed issues of student resistance and political strife in our contact zones. Do you sense teachers in the sciences share similar struggles?

JOHN TRIMBUR (JT): Couple things. I was at Worcester Polytechnic Institute (WPI) for 20 years and worked with Herb Beall on WAC/WID type stuff, which led to publications like the chemistry book, but I also worked with other engineering faculty and students. One of the graduate requirements at WPI was to do a junior-year project, three-quarters of a year long, that integrated science, technology, and society. I advised a number of those, including going to London and Puerto Rico, where students would work with nonprofits, government agencies, some private companies. Laying out bike paths was a typical project, or developing IT programs for nonprofits that didn't have the resources. So, against that background—the politics are different. One issue is how readily engineering and science students identify with professional expertise. In the projects that we did, it took a while for the students to get a sense that there were multiple stakeholders, because there was a sense that there was a problem, and professional people solve problems. Research done at an engineering school found that engineering students didn't like problem formulation—they wanted to go directly to the solution. That is one way of talking about what I was seeing: the politics were skipping over politics. In that sense, it relates to the issue of neutrality because

WPI students really did think that neutral technocratic forces were able to fix things. There was the "give back to the community" rhetoric but often students had a hard time seeing conflicts rather than problems. They didn't have the patience to go through the kinds of writing that were analytical or interpretive. That is when it dawned on me that being dismissive of certain kinds of writing coming out of humanities and the social sciences—thinking it was "splitting hairs" or "reading too much" into it, that kind of thing—you wouldn't have to worry about a lot of things if you just solved the problems. But for the students, this dismissal was also a form of alienation, and was disempowering, because what it ultimately meant was that they were being trained for midlevel management, and it was the kids who went to elite schools and majored in semiotics who were going to be their bosses and who knew how to formulate problems, to do interpretive work. That is how I'd explain my experience there.

DR: At some point you'd think that people less prone to think about politics self-select into these disciplines anyway, right? Are the disciplinary differences the lack of texts and textual interpretation, or how much is just epistemology of how knowledge is made? Thinking about student resistance in rhetoric and composition—and about how composition is a middle-class enterprise—getting students to be critical of the very system they are benefiting from seems to be problematic in engineering and business.

JT: Where it broke down a little bit was that there was no required first-year composition course at WPI. I just taught electives. Do you know that piece by Carl Herndl, Barbara Fennell, and Carolyn Miller about Three Mile Island and the *Challenger* disaster?[6] I think it was through looking at the actual memos that were being passed back and forth, that students began to see there really were conflicts in the workplace. That's one way to begin a critical professionalism. They have to see it through the experience of people on the ground.

DR: Karen Kopelson writes that students "come to us believing that academia is the quintessential realm of objectivity, that anything overtly political or opinionated is 'biased,' and that 'bias' is most certainly something to be avoided by authors, teachers, and other authorities."[7] It seems that most people outside universities expect the professoriate to be unbiased. Why? Where does this notion come from? What do you chalk this up to?

JT: Well, I think it comes from science. Over a long haul, the ideas of neutrality and objectivity are interrelated historically in the formation of modern science. I was thinking more about this: it is also about progressive initiatives going on in the university, like the raising of the question of implicit bias. I think the same set of presuppositions are there that bias—even though we all have it—is distorting, and part of what science does is remove that, and that is why methodology is critical. But then I started thinking, this is really Cartesian, as Richard Rorty would say, polishing the "mirror of the mind" in order to get more accurate reflections, to polish away that bias.[8] Cultural sensitivity trainers always talk about the work you have to do. And typically that means on an individual level, not about structural racism or sexism or xenophobia, but working on himself or herself individually.

There is no question in my mind scientists are well aware that the production of scientific knowledge operates rhetorically through persuasion. They talk all the time about telling a story when writing an article. And it is not a narrative. How are they going to get across the novelty of their findings? But at the same time they also see politics, emotion, personality, as contaminating. And, science has sold that methodology, and established that authority in the production of knowledge. In journalism, too. A lot of what we do in rhetoric is trying to show students that there is no such thing as "objectivity" but it is an achieved rhetorical effect.

DR: What do you think rhetoric and composition as a field has to contribute to our current conversations about political transparency of professors?

JT: I think things can happen through WAC/WID programs when faculty in rhetoric and composition find allies and work with other faculty, and then become influential. Through those collaborations you really can have discussions about the production of knowledge, so that is one means. But there is also the issue of how the doctrine of neutrality has become a measure employed against things that are constructed as "political correctness." That comes up with these new surveillance organizations like *Professor Watchlist* and *Canary Watch* that raise questions of free inquiry and academic freedom. What would a public campaign to see that all knowledge is situated look like? [Shared laughter.] What would a PSA be?

DR: There is the role of our field in the public intellectual conversation, versus how we're proselytizing to other fields within the university. In my experience with WAC/WID, we teach them how to teach writing in their own courses. Give them the necessary skills. But in a workshop that is five days long, the sheer epistemological conflicts are not able to be reconciled in that time frame. When you see the participants unabashedly adopt Carolyn Miller's "window pane" view of language,[9] as separate from knowledge making, you realize this is much more than a workshop. Our goal is to get them to see the value of writing, but I'd love to have larger epistemic conversations—but a lot of people in these disciplines haven't been given the training to even reflect on these processes in their field. Even from an early graduate level, they've come so far unreflectively.

But I am interested in your opinion on *Professor Watchlist*, which is co-opting this idea of neutrality as a method of surveillance, and in our field—which lacks political diversity, I think that is fair to say—it seems that our field has coded neutrality to mean a conservative ideology, because, perhaps, it has been co-opted by conservative groups. What can we do to educate on the public perception of what it means to teach in the humanities? I'm not sure how that happens.

JT: I think the lever there is one of negotiating differences. That is the civic role of rhetoric. And I think that has potential public appeal. That it is not the old humanistic approach of inculcating value and cultivating sensibility, cultivating taste—it is not that. I think that the idea of engaging cultural, linguistic, and ideological differences is a mission of rhetoric. There is some public sympathy for that role of rhetoric, which is undercut to some degree by "What can you do with that?" and the anxiety about college costs, loans, and the general precariousness of people coming out of college with degrees or having spent time in college without getting a degree, which is a significant percentage. So, I think the role of the humanities is being undermined by this market mentality. I see it on the level of individual students who want to change their major from marketing to a BFA in creative writing. Their parents—because they love them [laughs]—are fearful. Or the kids whose parents want them to go to med school but who really want to major in medical anthropology. I think that the market has put constraints on people's sense of possibilities, the way it is bearing down. So, I think bringing back non-market ways of thinking, more public thinking, is critical. The health debate ("Medicare for all") is about that in a lot of ways, where the public can see things in terms of the public good.

DR: I want to circle back to Maxine Hairston's 1992 article "Diversity, Ideology, and Teaching Writing" (CCC 43.2) and the subsequent responses the following year (CCC 44.2). So, do you see that attitude manifesting in our field, at conferences, in our journals?

JT: This was really a beef between liberals and radicals. There is no question that Maxine's values are not neoliberal, but old Democratic Party, New Deal liberalism—Ann Richards style. It was partly a generational thing. I think it was two readings of diversity. Maxine had the dominant liberal—and I think it is still dominant—view of diversity as "sharing time in the metropolis." That has now become institutionalized and taken up by higher education and corporations, a cosmopolitan vision of multiculturalism and a celebration of different identities. In retrospect, the people that Maxine called out—me, Jim Berlin, Pat Bizzell, Dick Ohmann, and others—for politicizing the composition classroom were interested not just in these cultural differences but in understanding the conflicts that arose from them and how conflicting perspectives could be negotiated in the classroom. I think Maxine didn't want there to be conflict in the classroom. So I think there was a polite, middle-class fear of the unruly, the impolite, what might bubble up, and we should all just respect each other and take turns speaking.

Like most controversies in composition, this never got resolved. The graduate students at Emerson are always asking, "Well what happened in the debate with Maxine? What happened in the taxonomy wars? Who won? Did social construction or cognitivism or expressivism win?" It is not like that—it just *stops*. I think Maxine's worldview is still dominant in

CCCC, but there has also been more self-reflective work on how you deal with conflict in the classroom, and how can you manage what seems to be risky and threatening about it.

DR: If the field doesn't resolve these issues, necessarily, do you see any manifestations of these now? Or do you see them as so internalized and calcified in the field that it is not really an active conversation?

JT: I haven't been to CCCC in the last couple of years, but my sense is that the liberal/neoliberal diversity has become a dominant ideology. And that has certain kinds of limits. One example is the Steven Salaita case, when his appointment at the University of Illinois at Urbana Champaign (UIUC) was rescinded because of Salaita's impassioned tweets protesting the Israeli military attack on Gaza in 2014. There was a group of people trying to get CCCC and NCTE to make a statement, as AAUP, MLA, and other professional associations did, about how UIUC had violated norms of academic freedom and fair hiring practices. It was clear to us that the organization was very uncomfortable about making a public statement. It was also clear that the civility doctrine UIUC applied to Salaita fed into ideas of faculty neutrality, offering a method to examine faculty discourse performances. The interactions we had with the executive committee made it obvious they didn't see what was in the Salaita case for CCCC and that any association was potentially damaging to the organization's brand. I'm not a member of CCCC anymore. A number of us decided not to renew our memberships.

DR: Do you feel comfortable talking about that?

JT: Yes, absolutely. I've tried to tell the story in the collection *Unruly Rhetorics*, edited by Jonathan Alexander, Susan Jarratt, and Nancy Welch, that was recently published. At first I thought not renewing my NCTE/CCCC membership was simply a personal matter because I felt fed up. But then I realized there were another ten or eleven people who did the same thing, so that it constituted kind of a moment, and by 2016 we did get the issue into the executive committee, there was a discussion about it. Nothing happened and nothing is going to happen. But it did raise the question of what is the organization's capacity to make statements about public issues in a way that MLA or AAUP does.

DR: Wait, are these things connected? Questioning the capacity of CCCC and not renewing memberships and the Salaita case?

JT: That's what it turned into. We just wanted CCCC or NCTE to make a statement about the Salaita case. NCTE did make a statement on academic freedom in November 2014. This was a very weak statement and clearly avoided any mention of the Salaita case. We also asked the editors of *CCC* and *College English* to publish an open letter explaining why we didn't renew our memberships and what we thought was at stake in the Salaita case. They declined to do so, though Jonathan Alexander did bring the issue to the *CCC* editorial board about the capacity of the organization to respond to pressing issues. There was also a roundtable at the 2017 CCCC, organized by Bruce Horner, that was about the capacity of the organization to respond to public issues. That issue keeps floating around, and inevitably raises questions about neutrality and CCCC's public face.

DR: That circles back to the previous question about Hairston. You mentioned civility, the kind of safer liberalism, one where inclusion is institutionalized but not intended to provoke conflict, so it seems like in a way, I'm thinking about myself as junior faculty going to CCCC and going as a graduate student and not seeing the type of conflict we would read about in graduate school that seemed to happen so much in the 1980s and 1990s, and now going now and seeing the debates as relatively innocuous. It made me think, was that just the specific postmodern moment, or was that just because that type of liberalism has become institutionalized? In the sense that it *is* the organization now? From my perspective, it's not that I was craving a free-for-all or anything . . . [shared laughter].

JT: Right! Where's the beef?

DR: Exactly, right? We present, we all agree with it, and we all go home. That kind of consensus I know is performative because I know a lot of people who don't subscribe to the actions and behaviors or presentations or keynotes or anything like that. So anyway, that's a whole other conversation. I'm looking forward to that collection. So the most recent CCCC in Kansas City, the statement that was released for that.[10] I was thinking about that. For the nature of this collection we have to put some scope on it. Neutrality is this amorphous concept. It is interesting to think about NCTE and CCCC as operating within that more conservative perspective of neutrality. For business purposes, almost.

JT: Yes, I think so.

DR: Because their decision ultimately has benefits for them financially. It is typically in the best interests in the organization to stay conservative. Hey, maybe neoliberalism has infected us, too. Let's move on for the sake of time. So when you hear Paulo Freire's *Pedagogy of the Oppressed* and you read his assertion that there is no such thing as a neutral education process, is it fitting that we adopt that mentality to our specific postsecondary moment?

JT: Yes. That's a noncontroversial statement.

DR: In what way?

JT: I think people recognize that. Another formulation that is similar but not so loaded politically, was the argument that Ken Bruffee would always make, or a way of thinking, which is "how we teach is what we teach," which emerged out of his rethinking of classroom practices and how collaborative learning fit in. But, I think, to start, for me, the university is not neutral. It is procapitalist. They are nonprofits increasingly run on a market model. To then say the university is a free marketplace of ideas is to naturalize that model and put it off the agenda.

For me the biggest revelation of non-neutrality occurred in the late 1990s, when I realized I had been teaching and enacting an English-only language policy for about thirty years. Another non-neutral way in which colleges and universities operate is the tacit policy that English is the only means of teaching and learning. That has been a lot of my preoccupation over the last twenty years, about language politics in composition and higher education in general. I feel like I'm not neutral, for example, in the way we talk about the writing classes at Emerson, that we think we're teaching writing, we're not teaching English. We recognize that students write in languages other than English and have sections set up for students who want to compose in multiple languages. That's why I think these questions could be put another way: is there anything good about neutrality? [Laughs.] All that I'm seeing is what neutrality is being used to screen. But I would also say there are positive political uses of neutrality. Here I am thinking of the whole neutral nation, non-aligned nations movement during the Cold War era, symbolized by the Bandung Conference of 1955, where Indonesia, Egypt, and other countries emerging out of colonialism—India, Pakistan—were trying to find a non-aligned but anti-imperialist place in the Cold War world. I don't want to give the impression that this kind of neutrality is false consciousness, you know . . .

DR: Well, you know, this entire collection . . . I have visions of writing a conclusion where it almost seems more useful, the very presence of the term "neutrality" seems to cause more harm than good. In the sense that it is generating some false sense of what is possible.

JT: Yes.

DR: But also to me this is where the term breaks down. You're talking about your English-only class, which was the presumption . . .

JT: Like I had no idea . . .

DR: And I'm curious to see thirty years from now the assumptions we make . . . I'm sure I have many of them. But the idea of English-language-only instruction is deemed to be neutral by specific parties, in the sense it would be naturalized in a more conservative mindset—"Well of course, higher education serves a larger social function of serving the community"—so it almost seems as though neutrality is unproductive because whatever is naturalized in our own estimation seems to be rendered neutral, as opposed to through consensus.

JT: I think so, yes, yes.

DR: So then it gets deployed in manipulative ways to normalize what your own specific ideology is, or to downplay those of others. Makes me think about a question I have here on what comes to mind when you hear the word "neutrality," and I think we've addressed that. But when I say the topic to another person they typically cringe, either because they don't think it is possible or because it is some sort of artificial construction based upon a modernist past. But the main goals of the collection [in the present volume] is to add nuance to the conversation about what people mean when they say "neutrality," in the sense that a lot of universities have statements of political neutrality. Of course, it is a public university, so they would never advocate one specific person or party all the way from municipal to federal. And, of course, they would say that—and of course you would want that. But you were talking about how Freire's statement is non-controversial because universities subscribe to some sort of market ideology, but that to me is where the neutrality conversation becomes unproductive: in a lack of distinction between what Freire was talking about—the larger ideology of social structures—versus the actual professor wearing a pin on his lapel in 2016. Those are two different types of conversations. And it seems as though when rhetoricians speak of politics we discuss it on an ideological or organizational, Foucauldian level, and we see that everything is innately political in that respect, but that doesn't necessarily help us think about if we're going to be rah-rah for Hillary Clinton in our classroom. Those strike me as two fundamentally different conversations but they get conflated. So how do we avoid that? Or should we avoid it?

JT: I think that is a real issue. I remember once in the 1990s, around the cultural-studies moment, I gave a talk at some graduate program, and we were talking about the grad students' goals of their writing courses and one said their goal is to show students how they're implicated in the "death machine." [Shared laughter.] And I thought, "Aw, that's so sweet, but . . ." So I think there is—and I'm not sure if this is me or a normal leftist position—but my position for a long time has been that, while it is true that education and teaching are all political activities in the most general sense and must be dealt with as political realities, I think it is a mistake for leftist teachers to think about teaching as their primary political work. And that is not to say that I think you should be neutral, but you have to work through your discipline, in the sense of exploring the political issues that not only you individually but the work in a field of study raises. For example, Emerson College, where I teach, is a left-liberal university. But on November 9, 2016, the day after Trump's election, one of our MFA instructors comes to class with a "Fuck Trump" t-shirt on. I mean, I went to class, students were crying, it was very emotional, and we had lots of discussion. But it was a mistake, I think, to wear the "Fuck Trump" t-shirt.

DR: *Why?*

JT: Because—well, that's the question. Everybody knew right away that it was a mistake. In the most local sense, we knew there were going to be a lot of discussions in classes, that students were upset. We were worried that the processing that faculty felt they should do with their students would also make either Trump supporters or students from Trump-supporting families feel stigmatized. And, so I think that the "Fuck Trump" t-shirt was bad manners, in that sense. But, I totally get it.

DR: So, you were talking about filtering politics through your discipline, would that essentially mean, when you have a student who makes a controversial or neo-Nazi argument, let's say, by filtering through your discipline do you mean to ask them to think about their statement rhetorically, and ask them to think about why it is valid?

JT: Usually, I rely on some simplified version of Toulmin's notion of warrants: What's the argument? What are the underlying assumptions that enable you to connect claims and evidence? How do these assumptions compare to assumptions others might have? What are the advantages and disadvantages, to whom? I'm teaching a class on transnational English currently, and we were reading about the West Indian migrations to the UK in the 1950s, when, one student brought up the idea that West Indians were taking away jobs from White workers. There were some empirical things I could say, such as the West Indian migration resulted from labor shortages following WWII. Then other students began to talk about how race has been used to divide workers. All of that somehow is to me the pedagogical question: How do you go from the first student's statement without correcting or calling him out to enable a conversation that explores and negotiates those differences?

DR: The challenge here—if we're doing Toulmin or Rogerian argument or whichever structure we teach—is that these structures are political as well, so you're filtering through the very idea of warrants, the validity of assertions, and so on. There are some students we have where these ideas themselves are impinging on their ideology, including students from a religious background, in that we are restricting some types of data that are useful in a specific argument. And I know of the scholars who write about religious fundamentalism in the classroom who talk about just that very thing. Even the most "neutral" forms of argument, like Toulmin, or backing up an argument with data, is a form of coercion.

JT: And I would say Toulmin is not neutral. That is a vision of knowledge production. And the tools to talk about it require students to be analytical and open to intellectual inquiry. I have taught religious fundamentalist students who want to do term papers disproving the virgin birth and Nation of Islam students who want to prove it's wrong to eat pork—which to me are both matters of religious belief. We had a case at Emerson where a student refused to read *Angels in America* because he already knew it was sinful. I felt that it was not coercive to make reading the play a condition to continue in the class, or he could withdraw and go into another section another semester. There was a way in which we couldn't be neutral about that. So, I think things that may feel coercive to students are, from another perspective, not coercive.

DR: Let's end on Dewey then [referencing prior conversation about a mutual admiration of John Dewey's work], because Dewey was my entry point into the field, and I do think his vision of pragmatism can assuage some issues. And when I read the "Habits of Minds,"[11] I see Dewey everywhere, even though he's not specifically referenced. It seems like it got framed like, Let's go to "habits" and keep things neutral. Again, that's where the term "neutral" breaks down though . . .

JT: Actually, well, I do think it is a curious rhetorical turn, to use "habits," which means avoiding something else.

DR: Right, that's how I coded that, as "Well, if we talk about external habits, then we've created some safe space distance between physicality and our specific politics." It seemed an attempt to break free from the mess of critical pedagogy.

JT: Yes, I think, yes, definitely that. Which is interesting, because there is also Bourdieu hovering over with "habitus." Which would be another way to think about and read out some similar kinds of educational situations and goals.

DR: So do you think "habits" is perhaps the way out of some of these debates or does it introduce more problems into the classroom?

JT: You know, I can say I'm only vaguely familiar with the framework, and so my initial reaction to the emergence of the term "habits," like you were saying, is trying to neutralize rhetorical behavior by renaming it. In that sense, it reminds me of the other pragmatist term that I've relied on, and still rely on, when negotiating difference: "conversation." The weakness of Rorty's "conversation" is that it doesn't really pay attention to the distribution of representational resources, and how that affects the conversation. I've been really influenced by pragmatism. It started with [Kenneth] Bruffee—I went to his Brooklyn College Institute for Training Peer Tutors in 1980 and that was where the conversation with him all started. At that time he was just starting to read Rorty, so that was going on, and then I read Dewey. I have a real fondness for the American pragmatists, but I think the limit to me is the limit of acknowledging the class-base of expertise, that there is a tendency to see a public that is separate from class structures that people can just kind of have access to. That's where the idea of "really useful knowledge" from British nineteenth-century, radical, working-class education, which was a critique of utilitarianism, has some affinities to pragmatism in certain ways, without the philosophical depth that Dewey and Rorty have, but with the class inflection that the point of knowledge is to "get out of our present troubles." I like Dewey and Rorty's epistemological moves. But, to go back to the students and their identification with professional expertise: I really am interested in critical professionalism, critical vocationalism, as a way of intersecting with undergraduates. That is not a traditional humanities approach although it does come out of the humanities.

DR: Does that relate at all to Russel Durst's notion of reflective instrumentalism?

JT: I've taught sections out of *Collision Course*[12] a lot because it deals with a problematic moment where the process movement is turning into critical pedagogy. And the case study of Sherry [Sherry Cook Stanforth] is heartbreaking, because we've all been there and we all know her and we've all done it ourselves.[13] But I think my main reservation—and this comes in part through the piece that Min-Zhan Lu and Bruce Horner did on careers[14]—is that Russel is overcorrecting. I mean, he's a good liberal, I mean self-described. One of the funniest parts in the book is when he is visiting Sherry's classroom and talking about affirmative action and the students are saying it is unfair, White people get screwed all the time, etc., etc. And he's listening, listening—Russel is an ethnographer, right. But he can't stop himself, so he stands up and says, "It's not true! I've been at committee meetings and affirmative action isn't unfair to Whites." [Laughter.]

DR: Doesn't that epitomize our roles in a lot of ways, though, right? Having to abide by the processes but just feeling like . . .

JT: Yeah, I just think it is a wonderful breakdown in ethnographic method and probably did no good—the students were probably more dismissive of it and Sherry afterwards. He just couldn't let it go—he couldn't be neutral.

DR: That I think is the microcosm of what rhetoric and composition instructors feel. Especially in ethnography, this kind of observational-type approach to teaching and not being able to interject or not knowing when. Authors talk about this strategic interjection, timely interjection, *kairos*, etc. But yeah, that is really good. So, any final thoughts? If you imagine this collection maybe being used in a graduate course in rhetoric and composition and students are thinking about neutrality, are there any final thoughts you would want to share with emerging teachers? Or new teachers? To help them think through these things? Because for this generation, the *Professor Watchlist* is normal.

JT: It is normal. And it is not going to go away at least for the coming period. What I learned from Bruffee is that it is a matter of working out what the authority of the teacher is. And I think bouncing off of the complexity that emerges when you start to talk about neutrality, and to see both what it screens and hides and what it authorizes. New teachers do worry about being biased. They know they have strong opinions. When we read, say, Richard Miller and "Fault Lines along the Contact Zones,"[15] they get frustrated because Richard never tells them what to do. He gradually discloses more information and makes things more complicated. Getting students to negotiate differences—and that is a Deweyan notion, too—that gives them a methodology to think their way out of "you're either neutral or biased"—one or the other—and that kind of plus/minus thinking doesn't help, it stymies, and leads to mood swings, that you're going to do one or the other, rather than seeing there are alternative ways of dealing with students. And then I think the key thing: textual material is central, sending students back to the text, not as a way of ensuring neutrality or absence of bias, but as a way of clarifying everybody's situation, their positionality in the whole thing, so that ultimately you could ask—at the end of collaborative learning—the question, "Why do you think people like me think that way?" Where you're not posing yourself idiosyncratically as an individual but someone who imbibes a certain kind of training, and social status, and habits, you know, non-neutral ways of doing things, that those are discussable.

DR: That seems to me to promote a certain kind of vulnerability in the classroom on the behalf of the instructor. Do you think vulnerability is key? Vulnerability can be positioned against neutrality where neutrality is something to hide behind . . .

JT: I suppose. I never experienced it that way. I think that what the students saw was getting them to talk about my discourse, not about me. I don't care how they talk about my discourse. I want them to talk about it. It would be more vulnerable for students, makes graduate students feel a higher risk, because they feel less consolidated between their authority and their discourse. And at Emerson they are largely MFA, not in doctoral programs, so they are already pulled between literary and academic worlds in terms of the way they're teaching.

DR: Thanks for your time, John. This has been really interesting.

JT: Not a problem, no—this has been very stimulating.

DR: Good. Excellent.

NOTES

1. Trimbur writes consistently on translingualism now, but readers interested in the core concerns of this collection will find value in reading through Richard Bullock and John Trimbur, eds., *The Politics of Writing Instruction: Postsecondary* (Portsmouth, NH: Boynton, 1993), and John Trimbur, "Agency and the Death of the Author: A Partial Defense of Modernism," *JAC 20*, no. 2 (2000): 283–298.

2. Maxine Hairston, "Diversity, Ideology, and Communication," *College Composition and Communication* 43, no. 2 (1992): 179–193.

3. John Trimbur, "The Steven Salaita Case: Public Rhetoric and the Political Imagination in US College Composition and Its Professional Associations," in *Unruly Rhetorics: Protest, Persuasion, and Publics*, eds. Jonathan Alexander, Susan C. Jarratt, and Nancy Welch (Pittsburgh: University of Pittsburgh Press, 2018), 183–206.

4. Herbert Beall and John Trimbur, *A Short Guide to Writing about Chemistry*, 2nd ed. (New York: Pearson, 2000).

5. Herbert Beall and John Trimbur, "Writing in Chemistry: Keys to Student Under-life," *College Teaching* 41, no. 2 (1993): 50–54.

6. Carl G. Herndl, Barbara A. Fennell, and Carolyn R. Miller, "Understanding Failures in Organizational Discourse: The Accident at Three Mile Island and the Challenger Shuttle Disaster," in *Textual Dynamics: Historical and Contemporary Studies of Writing in Professional Communities*, ed. Charles Bazerman and James Paradis (Madison: University of Wisconsin Press, 1991), 279–305.

7. Karen Kopelson, "Rhetoric on the Edge of Cunning; Or, The Performance of Neutrality (Re)Considered as a Composition Pedagogy for Student Resistance," *College Composition and Communication* 55, no. 1 (2003): 115–146; quotation on page 117.

8. Richard Rorty, *Philosophy and the Mirror of Nature* (Princeton, NJ: Princeton University Press, 1979).

9. Carolyn R. Miller, "A Humanistic Rationale for Technical Writing," *College English* 40, no. 6 (1979): 610–617.

10. This is in reference to the "CCCC 2018 Statement on NAACP Missouri Travel Advisory," released by program chair Asao B. Inoue, viewable at cccc.ncte.org/cccc/conv /2018naacptrvadvstatement.

11. Council of Writing Program Administrators, National Council of Teachers of English, National Writing Project, *Framework for Success in Postsecondary Writing* (CWPA, NCTE, NWP, January 19, 2014).

12. Russel K. Durst, *Collision Course: Conflict, Negotiation, and Learning in College Composition* (Urbana, IL: NCTE, 1999).

13. Sherry Cook Stanforth authors chapter 7 of Russel K. Durst's *Collision Course*, tracing the conflict she and her students feel between their home and school discourses—conflict that she by her own admission would like to avoid but cannot.

14. Min-Zhan Lu and Bruce Horner, "Composing in a Global-Local Context: Careers, Mobility, Skills," *College English* 72, no. 2 (2009): 113–133.

15. Richard E. Miller, "Fault Lines in the Contact Zone," *College English* 56, no. 4 (1994): 389–408.

SECTION II

Praxis

6

STRANGERS ON THEIR OWN CAMPUS
Listening across Difference in Qualitative Research

Kelly Blewett, with Tyler S.

Teachers are expected to perform neutrality, but what Arlie Russell Hochschild calls *empathy walls* certainly exist in higher education. Hochschild defines an empathy wall as "an obstacle to deep understanding of another person, one that can make us feel indifferent or even hostile to those who hold different beliefs" (Hochschild 2016, 5). Performing neutrality may seem a way to avoid confronting difference in the classroom. Yet behind this performance, teachers may feel wary, especially if the teacher leans left politically and culturally, but senses that students—and the community surrounding the campus—lean right.

In my own qualitative study of first-year writing, a master's student in her second year of teaching writing indicated she had already tired of seeing what she regarded as the conservatism of the city in which she was teaching show up in the students' writing. To mitigate these unwelcome reminders of the gap between her own politics and those of (some) students, she decided to simply declare certain topics off limits, such as gay marriage, gun control, and political correctness. Liberal/conservative divides, in fact, dominate much of our field's discussion of student resistance, particularly as it relates to critical pedagogy (for example, Durst 1999; Greenbaum 2001; Ratcliffe 2005).

Just as Hochschild, a progressive academic from California, felt like a "stranger in her own country" when interviewing Tea Party members in Louisiana, so I argue that many teachers feel like strangers on their own campuses. Further, my contention is that the desire to ignore, quarter off, or disregard the beliefs, values, and preferred writing topics of conservative students may be heightening empathy walls within our classrooms. By instead considering how to build empathy bridges, as Hochschild proposes, we might be able to find mutual common ground, decrease fear, and increase the sense of connectedness between students and teachers. Increasing feelings of connectedness and empathy

DOI: 10.7330/9781607329992.c006

are particularly important in our current political climate, when anxiety, frustration, distrust, and contempt are rapidly circulating. I will shortly be discussing a qualitative study conducted in the fall of 2016; a few months prior, during the summer, a Pew Research Center poll indicated that more than four in ten Democrats and Republicans "perceived the other party's policies as so misguided that they pose a threat to the nation" ("Partisanship" 2016). Where can common ground be found amidst so many differences? One answer is at the site of qualitative research.

Qualitative research is less encumbered by entrenched roles and authority structures than teaching, particularly when informed by feminist methodologies that seek to challenge dominant systems of representation (Sheridan-Rabideau 2003; Kirsch and Ritchie 1995), and therefore presents different, perhaps easier, spaces for engaging difference. In this essay, I describe an unexpected connection fostered between myself (a researcher and doctoral candidate who identified as liberal) and Tyler (a participant and student who identified as conservative). The purpose in detailing this exchange is to demonstrate the unanticipated effects that unfold when diverse teachers and students connect. My aim is to suggest, and demonstrate, that by finding ways to identify with students and establish trusting relationships with them, teachers might find useful applications to the classroom.

In the following sections, I describe how my interviews with Tyler both followed and defied interview protocols, how trust was established, and what revelations Tyler made in this space. Next, Tyler will have an opportunity to respond to my portrayal of our research experience. Finally, in the discussion, I'll offer a few thoughts about how this research engagement changed me as a liberal-identified teacher and what it might suggest for other teachers who are struggling to perform neutrality, who feel ill at ease in classrooms in which they suspect that their deepest political commitments are not shared by their students, who feel—as many of us might—the height and complexity of an empathy wall.

INTRODUCING TYLER AND THE RESEARCH SITE

Tyler, a 23-year-old veteran who was returning to college following four years in the Marines, was one of eight focal students in my study. While the site of the study was a first-year writing course, I was also interested in how students adapted to life at the University of Cincinnati (UC), an urban public institution whose writing program serves nearly six thousand students every year. Tyler intended to study business but switched to communications in the middle of the term. The oldest of five children, Tyler grew up on the West Side of Cincinnati.

When initially asked to describe himself, Tyler replied, as though this fact explained everything, "I went to Elder." Elder is a private, male Catholic high school on the West Side. After graduation, Tyler became the first in his family to go to college, but dropped out to enter the military. Tyler felt deeply indebted to his parents and was aware of the many sacrifices they'd made to care for him:

> When I was a kid, they grinded. All my friends have no clue, because all their parents . . . had them later in their lives, and careers, and all this. My dad at one point was working . . . he'd go in at six, and he would finish his job at around five. Then he would go to his other security job from six until nine. And then he would go to where you do the corn and the funnel cakes. We used to have the Festival of Lights account for corn and funnel cakes. So he would go from the second security job to the Festival of Lights. For years, the dude was working nineteen-hour-days for months.[1]

In the spring of 2016, Tyler was ready to return to UC, this time with the military footing the bill. He registered for his classes from Camp Miramar in California: "I was doing everything over the phone and I hadn't been in school in a long time so I didn't even really know where to begin." He had no expectation for what first-year writing would be like, but in the Marines Tyler had developed a strong set of writing skills that he anticipated would serve him well in college. He said, "I think that I'm pretty well spoken and that comes out in my writing. I write pretty smooth."

In fact, Tyler positioned himself as something of a writing coach for the men he supervised in his unit. Offering both formative and summative assessment on writing and speaking, Tyler worked with those in his unit closely:

> I had a Marine of mine who could not communicate, period. Wasn't a good talker, we worked on that. I would make him present things to me all the time because he would get so nervous and that's how we would knock that out, more or less. He never sent a thing without sending it to me or one of my peers. We would look over everything and give him feedback, but not hateful feedback. We would make sure that we were pretty positive about it. We all knew [he] was not a good writer, that's fine. We're going to work on that together.

Perhaps because Tyler's beliefs about feedback mirrored my own, or perhaps because Tyler was four years older than my other study participants, or perhaps because relationship-building is so central to both teaching and qualitative research, I found myself telling things to Tyler to help me establish a rapport with him. Lad Tobin (2010) would position these tidbits of shared information as the sort of "purposeful self-disclosure" that is essentially rhetorical in nature. My disclosures emphasized our commonalities: my husband's service in the military, and my own experiences as a military spouse. I shared that I was gifted a social manual when my husband and I married. We laughed when I said I didn't read it but we understood what I meant when I·said that I followed the rules anyway.

In making these disclosures, some might say that I was making my identity stable and legible to Tyler and also might note that the identity I performed was highly normative: able-bodied, middle-class, hetero-sexual, White, married. I didn't worry overmuch about these disclosures. Surely part of the reason I was able to make them is that I anticipated correctly that they would be welcomed by my audience. Teachers whose identity characteristics are non-normative may not be able to make the same assumption (Kopelson 2006; Gutiérrez y Muhs et al. 2012).

I had determined, through this brief initial interview, that I genuinely liked Tyler. I liked his frankness, his articulateness, his willingness to participate in the study, his desire to perform well in school, his commit-ment to his family and his community. From this foundation, I came to trust Tyler and, of course, I wanted to prove myself a trustworthy person for him.

Trust has been studied from a range of disciplinary perspectives, and some general themes have emerged. To be trustworthy one must be per-ceived as both caring and credible. Trust is established between people and heightens the expectations that they have for each other. As philoso-pher Katherine Hawley puts it, "trust is at the center of a whole web of concepts: reliability, predictability, expectation, cooperation, goodwill, and—on the dark side—distrust, insincerity, conspiracy, betrayal, and incompetence" (Hawley 2012, 3). Neutrality—an openness to listening, a making of space for the student to explore their own ideas—can be a natural precursor of trust.

As much as I liked Tyler, the additional three hours we spent together were characterized by a kind of push and pull. On many topics, we sim-ply didn't agree: the protests in the National Football League, the value of political correctness, the candidate for whom we would vote for in the 2016 presidential election. As Kenneth Burke has written, "but put iden-tification and division ambiguously together, so that you cannot know for certain just where one ends and the other begins and you have the characteristic invitation to rhetoric" (Burke 1969, 25).

In discussion, I didn't call attention to our disagreement. Instead, I drew attention to places where I thought Tyler's views didn't stick neatly together (see Stubblefield and Chisholm, chapter 15 in this collection, who make a similar move when engaging students). For instance, how could Tyler say he wanted a supportive feedback environment, and then say that political correctness was a waste of time? It seemed to me that political correctness was foundational to a supportive environment. As we had these disagreements—edged our way into various contact zones—there was a directness to the exchanges that I found both invigorating and unsettling. I was unsettled because I wasn't sure if I was overstepping the boundaries of my researcher role.

Irving Seidman, who has written a manual on qualitative interviewing, would say that I'd gone too far in engaging Tyler—that I'd shifted our relationship from one that was *I/Thou* to one that was *We*. In a *We* relationship, Seidman writes, there is an equal exchange of ideas (Seidman 2013). The line between *I/Thou* and *We* is blurry, and some feminist researchers argue that all good research should begin with a *We*. Exactly how much someone should share of themselves in qualitative interviewing is debatable. Seidman recommends "enough to be alive and responsive" but not enough to redirect the interview (Seidman 2013, 97). I was torn, though, because it was in these moments of redirections that the exchange between myself and Tyler seemed most vital. Tyler seemed to think so, too. "We do good work together," he commented after one of our discussions, and held out his hand for me to shake. As the political intensity of campus life escalated throughout the fall, I also did a lot of listening to Tyler. What I heard genuinely surprised me.

TYLER'S ADMISSIONS AND KELLY'S RESPONSES

I heard about Tyler's disappointment in college as an experience. While he thought there would be a free exchange of ideas, it turned out that people seemed to really "tiptoe" (his word) around hot topics. The environment seemed alienating. "It seems like the whole class is on this side, and then I'm over there on some of these conversations," he said. The lack of direct exchange left him puzzled.

> I don't know why we're tiptoeing, and I keep seeing that. It's not just in English. It's in a couple of different classes where some topics are stifled, and it's strange to me because this is college. Where ideas should be, like there's an acceptance thing going on at the same time. But not accepting if it's not in this progressive kind of field. We'll avoid topics. It's a little too iffy. Let's not talk about that, and it's like, well that's weird. But it's just not comfortable.

Like what? I asked. Like race, he answered. To Tyler, our campus was a place where his own identity characteristics—a West Sider, a former Marine—were not particularly welcome. I listened as he talked about feeling out of step with the other men on campus, feeling that he was a throwback to an older model of masculinity. "I couldn't even talk to him about guns or sports," he said of another man in his composition classroom. "Are those your only interests?" I asked, "Guns and sports?" He agreed they were not. I listened as he attempted to analyze what exactly it was about his self-presentation that threw people off: "I need to be friendlier[. . .]Seriously, there's just something about my face[. . .]I need to come across as less stern." I listened as he talked about his attempts to feign political neutrality around campus, his attempts not to take up too much room or to make trouble. I listened as he talked about his concern that women on campus were uncomfortable with him, especially in his composition classroom. "I can't make her talk to me!" he said. "I just knew that as she was looking at me, she didn't want me here." He went on, "girls are very darty-eyed around me." And finally, I listened as he asked: "Do you think I'm sexist?"

With this question, I felt that Tyler was inviting me to comment on his identity performance, on aspects of his gender presentation that might be threatening, but that he couldn't see. I felt a true obligation to Tyler to help him see himself as others might see him, to see how his imposing frame and traditional masculine presentation might be interpreted as aggressive. I wanted to show Tyler these things, and I began by relating with him. "Everyone has work to do," I finally said. "For instance, I've been thinking about how much I have not seen as a result of being White." Tyler replied, "Being White isn't any different than being Black." Feeling my blood pressure rise, I countered that this was factually untrue. Tyler shrugged.

What I realize now, looking back, is that Tyler and I had entered a very particular kind of conversation, one where we were both being vulnerable with each other, where we were struggling to talk across difference, where we were surprised by what the other person seemed to just take for granted. I had become what Wendy Wolters Hinshaw calls "an uneasy listener" (Hinshaw 2011, 276). She writes, "It's not easy to balance our commitments to social justice with the need to listen to and acknowledge students' potential resistance to them." Hinshaw recommends teachers "address [students] relationally rather than confrontationally" (276). These relational conversations—which happen in trusting spaces—can be galvanizing for teachers, or at least that was the case with me. Because I had a trusting relationship with Tyler, I reacted more strongly to his impulse to disregard the notion of White privilege than I think I would have typically. Certainly the view that Tyler espoused is not unusual in first-year college students (Ratcliffe 2005). Yet it felt so to me, as someone who has been thinking about race in my city and my country. In a sense, listening to Tyler only sharpened my own commitment to making him rethink his positions. While it might be comforting—and cliché—to think listening can change everyone a little bit, actually sometimes listening only clarifies disagreements.

In a well-known example of talking across difference, six women, three leaders from each side of the abortion debate, met for over 150 hours. They came together following a shooting at an abortion clinic. All wanted to find common ground. They met for five years. At the end of the meetings, not one woman had changed her position. In fact, their previously held convictions only solidified and sharpened through dialogue (Fowler 2001). This was also the case with me and Tyler. In hearing that Tyler did not regard life in Cincinnati as being substantively different if one was Black or White, I was driven back into scholarship on teaching about race. If anything, I became only more dedicated to the ideals I held before engaging Tyler. There was, however, a change. I didn't see Tyler as an abstraction. We were not, to use the language of Hochschild, on different sides of an empathy wall.

Instead, I felt close with Tyler himself, and a desire to see him flourish. I felt, too, a shared sense of what the university could and should be for students. The university, for me, is not a place where students should leave thinking the same thing; it is a place where they should leave understanding why they think the way they do. Hearing Tyler talk about his feelings of alienation on campus and how he hides his actual perceptions so that he's not regarded as "a punk" (as he put it) by teachers and peers made me realize that for Tyler to have the kind of college experience he wanted—and that I wanted for him—he would have to find ways to engage. He would have to feel more comfortable and more seen. "I'm a 'they,'" he said at one point, as he recalled watching a group of students ridicule a man who was wearing hat emblazoned with the words "Make America Great Again."

Months later, when I would invite Tyler to participate in writing this book chapter, he'd tell me that he no longer went to UC, that he dropped out and entered the police academy. He was concerned about making the Servicemen's Readjustment Bill (commonly known as the GI Bill) stretch as far as possible. He could get more value from it by going to the police academy right away, he said. Meanwhile, he was also working a night job to make extra money to pay for his wedding to

Katie, his girlfriend from high school. He cleaned carpets with a team of men in their late forties and fifties. "I do the stairs," Tyler said, "since my back isn't messed up yet." Tyler's approach to his education, including this decision to delay college until after the police academy, reflects his desire to achieve financial stability, an important motivator for many students, as Evans in chapter 2 in this collection points out.

He confirmed for me at the time of our meeting—which, while scheduled for only an hour, stretched to nearly three—that our conversations had affected him. They had made him more aware of how uncomfortable and constrained he felt at times at the university. He'd felt better after he talked with me and had been hopeful that I would communicate to a broader audience what it was like for him on campus. Below are his thoughts in his own words.

TYLER'S RESPONSE

Initially I was interested in this project because I wanted to help Kelly with her dissertation. I didn't expect we'd have a lot in common. Honestly, I don't expect to really agree with anyone in an authority role in higher education. My teachers in high school at Elder prepared me for that. But it was cool talking to Kelly. She seemed receptive to what I had to say. I hoped that by sharing with her how weird it was for me on campus, especially as the election got closer and people seemed to be stereotyping each other a lot, she would do something about it, maybe even talk to my teacher. I thought maybe things could change.

There are parts of her chapter that I don't agree with, like the idea of a writing course centered on race. I think it would be hard to take a position in writing with which your professor would disagree. They're the one grading you, right? You don't want them to think of you as that punk kid. It's like you're with a boss. You don't say something to make the boss mad. Kelly was really the only person I felt I could talk to about this kind of stuff, partly because she wasn't my teacher and she wasn't grading me. I do trust her, and I hope this chapter encourages more space for conversations like we had.

I'm no longer in college, but I am excited to go back once I get into a comfortable job policing. Kelly had a big influence in my wanting to go back because at the time our meetings started I was getting frustrated with the way things were going. It was during the election, to be fair, but still these classes were getting hostile. I had a professor stand in front of the class and go on a 10-minute rant about how stupid someone had to be to vote for Trump. At first, I thought it was funny. It didn't matter to me at all what he said, because it was a class about composing music for video games. The humor, though, went away quick because his rant went on for too many days and he would go straight into the lecture I was actually paying money to hear. He also left zero room for discussion or counter arguments, so what was the point? Anyway, my meetings with Kelly became a comfortable place for me to explain my frustration. I was there to talk about the importance of professor feedback, which we did, but still I had to tell someone this was going on because it just felt goofy. Like, who the hell does this dude think he is? Because Kelly would listen, given I didn't seem to have space in the classroom to be heard, this definitely had a lasting effect on my desire to continue college.

After reading all that Kelly has written it really feels like she got what I was saying, which is awesome. I had forgotten about a lot of stuff we talked about so it is cool to look back over it and see how she interpreted it. I definitely think there's a liberal/conservative divide everywhere, and not just on campus. But in the fall of 2016, this divide just really stuck out to me because it was political overload going to class every day. I also think the divide is completely normal and acceptable as long as we can still have open conversation about it instead of using whatever power we have to silence people we disagree with. Connecting with Kelly—and writing this chapter—has been fun. I like being able to talk to a person who will listen and maybe even stop her professor colleagues from making the classroom about themselves and not the students.

DISCUSSION

In this essay, I, along with a conservative-identified student Tyler, have discussed how we communicated across a liberal/conservative divide by establishing a trusting researcher/participant relationship. While on the one hand it may seem unsurprising that two people who seem to have a lot in common in terms of their identity presentation could make this kind of connection, I sense such connections are rarely fostered on college campuses or in public life. As I've worked on this essay, it seems that everywhere I turn I hear people lamenting the fraying of our national cloth (see American University Radio 2018).

Yet this frayed fabric is not worse than that of the debates surrounding women's reproductive rights in the nineties. And those speakers, after realizing that they would never change each other's mind, continued talking anyway. They wrote: "As our mutual understanding increased, our respect and affection for one another grew" (Fowler et al. 2001). So this essay, then, is ultimately a call for teachers to practice building relationships with students across various divides, including the liberal/ conservative divide. We may find that we are changed through these efforts, though not in ways that make us more similar to the students we are engaging.

Briefly, I describe three ways that forging this empathy bridge changed me as a liberal-identified teacher. First, I became more open to teaching about race, a topic I had previously avoided. Perhaps I, like the graduate students studied by Brewer (chapter 1) and Holt (chapter 10) in this volume, felt wary of engaging in political critique. Yet because large-scale racial inequality can be demonstrated and because I think a student like Tyler would benefit from such a course, I anticipate that I will be a more demonstrably ideologically driven teacher than I was before our conversations. Second, I also understand my campus differently. Tyler's identification as a West Sider informed his interpretation of the university, which he regarded as an East Side institution. Early in our interviews, Tyler said, "My girlfriend is from Norwood. My family is huge, [I have a] big group of friends, [and] my kids will go to Elder. I'll always live on the West Side. I've just got strong ties here that I can't leave again." Even though I'd grown up in Cincinnati, I'd underestimated the differences that neighborhood affiliation can play in one's university experience. Since talking to Tyler, I have considered how geographic location can used as a shorthand to communicate values, class, and racial information (see Davila and Dickinson 2016). Finally, I also realized that, as Hochschild promised, there were ample areas of practical agreement in spite of the ideological divides between Tyler and me. Specifically, the way that Tyler and I both saw the university as a place where ideas and identities should be freely communicated will linger with me. I find myself, as I think about this view of the university, returning to Joseph Harris's vision for a cosmopolitanism that enables diverse parties to traverse university grounds freely; for our campuses to feel like a public, rather than communal, space (Harris 2012, 147; for a critique of the cosmopolitan metaphor, see Richards's chapter 5 interview with John Trimbur, as well as Holt's chapter 10, both in this volume).

I have reservations, of course, about the ability of this story to transcend the bounds of my own Midwestern campus. It may be easy for someone who is read as part of the majority to foster conversations with conservative-identified students. Perhaps Tyler only trusted me because I looked so much like him. In other words, my identification with Tyler was not a "troubled identification" (Ratcliffe 2005, 1). Additionally, having these conversations apart from actual classroom dynamics likely created unrealistically harmonious conditions between the speakers. If

Tyler were in a class that I was teaching about race, our dynamic and appraisal of each other might in fact be quite different, even adversarial. It may be that a better teacher or researcher would have tried to be less stable than I was in my presentation of my identity. Perhaps, knowing that I was offering myself as a text for Tyler to read and identify with, I should have foregrounded aspects that made it less possible or desirable to form the kind of trusting bond that led to our most engaging exchanges. And yet . . .

What was significant about listening to Tyler was that his most arresting insights—such as his interpretation of how his masculine presentation was received by women on campus, which I could not have predicted—were offered only after a trusting relationship had been established. Part of what contributed to the establishment of trust was a combination of identification and performing neutrality. Perhaps, then, the relationship between these two concepts—trust and performed neutrality—merits additional theorization.

Performing neutrality and fostering trust are connected, I've come to think, because as teachers make room for students' perceptions without seeming to respond negatively, students trust them more. They feel more open and relaxed—more of what cognitive scientists call the *feeling aspect* of trust. Cristiano Castelfranchi and Rino Falcone explain: "Trust as a feeling is characterized by 'letting oneself go,' of relaxing, a sort of confident surrendering" (Castelfranchi and Falcone 2010, 140). They continue:

> Affective components of trust result in a felt freedom from anxiety and worry; X feels safe or even protected; there is no suspicion or hostility towards Y, which is appraised/felt as benevolent and reliable ('S/he will take care of . . .'). Toward a benevolent Y, we are benevolent, good-willing; toward a good/skilled Y, we are not aroused, alerted, cautious, worried. (Castelfranchi and Falcone 2010, 140–141)

This kind of trust, they write, seems to be the consequence of "an intuitive appraisal" on the part of both parties (140).

Neutrality, for me, has come to mean not only a performance for students but also an orientation to students. Research and experience demonstrate that actual neutrality—an objective, third-party position—doesn't exist. To feign neutrality in any role is to play, as Donna Haraway memorably put it, "the god trick" (1988, 581). Yet the expected performance of neutrality has become, as many chapters in this text point out, commonplace. Instead, what interests me is how teachers can engage students across various divides. I also wonder: as we create space for students to explore their own beliefs and opinions through the expected performance of neutrality, is it possible for us to also be preparing ourselves to be uneasy listeners, to be open to hearing things that might make us uncomfortable, to forming identifications and connections across difference? The potential benefits of this approach are manifold, as Hochschild writes: "We, on both sides, wrongly imagine that empathy with the 'other' side brings an end to clearheaded analysis when, in truth, it's on the other side of that bridge that the most important analysis can begin" (Hochschild 2016, xi).

It may be that qualitative research is a space uniquely situated for building these kinds of bridges that will, then, make it easier for teachers to be more understanding of and committed to their students in the classroom. In particular, feminist research engages a promising approach: one that "works the hyphen" between participant-observer (Bruggeman 1996; Fine 1998), one that builds a relationship with participants by pursuing mutuality, one that is willing to explore and acknowledge positionality (see also Johnson and LeBouef Tullia, who discuss a similar overlap between intersectionality and relationality in chapter 14 in this volume). While my study did not initially seek to study listening across difference, qualitative research can uniquely create these spaces. Perhaps, then, engaging in qualitative research is ultimately a way to assuage resistance.

As of this writing, the question of teacher neutrality seems more fraught than ever. The 2016 presidential election caused many issues to rise to a boil, including the perceived problem of progressive teachers trying to get students to lean left. The establishment of *Professor Watchlist* explicitly gathered teachers accused of spreading progressive ideology in one place. Many professors, including writing studies' John Duffy, were dismayed by the move. "People who detract from university campuses should just come to my campus," said Professor John Duffy of the University of Notre Dame on *All Things Considered* (2016). "They'd find there's nothing to be afraid of." My hope is that in offering this glimpse into the possibilities provided by qualitative research, my essay might continue the work of Duffy and Hochschild, to suggest that building empathy bridges on campus through honest conversation and fostering trust may be a way to decrease fear, increase compassion, and find the possibility for practical cooperation.

NOTE

1.   All quotes from Tyler are from transcribed audio recordings and contemporaneous notes collected through one-on-one meetings during the fall 2016 semester.

REFERENCES

All Things Considered. 2016. "Professors Take a Different Approach in Responding to Leftist Propaganda Claims." 10 December 2016. https://www.npr.org/2016/12/10/505 109280/professors-take-a-different-approach-in-responding-to-leftist-propaganda -claims. Accessed 26 April 2018.

American University Radio (WAMU 88.5). 2018. "In Conversation: Ambassador Susan Rice." 12 March 2018. *1A* Accessed 26 April 2018. https://the1a.org/shows/2018-03 -12/in-conversation-ambassador-susan-rice.

Burke, Kenneth. 1969. *A Rhetoric of Motives.* Oakland, CA: University of California Press.

Bruggemann, Brenda Jo. 1996. "Still-Life: Representations and Silences in the Participant-Observer Role." In *Ethics and Representation in Qualitative Research,* ed. Peter Mortenson and Gesa E. Kirsch, 17–39. Urbana, IL: NCTE.

Castelfranchi, Cristiano, and Rino Falcone. 2010. *Trust Theory: A Socio-Cognitive and Computational Model.* Sussex: John Wiley and Sons.

Davila, Bethany, and Hannah Dickinson. 2016. "At a Distance: The Encoding of Place in the University." *Composition Studies* 44 (2): 94–115.

Durst, Russel K. 1999. *Collision Course: Conflict, Negotiation, and Learning in Composition.* Urbana, IL: NCTE.

Fine, Michelle. 1998. "Working the Hyphens: Reinventing Self and Other in Qualitative Research." In *The Landscape of Qualitative Research: Theories and Issues,* ed. Norman K. Denzin and Yvonna S. Lincoln, 130–155. Thousand Oaks, CA: Sage.

Fowler, Anne, Nicki Nichols Gamble, Frances X. Hogan, Melissa Kogut, Madeline McCommish, and Barbara Thorp. 2001. "Talking with the Enemy." *The Boston Globe,* 28 January 2001. Reposted on *Feminist.com.* https://www.feminist.com/resources/artspeech /genwom/talkingwith.html. Accessed 26 April 2018.

Greenbaum, Andrea, editor. 2001. *Insurrections: Approaches to Resistance in Composition Studies.* Albany: State University of New York Press.

Gutiérrez y Muhs, Gabriella, Yolanda Flores Niemann, Carmen G. González, and Angela P. Harris, editors. 2012. *Presumed Incompetent: The Intersections of Race and Class for Women in Academia.* Logan, UT: Utah State University Press.

Haraway, Donna. 1988. "Situated Knowledges: The Science Question in Feminism and the Privilege of Partial Perspective." *Feminist Studies* 14 (3): 575–599.

Harris, Joseph. 2012. *A Teaching Subject: Composition Since 1966.* 2nd ed. Logan, UT: Utah State University Press.

Hawley, Katherine. 2012. *Trust: A Very Short Introduction.* Oxford: Oxford University Press.

Hinshaw, Wendy Wolters. 2011. "Making Ourselves Vulnerable: A Feminist Pedagogy of Listening." In *Silence and Listening as Rhetorical Acts,* ed. Cheryl Glenn and Krista Ratcliffe, 251–277. Carbondale, IL: Southern Illinois University Press.

Hochschild, Arlie Russell. 2016. *Strangers in their Own Land.* New York: New Press.

Kirsch, Gesa E., and Joy S. Ritchie. 1995. "Beyond the Personal: Theorizing a Politics of Location in Composition Research." *College Composition and Communication* 46: 7–29.

Kopelson, Karen. 2006. "Of Ambiguity and Erasure: The Perils of Performative Pedagogy." In *Relations, Locations, and Positions: Composition Theory for Writing Teachers,* ed. Peter Vandenberg, Jennifer Clary-Lemon, and Sue Hum, 563–571. Urbana, IL: NCTE.

"Partisanship and Political Animosity in 2016." 22 June 2016. Pew Research Center. Washington, DC. http://www.people-press.org/2016/06/22/partisanship-and-political -animosity-in-2016/.

Ratcliffe, Krista. 2005. *Rhetorical Listening: Identification, Gender, Whiteness.* Carbondale, IL: Southern Illinois University Press.

Seidman, Irving. 2013. *Interviewing as Qualitative Research.* 4th ed. New York: Teachers College Press.

Sheridan-Rabideau, Mary. 2003. "Part Two: Introduction." In *Feminism and Composition: A Critical Sourcebook*, ed. Gesa E. Kirsch et al., 75–77. Urbana, IL: NCTE.

Tobin, Lad. 2010. "Self-Disclosure as a Strategic Teaching Tool: What I Do—and Don't—Tell My Students." *College English* 73 (2): 196–206.

7

BELIEVING CRITICALLY
Teaching Critical Thinking through the Conversion Narrative

Christopher Michael Brown

Since the rise of social-epistemic and cultural studies pedagogies in the 1980s and 1990s, the trope of teaching as transformation—of both students and society—has come to exert significant influence in composition. In a familiar version of this narrative, students who are compliant with the discourses of mass culture learn to recognize, name, and resist the modes of subjectivity that these discourses impose on them and, in some cases, to discover more empowering subject positions from which they can enact change in society (Myatt Barger 2012, 79–80; Newkirk 2004, 263–264; Paine 1999). Newkirk refers to this transformative narrative as one of "conversion," a "dogma" that colors the field's perception of good writing. Over time, the tendency of such approaches to provoke resistance from students has led scholars to question their ethical value and pedagogical effectiveness. Some argue that strains of writing pedagogy with transformative or emancipatory agendas rely on a condescending view of students as the unenlightened "other," neglecting their diverse interests, knowledge, and educational needs (Myatt Barger 2012, 81–82; Newkirk 1997, 101–102; Yoon 2005, 721). Others question the feasibility of efforts to liberate students from their ideological commitments, which provide a relatively stable sense of identity and community to language users (Alcorn 2002, 21; DePalma 2011, 223; Rickert 2007).

Though most of these critiques issue from scholars who claim some form of adherence to critical pedagogy, their skepticism may signal a waning commitment within the field to the goal of student transformation. Alexander and Rhodes (2014) observe that the economic challenges of the past decade have led composition to shift its focus from cultural critique and transformation to questions of college readiness and career success, as evidenced by recent interest in writing assessment and transfer of skills (Adler-Kassner and Wardle 2015; Yancey,

DOI: 10.7330/9781607329992.c007

Robertson, and Taczak 2014). In light of these developments, this chapter considers how ideological commitment might support pedagogical efforts to prepare students for success in college and beyond. Extending Jeffrey M. Ringer's (2013) argument that all inquiry is rooted in belief, I argue that ideological commitment may prompt thinkers to question and revise received knowledge in order to gain a clearer sense of the truths to which their ideologies lay claim. For this reason, I suggest that pedagogical approaches that seek to convert students along particular ideological lines may be less effective as a method of engaging students in critical thinking than approaches that enable students to develop lines of inquiry rooted in positions to which they have converted.

A pedagogy that enabled students to develop lines of inquiry from the premises of their own ideologies would stimulate critical thinking by remaining "neutral" toward those ideologies. By *neutral* I do not mean that the instructor or pedagogy would be operating free of ideological commitment but that students' own commitments, by serving as the grounds for their inquiries, would provide the impetus for critical thinking. To that end, I show how an assignment I call the "conversion narrative," rather than seeking to convert students from or toward a particular position, allows critical thinking to emerge from students' inquiries into their own experiences of conversion. Charles Griffin (1990) observes that a conversion narrative accounts for how its author came to hold a certain value or belief by reconstructing the sequence of events that led to changes in her perspective, clearly delineating how each event impacted her developing views—a strategy of narrative development that Kenneth Burke termed *syllogistic progression form* (Burke 1968). Drawing from two case studies of first-year composition (FYC) students, I show how focusing on the syllogistic form of the conversion narrative enabled me to provide critiques of student narratives that were grounded in the ideological commitments of their authors. In both instances, my feedback enabled students to examine the underlying assumptions that held together the various stages of their narratives, identifying along the way assumptions that needed to be in place for the narrative to follow through to its conclusion. In this way, the process of writing a conversion narrative encouraged students to think critically about that narrative, as an argument supporting their ideological commitments. To the extent that such thinking enabled students to construct more compelling, well-reasoned accounts of their conversions, the assignment also provided a "neutral" incentive for critical thinking—one that was rooted in students' own commitments.

TWO APPROACHES TO CRITICAL THINKING:
BERLIN V. AUGUSTINE

While the social turn in composition brought the concept of ideology to the fore of scholarly conversation and classroom praxis, this concept was later extended in directions that called into question the viability of pedagogies that made critique of ideology the focus of instruction. James Berlin argued that the subject of language is constituted by the manifold "signifying practices," or discourses, that circulate in a given time and place. These discourses do not provide a transparent window onto the world but, through the mechanism of ideology, advance particular interpretations of reality (Berlin 1996, 89). Here, the function of composition is to give students the analytic tools needed to recognize that the discourses that mediate their experience do not reflect timeless truths but emerge from—and are allied with—historically situated interests (101). While aligning himself with Berlin's belief that composition should advance progressive political goals, Marshall Alcorn complicates Berlin's understanding of subjectivity and, consequently, the means of achieving those goals. In Alcorn's psychoanalytic framework, the subject formed by a given set of signifying practices forms "libidinal" attachments to those discourses. Conferring a sense of identity on the subject, these attachments become the primary means through which she relates to herself and others. In this way, the subject's attachment to ideology can be likened to the bond shared between family members or lovers (Alcorn 2002, 28). Rational analysis of the ways that one's commitments are discursively constructed is insufficient in the face of such attachments, which "prestructure in advance any thinking [one] might do on a particular subject" (25).

Alcorn's corrective to Berlin shines a much-needed light on the intimate relationship between ideology and identity, which critical writing pedagogies often overlook in their zeal to liberate students from ideologies that are perceived to be harmful. At the same time, his argument focuses mainly on the limitations that ideology places on critical thinking—that is, evaluating knowledge from a distance necessary to question and, if necessary, revise that knowledge. Consequently, Alcorn does not consider the extent to which the boundaries drawn by ideology *promote* this kind of thinking, a possibility suggested by Jeffrey M. Ringer in his article, "The Dogma of Inquiry" (2013). Here Ringer shows how religious commitment, while placing certain limitations on thought, calls for a measure of self-reflexivity. He derives this insight in part from the Augustinian formulation, *faith precedes understanding.* Augustine's *Confessions,* the autobiographical account of his conversion to Christianity, reveals a thinker who was not content to accept received knowledge but moved continually to ask questions *about* that knowledge—to better understand the things he "knew" (352). Undoubtedly, the questions that guided Augustine's search for knowledge—for instance, about the nature or existence of God—emerged from the context of his faith (353). As such, the answers he reached tended to affirm that faith. From a social-epistemic perspective, one might say that Augustine's understanding was ideologically mediated: by determining the questions he asked, Christianity advanced particular interpretations of reality, or discourses, where others were possible. At the same time, Augustine's confidence that behind his interpretations was a reality he had yet to fully grasp prompted him to continually challenge and revise his answers to the questions that interested him (352).

The example of Augustine demonstrates that critical thinking is not an isolated activity but part and parcel of a process of inquiry initiated by the writer's ideological commitments. To the extent that the writer is committed to a particular belief, she will seek to understand the object of her belief—a process that entails questioning and, in some cases, revising existing understandings of that object. Ringer demonstrates this process of inquiry at work in an academic context through an analysis of Amy Goodburn's (2007) article, "It's A Question of Faith: Discourses of Fundamentalism and Critical Pedagogy in the Writing Classroom." Goodburn initiates her inquiry by outlining the tenets of critical pedagogy, which here entails an examination of the ways that social constructs like race, class, and gender influence students' reading and writing practices. Acknowledging her commitment to these principles, Goodburn observes that critical pedagogy has not given sufficient attention to another form of difference: religion. She proceeds to explore the interaction of students' religious identities with her attempts to implement critical pedagogy in the classroom (Ringer 2013, 355). Here, Goodburn's commitment to a particular ideology—critical pedagogy—prompts her to observe an omission in the areas where this ideology has traditionally focused its attention, to extend the insights of critical pedagogy to this new context, and finally to revise common understandings of critical pedagogy itself. As Ringer observes, it is Goodburn's commitment to critical pedagogy—and, I would add, her revision of existing understandings of critical pedagogy—that enabled this line of inquiry by generating her interest in the question of religious difference and providing her method for exploring this question (355).

Of course, there are important differences between the kind of critical thinking that supports inquiry and that are employed, in some cases, by critical-writing pedagogies. The former seeks to understand the object of ideological commitment (i.e., for Augustine, God; for Goodburn, critical pedagogy), taking for granted that this object exists and can be known. By contrast, the critique of cultural codes central to Berlin's pedagogy aims to *demystify* belief in this object—that is, to show that it is unworthy of belief. He explains that the goal of this exercise is to "make students aware of cultural codes, the competing discourses that influence their position-ing as subjects of experience" (Berlin 1996, 124). More specifically, stu-dents are guided in uncovering the contradictions that exist within the discourses of mass media and identifying the ideological assumptions that such media deploy in order to resolve those contradictions (140). Through this process Berlin hopes to empower students to resist the models of subjectivity upheld by these discourses (124). Regarding a les-son built around the 1980s television sitcom *Family Ties*, Berlin notes that students quickly catch onto the competing cultural codes in the show. The character of Alex Keaton, for instance, "rebels, but he does so in a socially approved manner, working hard to be rich. The adverse conse-quences of [Alex's] extreme selfishness are never addressed; indeed, in the ingratiating actor Michael J. Fox's hands, ruthlessness is made charm-ing" (131). Here, Berlin interprets Fox's performance as a vehicle for free-market ideologies that frame ruthless ambition as a virtue. His point seems to be that, in the world outside of television, selfishness like Alex's is not charming but destructive. By uncovering the unresolved contradic-tions within the character of Alex, Berlin's analysis seeks to undermine the ideology that this character embodies and—by extension—weaken students' investment in that ideology.

That Berlin's critique targets free-market ideologies suggests that his own ideological commitments lie elsewhere. Specifically, it is Berlin's stated commitment to progressive political change that drives his peda-gogy's interrogation of free-market ideologies (Berlin 1996, 122). This is evident from the guiding questions of Berlin's lessons—for instance, how economic circumstances influence the depictions of family life in popular television sitcoms (127–132). A desire for progressive political change is likewise indicated by his—and his students'—answers to these questions. In answer to the aforementioned question, for instance, he cites a student's observation that the *Family Ties* depiction of the upper-middle-class family as the "answer to all of life's problems" reflects the Reagan administration's emphasis on the importance of the family to social and economic well-being (132).

To the extent that students' thinking is prestructured by their ideological commitments, as Alcorn (2002) suggests, they must either already possess or acquire similar commitments to Berlin's in order to engage sincerely in such exercises. It is clear from anecdotes like the one above that some of Berlin's students *do* share (or appear to share) his commitments. As such, they engage enthusiastically with the lines of inquiry initiated in these lessons and come to conclusions that are consistent with a commitment to progressive politics. Students who do not share the commitments of liberatory pedagogies, however, may engage in the kinds of resistance described by Rickert, Alcorn, and others. Such resistance occurs, I suggest, because the lines of inquiry that students might pursue have been limited to questions that further the ideological commitments of the instructor. In chapter 9 of this volume, Heather Fester warns against this type of pedagogical move, suggesting that instructors must be alert to complexities in ideology in order not to "alienat[e] students against their own authentic motives" (151). Politically conservative students, for instance, may perceive the questions at the center of Berlin's pedagogy as irrelevant or even inimical to their own commitments. Consequently, those commitments become a stumbling block—rather than an impetus—to the process of inquiry that underpins critical thinking.

PRACTICING CRITICAL THINKING THROUGH THE CONVERSION NARRATIVE

Of course, the clash of student and instructor ideologies that critical-writing pedagogies often provoke is, potentially, a feature of all writing instruction. No teaching practice is neutral, in the sense of being *free* of ideological commitment, and the commitments that inform any given pedagogy inevitably pose restrictions on the types of inquiries that students can pursue. Yet, as Newkirk (1997, 107) asserts, the "ideological space of a composition course, while never unbounded, can be expanded or contrasted." In chapter 12 of this collection, Adam Pacton makes a similar proposal that we view "ideological neutrality as a direction rather than a destination" (195). In this spirit of moving in neutrality's direction, I suggest that a pedagogy committed to students' success as college writers would aspire to be "neutral" in a more nuanced sense than this word often connotes: enabling students to develop lines of inquiry on the basis of their own ideological commitments. With inquiry rooted in their own commitments, students might be more inclined to question and revise understandings they may have reached previously, on the basis of those commitments. In doing so, students would be practicing a mode of critical thinking that often characterizes academic inquiry.

One assignment that I have used to ground critical thinking in students' commitments is the conversion narrative. Here each student writes about a time in her life when she experienced a change of belief: any idea about what is true or real. As Faith Kurtyka has shown, compositionists have often framed narratives of personal transformation in opposition to critical thinking. Such narratives may simplify complex human experience, tend toward melodrama, and—in the case of religious narratives—offend readers whose beliefs differ from the author's (Kurtyka 2017, 100–101). Newkirk casts doubt on the value of the narrative of personal transformation as an FYC assignment, which may limit students to writing about a narrow subset of their experiences (Newkirk 1997, 22–23; Newkirk 2004, 264–265). Without discounting the potential problems of the genre, I would also emphasize the value of the conversion narrative as an assignment that grounds inquiry in the writer's own commitments. As Ringer (2013) argues, commitment to a system of belief, rather than bestowing certainty on the believer, may function as a starting point for inquiry, drawing her to seek a greater understanding of what she believes. The guiding question of the conversion narrative—Why do I believe?—functions as a vehicle for this search, inviting writers to investigate the experiences that helped to shape their commitments.

Through this process of investigation, writers of conversion narratives also confront challenges to their ideological commitments, which arise from the demands of Burke's *syllogistic form*. Describing the effect of form in literature, Burke writes, "a work has form insofar as one part of it leads the reader to anticipate another part, to be gratified by the sequence" (Burke 1968, 124). It is possible to expand on Burke's explanation by saying that every piece of information, or "premise," that a story introduces sets certain parameters regarding what *can* happen in the course of the narrative. In the movement from one premise to the next, the story raises questions in the reader's mind about what, given those parameters, *will* happen. The story achieves believability to the extent that its answers to these questions thoroughly acknowledge the boundaries set by the premises. Within the genre of the conversion narrative, syllogistic form is not simply a matter of establishing verisimilitude but showing that the author's beliefs have a logical foundation. If readers are to believe in the sincerity of the author's conversion, the information that she introduces regarding characters or plot must work collectively to demonstrate that her conversion was logically necessary (Griffin 1990, 153). This means that readers, applying common assumptions about human motivation, should be able to follow the complete sequence of premises to their conclusion in the author's conversion. Of every premise, the reader may ask: Given these circumstances, how might a reasonable person respond? As it unfolds, the narrative must answer this question to readers' satisfaction if they are to believe in the authenticity of the author's conversion. Thus, although the assignment allows students' inquiries to proceed from their own commitments, it does not thereby *endorse* those commitments. To the extent that the author must take into account readers' expectations as she develops her answer to the narrative's guiding question ("Why do I believe . . . ?"), she is challenged to examine the reasons behind her ideological commitments—indeed, to question those reasons.

RESPONDING TO STUDENT NARRATIVES

Focusing on syllogistic form—specifically, the logical development of plot and character—in the conversion narrative has offered me a "neutral" position from which to comment on drafts of narratives by students in my FYC classes. While the details that I focus on are inevitably colored by commitments I bring to my readings of these narratives, focusing on the logical relationship among the narrative's different stages enables me to ask questions that facilitate the process of inquiry already begun by the author. These questions, grounded in students' commitments, challenge them to recognize the unstated assumptions that their narratives deploy in order to account for their conversions and, consequently to revise their drafts to better account for expectations that readers might have for the narratives' logical progression.

A narrative by one student, "Vishal," explored the reasons why the author—a Hindu from birth—converted from a vegetarian to a non-vegetarian diet ("Vishal" 2017). The first draft of the narrative framed this period of Vishal's life as painful and conflicted. He notes at the beginning of the narrative that he was raised by a Hindu family "that was strictly about religion and enforcing all the rules of the religion." He then describes the difficulty of growing up as a vegetarian among friends who ate meat, which caused him to feel out of place. After eating a piece of chicken for the first time in high school, he was "haunted" by the knowledge that he had "crossed the line with my religion"—a feeling that he notices especially when he prays at the local temple. At the same time, he is so drawn to the flavor of meat that he begins to consider incorporating it into his diet. He seeks advice from his mother and a priest, both of whom remind him of Hindu beliefs regarding eating meat while emphasizing that this is a decision he must make for himself. Within a week of the latter conversation he resolves to give up his vegetarian diet, a decision that he says greatly improved his life by opening up a range of new foods and restaurants to him and giving him new opportunities to socialize and make new friends.

Because this story seeks to explain how Vishal overcame the struggle to give up vegetarianism, this draft left with me questions about the nature of this struggle. In conversation with Vishal, I explained that the only information he provides about his motivation for eating a vegetarian diet in the early part of his life comes from his statement that his parents strictly enforced the rules of Hinduism. Consequently, it is difficult to pin down the reason for the conflict he feels in giving up this diet. For instance, is he afraid of displeasing his parents? Are there spiritual reasons behind this struggle? These questions also hover over the resolution of the story, which claims that the enjoyment Vishal experiences as a meat-eater resolved his initial doubts about giving up vegetarianism. This statement remains silent on the spiritual dimension of Vishal's conflict mentioned earlier, leaving readers to wonder if those feelings were indeed put to rest. In response to these questions, Vishal at first expressed concern about going into the "complexities" of Hindu beliefs about eating meat. I explained that going into detail on this point might actually help the reader to understand why he struggled with this decision. As to the resolution of his doubts about eating meat, Vishal admitted that he still experiences these doubts—a fact not mentioned in the original draft, which states that "now till this day, that thought [of reverting to vegetarianism] has never come back to me." I encouraged him to incorporate some discussion of his doubts about giving up vegetarianism into the draft so that the reader understood that the feelings of acceptance from friends and convenience did not negate the worries that he experienced earlier in the narrative.

While all of these questions challenged Vishal to more clearly articulate the reasons for his decision to give up a vegetarian diet, they do so on the basis of information that he has introduced into the story in order to explain that decision. In that sense, the questions were intended to deepen his understanding of his decision to eat meat rather than to cause him to doubt that decision. Two additions to that draft are noteworthy for their contributions to the purpose of explaining his motivation for giving up vegetarianism. Whereas the previous paper simply noted that Vishal's parents strictly enforced his vegetarian diet, Vishal now provides more context about his religious upbringing. Specifically, he notes that he was born into the Swaminarayan sect of Hinduism and that his grandfather was "surrounded by many highly motivate [sic] priests." When he started to consider eating meat, he sought advice from his grandfather, who told him, "In the many years that I have been on this earth, I have never eaten meat. Which should go for you but in this case I have no say in what you do" ("Vishal" 2017). Regarding his grandfather's advice, Vishal recalls that "once he had told me all his stories and lectured me about this for weeks, I knew exactly what I wanted to do. He had motivated me to do what was best in my situation. Later . . . I stopped being a vegetarian and started to eat both meat and be a vegetarian" (2). This revised passage provides more context for understanding Vishal's internal struggle with the decision that he was about to make than was evident in the first draft of the paper. By noting the name of the sect to which he belongs, that he was born into that sect, and that his grandfather had ties to its priests, he helps the reader understand the depth of his roots in this religious tradition. Furthermore, his grandfather's advice is far more discouraging regarding Vishal's desire to eat meat than that offered by his mother or a priest later in the narrative. Given his grandfather's position within the Swaminarayan sect, we can better understand the conflict he must have experienced after receiving this advice and the "stories and lecture[s]" that followed. Finally, that these conversations took place over a period of weeks suggests careful deliberation on Vishal's part that was not as clearly indicated in his previous draft.

By clarifying the connection between his guilt about eating meat and his religious affiliation, Vishal helps readers to understand the nature of this conflict. With this understanding, the question as to whether and how this conflict was resolved weighs all the more heavily on the reader's mind. The second addition that Vishal made to the narrative begins to answer this question:

> To get over [my doubts] I had gone to the same priest again to talk to him again on the situation and this time he had told me, "God will always forgive, just keep that in mind." After that conversation, I had gone to my grandpa again and told him exactly what happened. He was very content with me because I had acted [on] something that was extremely important to him. Now till this day, I am still a meat eater but have certain thoughts that still run into my mind when I go . . . to my temple [back home]. ("Vishal" 2017)

With this addition, Vishal succeeds in establishing continuity between the first half of the narrative, in which he struggled with the decision to start eating meat, and the second half of the narrative, after he made that decision. Whereas the previous draft claimed that the enjoyment that eating meat had brought Vishal resolved his initial doubts, here those doubts continue to bother him even after he has started to enjoy the benefits of a non-vegetarian diet. This is understandable given Vishal's emphasis on his deep roots in Swaminarayan Hinduism at the beginning of the story. Indeed, we learn from this draft that Vishal continues to worship at his home temple, even after giving up vegetarianism—a fact not mentioned in the original version. By returning to the subject of his Hindu identity, Vishal also provides a (partial) resolution of the conflict he feels about eating meat that acknowledges the *source* of that conflict. Readers saw this conflict emerge in the first part of the narrative when he sought his grandfather's advice and was discouraged from changing his diet. It makes sense, then, for the resolution of this conflict to come in the form of the—albeit qualified—approval he now receives from his grandfather. With this revision, Vishal maps out the reasoning behind his decision to give up vegetarianism in a way that readers can follow and understand.

Many students engage enthusiastically with this type of questioning because they perceive it as connected to their own interests and commitments—a point I'll return to. This is not to claim that this approach solves the problem of student resistance to critical thinking. It does, however, offer resources for responding to resistance that are not available in some iterations of critical-writing pedagogy. One student who seemed to resist my questions about his first draft, "Alex," had written a narrative about a shift in his attitude about guns ("Alex" 2016). In it, the author explained how his upbringing in a "very socially and politically progressive neighborhood" led him to view guns and gun owners with suspicion. This attitude changed, however, when he enlisted in the military. The paper described an exhilarating experience during the weapons-training portion of boot camp, which took him back to the times he played with toy guns as a child. This experience, he claimed, completely changed his perspective: from one suspicious of guns and their owners, he became a recreational gun user and an advocate for gun rights. In our conversation about the paper, I pointed out that the draft didn't seem to account for *how* Alex's experience in boot camp led to a change in his views about guns. As a reader, I could understand why the enjoyment he felt using a gun for the first time would cause a conflict in his negative attitude toward gun users. But I wanted to know how the experience actually *changed* that attitude.

When I asked why his experience in boot camp caused him to begin viewing guns in a more positive light, Alex seemed frustrated. He answered, "Because a gun is like a tool. A carpenter uses a screwdriver, a soldier uses a gun" ("Alex" 2016). Significantly, this answer reverts to a general defense of Alex's beliefs, sidestepping the specific inquiry that he had initiated: Why do *I* believe that good people own and use guns? Based on this response, I inferred that my line of questioning had caused Alex to feel that his beliefs about guns were at stake. Within the iterations of critical-writing pedagogies surveyed earlier in this chapter, such moments can be experienced as a kind of deadlock. Discerning a contradiction between the commitments that guide the instructor's line of questioning and their own beliefs, students may withdraw from the conversation or become defensive. In order to avoid this outcome, I reminded Alex that the genre of the conversion narrative did not necessarily call for the author to persuade others of his beliefs but, rather, to show that he sincerely held those beliefs. I hoped that reminding Alex of the purpose of the assignment would clarify the motive behind my questioning, which was not to subject his beliefs to scrutiny—though I appeared to be doing just that—but to help him articulate the reasons for those beliefs.

Two revisions to the final draft helped to clarify the connection between Alex's attitudes about guns and his experience. The first describes the moment when Alex first used a gun in weapons-training boot camp. While a version of this passage appeared in the previous draft, Alex's revision explains the significance of this experience to his developing attitudes about guns: "I had never known anyone who had shot a gun, or been interested in them. But there I was shooting guns, next to 80 members of my boot camp division who had become like brothers to me over the rigorous training cycle which is boot camp . . . I had always thought that guns were bad, but here I was having fun for the first time in months, shooting guns and trying to beat all of my friends' qualification scores" ("Alex" 2017). Whereas the previous version of the paper had simply described Alex's enjoyment of weapons training, the revision frames that experience as an occasion of camaraderie between the author and his fellow soldiers. In that sense, the new passage provides context for understanding Alex's statement that guns have both good and bad uses: here, guns are used for the "good" purposes of friendly competition and forming relationships. Granted, this point will give some readers—myself included—pause: certainly, relationships can be formed without the use of dangerous weapons, which always pose a risk (however minimal) to the lives of users. Furthermore, if exercises like the ones Alex describes promote a sense of community among soldiers, their ultimate purpose is to train soldiers for combat. One may argue that the camaraderie that soldiers enjoy in these exercises comes at a steep price. However, I would point out that such objections are only possible because they proceed from a premise that both readers and

Alex take for granted: namely, that human relationships are, indeed, good. In that sense, the passage succeeds in establishing a logical—that is, believable—foundation for Alex's commitments, one rooted in premises that the audience shares.

CONCLUSION

Admittedly the approach to critical thinking outlined here requires a considerable reorientation from the goals that have traditionally defined critical-writing pedagogy. Pedagogies in the social-epistemic tradition, in particular, have encouraged resistance to ideology by examining the ways that dominant discourses limit and restrict our perceptions of what is good, true, or possible (Berlin 1996, 121). In doing so, these pedagogies sought to weaken the grasp of ostensibly harmful ideologies on students and, in some cases, to convert them to more progressive ways of thinking.

I have argued that such approaches generate resistance from students by grounding inquiry in the ideological commitments of instructors, a move that unnecessarily limits the lines of inquiry that students might pursue. Extending Ringer's argument that inquiry must be grounded in belief, I suggest that adherents of a particular ideology are more likely to question their ideologically mediated perceptions when doing so helps them to understand the truths to which their ideologies lay claim—a process that often characterizes academic inquiry. Finally, I have offered the conversion narrative as an assignment that facilitates critical thinking from an ideologically "neutral" position, enabling students to challenge and revise their ideologically mediated understandings by pursuing lines of inquiry grounded in their own ideological commitments. Assignments like this one may not produce the transformations in student consciousness to which critical pedagogy has traditionally aspired, but they do enable students to achieve a greater degree of distance from ideology than is possible when critical thinking is divorced from students' own ideological commitments. In this way, students are able to engage in a thinking and writing task that they will be expected to perform as they continue in their college careers.

REFERENCES

Adler-Kassner, Linda and Elizabeth Wardle, eds. 2015. *Naming What We Know: Threshold Concepts in Writing Studies.* Louisville, CO: University Press of Colorado.
Alcorn, Marshall W. 2002. *Changing the Subject in English Class.* Carbondale, IL: Southern Illinois University Press.

Alexander, Jonathan and Jacqueline Rhodes. 2014. "Reimagining the Social Turn: New Work from The Field" *College English* 76 (6): 481–487.

"Alex." 2016. In conversation with the author, March 2016.

"Alex." 2017. "The Story of My Obsession." Unpublished essay.

Berlin, James. 1996. *Rhetorics, Poetics, and Cultures: Refiguring College English Studies.* Anderson, SC: Parlor Press.

Burke, Kenneth. (1931) 1968. *Counter-Statement.* Berkeley, CA: University of California Press.

DePalma, Michael-John. 2011. "Re-envisioning Religious Discourses as Rhetorical Resources in Composition Teaching: A Pragmatic Response to the Challenge of Belief," *College Composition and Communication* 63 (2): 219–243.

Goodburn, Amy. 1998. "It's a Question of Faith: Discourse of Fundamentalism and Critical Pedagogy in the Writing Classroom." *JAC* 18 (2): 333–353.

Griffin, Charles. 1990. "The Rhetoric of Form in Conversion Narratives," *Quarterly Journal of Speech* 76: 152–163.

Kurtyka, Faith. 2017. "Learning How to Feel: Conversion Narratives and Community Membership in First-Year Composition," *Composition Studies* 4 (1): 99–121.

Myatt Barger, Julie. 2012. "Tracing the Trope of Teaching as Transformation." In *Disrupting Pedagogies in the Knowledge Society: Countering Conservative Norms with Creative Approaches,* ed. Julie Faulkner, 77–93. Hershey, PA: IGI Global.

Newkirk, Thomas. 1997. *The Performance of Self in Student Writing.* Portsmouth, NH: Heinemann.

Newkirk, Thomas. 2004. "The Dogma of Transformation." *College Composition and Communication* 56 (2): 251–271.

Paine, Charles. *The Resistant Writer: Rhetoric as Immunity, 1850 to the Present.* 1999. Albany: State University of New York Press.

Rickert, Thomas. 2007. *Acts of Enjoyment: Rhetoric, Žižek, and the Return of the Subject.* Pittsburgh, PA: University of Pittsburgh Press.

Ringer, Jeffrey M. 2013. "The Dogma of Inquiry: Composition and the Primacy of Faith" *Rhetoric Review* 32 (3): 349–365.

"Vishal." 2017. "Veg to Non-Veg," Unpublished essay.

Yancey, Kathleen Blake, Liane Robertson, and Kara Taczak. 2014. *Writing Across Contexts: Transfer, Composition, and Sites of Writing.* Louisville, CO: University Press of Colorado.

Yoon, Hyoejin. 2005. "Affecting the Transformative Intellectual: Questioning 'Noble' Sentiments in Critical Pedagogy and Composition." *JAC* 25 (4): 717–759.

8

IDEOLOGY THROUGH PROCESS AND SLOW-START PEDAGOGY
Co-Constructing the Path of Least Resistance in the Social Justice Writing Classroom

Lauren F. Lichty and Karen Rosenberg

The classroom remains the most radical space of possibility in the academy
—bell hooks (hooks 1994, 14)

While having on one hand to respect the expectations and choices of the students, the educator also has the duty of not being neutral.
—Paulo Freire (Horton et al. 1990, 180)

We teach because we want to change the world. As intersectional feminists, we teach to dismantle White supremacy, rape culture, transphobia, and xenophobia. We believe our most deeply transformational social-justice work (on campus) takes place in the classroom. We believe writing is critical to that practice. We believe that academic English—and the ways we teach and assess it—bears the marks of White supremacy (Inoue 2015). Like many in this collection, we are suspicious of the concept of neutrality because we believe that it rests too directly on complicity. However, we don't brandish this statement on our syllabus or rattle off our political commitments on the first (or last) day of class. Not because we seek to practice or perform neutrality. To the contrary, as we explore in this chapter, we reject the stance of professor neutrality in our co-teaching spaces. Rather, the ways we reject neutrality come not from our full-throated articulation of our beliefs but from our classroom processes and the curation of our course content. We frame this as nuanced non-neutrality.

The issue of professor neutrality feels both more urgent and more fraught in the current sociopolitical moment. We respect the decision

DOI: 10.7330/9781607329992.c008

of other teachers to perform a neutral stance in the writing classroom, especially for faculty who occupy marginalized identities. Kopelson (2003) makes a persuasive case for performing neutrality as a way of sidestepping student resistance and hostility. Indeed, we take seriously the risk of unproductive student resistance, whether that takes the form of student silence or hostility. We desire to create productive, engaged learning environments for students, as well as professional and personal safety for ourselves. We also share the analysis that oppressive power structures shape how our students view course content, course processes, and course instructors (Lichty and Palamaro-Munsell 2017). Our embodiment as White professors in academia is inherently non-neutral. Without intentional disruption, our performance of neutrality can further marginalize already minoritized students and capitalize on oppressive systems of power.

After years of pedagogical trial and error (more on that below), we offer reflections on how we make our ideological commitments transparent to our students while minimizing unproductive student resistance to course content or ourselves as teachers. We provide these reflections not as a "how to" for other instructors, but rather as a way of furthering conversation and inquiry about the stakes, strategies, and perils of attempting liberatory education during an era of US history in which White supremacy, patriarchy, and bullying rhetoric occupy the mainstream.

We practice an approach that lays bare: our own ideological commitments as they pertain to how power operates in our classroom, the course content, what constitutes evidence, and the student role in our learning community. Intersectional feminist praxis (Crenshaw 1991; hooks 1994), feminist composition studies (Siebler 2007), and community psychology principles (Kloos et al. 2012) shape our pedagogy. Crucially, we make our decisions about ideological transparency and nuanced non-neutrality based on our read of our own institutional context; we argue that analyses of classroom practice are incomplete without an understanding of how classrooms are nested within particular institutional locations.

Unproductive student resistance may emerge in reaction to our course content (gender), the extensive reading and writing assigned, or because our course is required. We seek to minimize student resistance using a variety of tactics, including unmasking student assumptions about what a legitimate university classroom "should" look like, de-centering professorial authority, legitimizing student experience as one form of valid evidence, providing productive outlets for student resistance, and enlisting students as active co-creators of the classroom learning community (Elbow 1973; hooks 1994; Freire 1970; Siebler 2007). In this context, students are not writing for the sake of becoming "good college-level writers," but as part of personal reflection, articulation of existing knowledge, and analysis of critical social issues. In asking students to co-create our learning community, we render the hidden curriculum and "language of exclusion" (Rose 1997) visible and make our ideological commitments to the nature of knowledge production, authority, and power explicit. We argue that our attention to process creates new space for first-year students to productively engage with ideologically charged material and experience transformative, slow-to-arrive "aha" moments.

Our discussion focuses on two facets of our analysis of ideological commitments, neutrality, and student resistance. First, drawing on insights from feminist pedagogy, community psychology, and learning theory, we argue that student resistance can be minimized by attending to developmental and contextual factors as we design our pedagogy. By supporting students to engage with challenging material from their unique starting places, their need to resist the material diminishes. Our approach requires faculty and students to co-construct bridges between students' existing cognitive schemas and the content introduced in the classroom. A hallmark of this approach is a deliberate "slow start" to the course, spending the first several class periods surfacing assumptions, learning and practicing language to communicate across difference, and practicing self-reflection through writing and discussion. We argue that this gradual introduction allows students to enter the learning community on their own terms, and that this diffuses potential resistances later in the term.

The second contribution this chapter offers is to nest the discussion of the classroom within institutions. Drawing on the social-ecological model (Bronfenbrenner 1979), we argue that any discussion of pedagogical possibility is incomplete without an understanding of the institutional location (e.g., department, division, campus, and outside community). We must "read" our campus culture to make calculated choices about how and when we make our ideological commitments visible. We discuss the ways that institutional nesting may enable or hinder our classroom work. By attending to this interplay between individual students, classroom process, and institutional context, we aim to co-create a path of least resistance for students in our writing classroom.

We ground our discussion of professor neutrality, ideology, and resistance first in our early-career failures and then in our experience co-teaching a first-year, themed composition course titled "Gender Under Construction" at the University of Washington (UW) Bothell.

OUR BACKDROP: UNIVERSITY AND COURSE CONTEXT

We attribute some of the success of our approach to the institutional location where we teach. UW Bothell, a commuter campus with just over 5,500 students, enrolls a underserved students as a majority: of students entering their first year of university, 60 percent are classified as from "diverse racial and ethnic backgrounds" and approximately 40 percent are first in their families to seek a four-year university degree (University of Washington Bothell, "Fast Facts 2017–2018"). The UW Bothell mission statement affirms the intention to "build an inclusive and supportive community of learning and incorporate multicultural content and diverse perspectives on ethnic and racial groups, gender, sexual orientation, social class, and special needs" (University of Washington Bothell, "Mission Statement").

At UW Bothell, Rosenberg directs the Writing and Communication Center and Lichty is an assistant professor in the School of Interdisciplinary Arts and Sciences. Our first classroom collaboration was in 2014 when Rosenberg led a reading-strategies workshop in Lichty's class. We discovered shared commitments and struggles around social-justice pedagogy. Taking advantage of co-teaching opportunities in UW Bothell's first-year curriculum, we developed a ten-credit course (equivalent to two classes) that fulfilled a composition requirement. We titled the course "Gender Under Construction" and used metaphors of (de)construction and (de)composition to analyze norms in college writing and gender performance across different social locations.

OUR PEDAGOGICAL BACKGROUND; OR IF AT FIRST
YOU DON'T SUCCEED, REFLECT AND REVISE

Since our co-teaching relationship is key to our practice of ideological transparency and nuanced non-neutrality in our writing classroom, we begin with a brief discussion of our individual learning curves (also known as our past failures), the establishment of our co-teaching relationship, and our articulation of the values, rationales, and tensions we bring to the social justice writing classroom.

Rosenberg Background

I (Rosenberg) cycled through several ineffective stances toward instructor neutrality en route to the co-constructed approach we describe in this chapter. Both because it provides a useful trajectory showing how we came to articulate the "ideology as process" approach we advocate here and because we seek to foster a praxis wherein we freely share and learn from our mistakes, I open with a teaching fail.

As a doctoral student in women's studies in the early aughts, the interwoven topics of neutrality, transparency, and authority preoccupied me as I negotiated my identity as a teacher. I hoped that performing neutrality (in my case not being read as a radical feminist) would increase my authority with my students.

I served as a teaching assistant for a section of an interdisciplinary course titled "The Question of Human Nature." The lecture portion of the course provided a sort of "greatest hits" of White Western European male thinkers: Plato, Aristotle, St. Augustine, Hobbes, Locke, and Martin Luther, followed by material on various "others," including women and people of color. After reading Thomas More's *Utopia*, originally published in 1516, the students worked in groups to design present-day utopias. After a bland preamble, a student explained that his group's ideal society would reinstate slavery. "Just like Thomas More talks about. Not based on race, but on economics. Like the poor people, the people who were just taking and taking, right? They would pay their way, because they'd have to. As slaves. We haven't decided if they'd be slaves forever or just for a while."

Stunned, but somehow still clinging to a fraying sense that I needed to perform neutrality, I asked, "What do others think?" Some students thankfully stepped in to point out the fatal flaws in this proslavery logic. Half the class, however, advocated some form of indentured servitude. For the following class session we read *New York Times* profiles of people who were poor despite their hard work, dedication, and good morals. I sought to build out an evidence base to argue against slavery, without ever simply coming out and saying, "this is wrong and is completely against my own morality."

Of the many missteps I took during this ordeal, two hold relevance for the discussion here. First, I neglected to co-construct ground rules or establish the fundamental terms of engagement. If I had, I might have had language to "call pause" on the proslavery talk and condemn the premise that slavery could serve as permissible elements of a present-day utopia.

My second error was my fealty to a notion of instructor neutrality that ultimately served to legitimize an oppressive ideology. As Kopelson

(2003) details, there are myriad skillful ways to perform neutrality in the writing classroom. I performed neutrality poorly. I left that class with a keen desire to develop a pedagogy in which I did would need neither to hide my ideological commitments nor to pretend to be a neutral professor of objective course content.

Lichty Background

The "slow start" pedagogy emerged from my (Lichty) training as a community psychologist, feminist activist, and three related teaching experiences. Community psychology distinguishes itself from other subdisciplines of psychology through its combination of core values (i.e., well-being, diversity and social justice, empowerment and citizen participation, sense of community, and empiricism), primary guiding frameworks (e.g., the social-ecological model), and commitment to community-based research for social change (Kloos et al. 2012). As a field, we are intrinsically non-neutral.

Despite attention to socially-just research, pedagogical instruction in community psychology training is less developed. I was not taught to consider how classroom topics may produce student resistance or create harm (for more on this, see Lichty and Palamaro-Munsell 2017). As a graduate student, I served as lead instructor of an undergraduate adolescent psychology course. I used a textbook with limited analysis of how power impacted development. I infused community psychology values into my pedagogical practice through social-justice-oriented in-class activities and discussions that surfaced differences in students' own lived experiences to complicate assumptions about access to resources and "typical" developmental processes. I never experienced resistance to the social justice themes that emerged through our in-class discussions.

Several years later I taught introduction to community psychology in Portland, Oregon. I planned to start with a discussion of values and social justice. Given the activist reputation of Portland, I anticipated rigorous discussions of systematic oppression and social change. I imagined this would be easy. Instead, I was met with dominant voices shouting back at the content. Rather than identifying how oppression operates and how that relates to ongoing stress and harms well-being, the class turned into a debate over whether anyone *really* had privilege or if we should just call it luck. Many of the minoritized students remained silent. Whether vocal or silent, I read these responses as non-productive resistance.

While in Portland, I simultaneously taught introduction to human sexuality. I adopted the same approach used in my adolescent development class: standard, mostly apolitical textbook paired with activities and discussions that surfaced troubled individual and community experiences and instances of pushing back on dominant White-cis-heteropatriarchal ableist themes. Students shared diverse values and discomforts. Students debated. Students listened. There was dynamic disagreement, but not the resistance I experienced in my community psychology class.

Teaching these courses in tandem forced me to consider the differences in my pedagogical practice across classes. I used similar activities guided by the same constructivist, critical, active-learning educational philosophy. I was the same short, blonde, young, White, queer-ish woman. So what was different? The entry into the content.

Every student has a relationship to adolescence and sexuality because they consciously lived them. These topics are discussed across the public sphere. Exposure to these topics creates a baseline awareness and foundation for entering classroom conversations. This sense of familiarity and perceived neutrality opened the door to student participation. My community psychology class, on the contrary, pushed against foundational belief systems, debunked meritocracy and just-world beliefs, and centered social (in)justice themes that threatened dominant narratives of power and privilege. These are not topics widely covered in the public sphere. I did not adequately consider student readiness to engage with course content and processes that could question core beliefs about the world and themselves that they perhaps held less consciously.

I began reimagining the beginning of classes as the opportunity to develop the shared foundation that seemed to occur naturally in the adolescence and human sexuality courses by surfacing and building off lived experience. We need to ease into content that asks students to consider radical revisions to their worldviews. We need shared language and space to process.

BRINGING OUR BACKGROUNDS TOGETHER: TOWARD NUANCED, STUDENT-CENTERED NON-NEUTRALITY

Together, our experiences speak to the complexity of neutrality stances. For our classrooms to foster compassionate, critical, transformative growth, nuanced non-neutrality is necessary. It must be introduced slowly through processes that meet students where they are at, give them a shared reflective practice, allow space for unveiling assumptions and engaging productive resistance, and incrementally challenge existing worldviews.

Slowing down often requires sacrificing content in service of process. When Lichty suggested spending almost three weeks (of a ten-week term) on our slow start before introducing gender-themed readings, Rosenberg pushed back. Lichty reminded Rosenberg that the material we intended to cover was likely to challenge students' core beliefs. Recognizing that gender categories are as much an artifact of culture as biology, and that even biology doesn't reflect a two-category model (Fausto-Sterling 2012), can quickly unravel the gender binary many rely on to make sense of the world and threaten one's sense of identity. If we wanted to create a learning community where we could challenge dominant ideology, then we needed to tread gently and offer the students a bridge between their cognitive schemas and course content.

Similarly, we anticipated that our approach to teaching composition and rhetoric would deviate from their past writing courses. We view writing classrooms as spaces of liberatory potential. However, students enter college with (often negative) beliefs about themselves as writers and the purpose of writing. Student apathy, resistance, and expectations that either conflict with our pedagogy (e.g., expecting grammar drills) or outcomes (e.g., expecting to be "finished" with their formal writing education after a single composition course) reflect common challenges in the writing classroom (Durst 1999).

We used a slow start to identify existing mindsets, meet students where they are at the start of the term, and build a brave space (Arao and Clemens 2013) for surfacing assumptions and engaging with personally challenging material related to *both* gender *and* composition.

THE "SLOW START" APPROACH TO NUANCED NON-NEUTRALITY IN THE WRITING CLASSROOM

Our slow start consists of (1) establishing and practicing norms for respectful, critical conversation, (2) valuing personal lived experiences and existing knowledge, (3) surfacing and examining assumptions about substantive topics and class processes, and (4) providing incrementally more challenging content to deepen engagement and reflection. By slowly introducing more complex content, students incrementally expand their worldviews, rather than being jarred by alternative frames and throwing them into intellectual fight or flight. Process-oriented writing (Elbow 1973) is a foundational strategy through which students surface their assumptions, express their feelings, analyze content, and document their insights. We apply the "slow start" practice at the start of a new term and with the introduction of each new content area (i.e., unit). We intend to build an empowering setting (e.g., Aber, Maton, and Seidman 2010) that promotes student agency and builds capacity for participation.

The slow start draws from Vygotsky's Zone of Proximal Development (ZPD; see Chaiklin 2003 for a review), sociopolitical development (e.g., Watts, Griffith, and Abdul-Adil 1999; Watts, Williams, and Jagers 2003), and related concepts of readiness, critical consciousness raising (Freire 1970), engaged feminist pedagogy (e.g., hooks 1994), and community-based participatory research practices (e.g., Israel et al.1998; Minkler 2005). We offer an explanation of the links between ZPD, consciousness raising, and feminist pedagogy and our practice, followed by a detailed example of our slow-start process.

Vygotsky's ZPD suggests each of us has a range of skills, knowledge, and developmental capacity we can access on our own, but when someone with greater knowledge or skill provides scaffolding and support our opportunity for growth extends. This is our ZPD—what we can achieve through the collaborative support of another. ZPD may apply to discrete skills or tasks and periods of psychological development that represent functional and structural shifts in how we think or operate in the world (Chaiklin 2003). By introducing new social justice frameworks and processes, we invite students to shift their mental models and practices. If we attempt to engage students in such radical shifts without support or scaffolding, then we are likely to fail. So what can we expect will be our students' individual ZPDs? What scaffolding will they need? Reflecting on this requires consideration of the ways oppression and power are transmitted and maintained.

We are all socialized into systems of oppression (see Harro 2013 for a useful model). These systems are more or less visible to us based on our positions of privilege across intersecting identities as well as our exposure to social justice-driven spaces. Not all students have discussed these topics before. Furthermore, White supremacist heteropatriarchal ideology is threaded through not only the content of formal education but also its rhetorics and accepted ways of writing (Inoue 2015). In other words, each student's awareness of and preparation for engaging in social justice-centered analysis and discussion will vary (we could call this the variability in social justice ZPD).

Freire and hooks also call on us to remember the humanity of learners. Social justice-related topics shape our personal lived experience. Surfacing the existence and effects of oppressive systems can prompt anger, fear, sadness, and resentment. For those becoming aware of these systems for the first time, they may need space to reconcile cognitive dissonance, cope with strong feelings, and reorganize their understanding of the world and their place within it. For students already aware of these systems, they may internalize oppression and/or experience strong feelings about how other students engage in this consciousness-raising moment. Understanding that the material will elicit emotional reactions and impact students' capacity to process and meaningfully engage, we scaffold our activities to make space for resistance in discussion and written reflection and invite emotions to become part of our compassionate, non-neutral classroom.

ILLUSTRATING THE SLOW START: EXCERPTS FROM CO-TEACHING GENDER UNDER CONSTRUCTION

We begin our class with three weeks of activities intended to develop a shared understanding of the university context, classroom expectations, perspective-taking, and conversation. These initial classroom activities—all introduced before we broach material on gender—demonstrate an approach that accounts for our students' cognitive and developmental processes. Thus, we do not declare, "down with White supremacist patriarchal power structures," but we set up our writing classroom as one that embodies principles of feminist pedagogy.

First Day

We open class by centering the importance of ourselves as whole people and learners. We (the professors) introduce our identities, social locations, and pathways to college and our current positions. We highlight how our social locations influence our lived experience and opportunities. We use a show-of-hands activity to invite students into this conversation. We discuss the diversity in the room, the ways our differences enhance new learning, and how we need to honor our many obligations outside of school in order to build a supportive learning community.

Students deepen their personal presence and experience their first writing success through the six-word memoir exercise (see *Six Word Memoirs* for details). After individual practice, students share their work with a peer, including what they seek to communicate, what they feel they did well, and what they would like help on. This promotes ownership over writing and collaborative learning. After a round of revision, each student reads his or her six-word memoir aloud. This exercise centers student lives and stories as meaningful topics of writing and discussion in class. It also gradually moves students into active participation.

Students—new to college—next engage in an activity to surface their assumptions about college classrooms. Students write about what they expected to find in their college classroom. They then work in groups to draw a picture illustrating what they thought their classroom would look like. Over the three years we have done this exercise, every drawing has had a male professor lecturing to students sitting in a large hall. Students are rendered as faceless or inhabiting stereotypes such as "the jock" or "the nerd," and every year we have at least one group that draws students sleeping in class. We ask them to discuss the differences between their drawings and what they observe in our classroom. Students note that we are women, that there are two of us, that we are not lecturing (and they are actively participating), and that our classroom is not a lecture hall. We point out that we are White, which likely does conform to their assumptions. We then ask them to write about why they think we asked them to do this exercise. They frequently respond along the lines of "our assumptions may not be correct."

We tie their analysis to a key premise of the class: we are all knowledge producers and contribute to create our learning community. We deliberately decenter our own authority, state our own critiques of dominant power relations as they pertain to both professionalized and "common sense" ways of knowing, and emphasize our commitment to serve as "guides on the side" rather than "sages on a stage" (King 1993).

First Unit

Defining expectations for participation is fairly standard practice in college classrooms. Our slow-start pedagogy calls on us to engage deeply around these practices—to discuss what is happening intra- and interpersonally when conversations get real. Our classroom becomes a site for recognizing that the personal is political. The varying levels of practice seeing, naming, and engaging with oppression-related topics mean we need to consider where and how we enter these conversations and what kind of container we turn our classroom into: What practices will we share? What commitments will we make to ourselves and each other? This work draws from nonviolent and compassionate communication principles that emphasize observing what is happening, naming our feelings, identifying our needs related to those feelings, and expressing a request to allow deeper connection and understanding (e.g., Rosenberg 2003).

The first text we ask the students to read is a book on communicating across difference (Cullen 2008), which serves as the foundation of our classroom discussion norms. Written for a general audience, Cullen offers us a shared language for discussing power and oppression and concrete practices for slowing down conversation and attending to what is happening within and between us, attending to intention, impact, and accountability.

Cullen provides a gentle introduction to our conversations about respect in the classroom, power and privilege, unintentional harm, and accountability. Students write responses to the text outside of the class. In class, they discuss their responses in small groups and highlight important lessons and challenges to raise during class discussion. Finally, they revisit our syllabus with these new insights in mind. We revise our classroom practices, deepening our commitments to listen, learn, and demonstrate respect for one another.

After reading this text, students read the introduction to *Composing Knowledge* (Norgaard 2006). This text highlights the co-construction of knowledge and invites students to join ongoing conversations as knowledge producers (as opposed to merely consumers). Norgaard emphasizes that our understanding of the world is up for continued renegotiation through engaging writing and rhetoric as "critical literacy," "community," and "inquiry." Norgaard posits that reading and writing are fundamentally relational practices with material impacts. Students engage with these ideas in conversation with Cullen and our ongoing classroom practice. By positioning our students as powerful knowledge producers with commitments to co-create our classroom learning community while caring for and supporting each other, we lay claim to an intersectional feminist pedagogy through the processes we enact in the classroom (hooks 1994).

Whole Course

We developed two formal arcs of content and assignments related to gender and writing and rhetoric. These arcs contain three units that operate in tandem: (1) surfacing students' gendered assumptions and cultural norms through personal storytelling and reaction to texts, (2) developing an op-ed in response to cases that push against dominant narratives, and (3) engaging them as experts on their own campus by reviewing and writing a white paper advocating for gender-based violence educational intervention on campus.

For example, in the first gender unit, students explore their gender-based assumptions and cultural norms through personal storytelling. Their major writing assignment follows a series of activities examining gendered cultural artifacts that belong to the professors (but the students do not know that up front) and then students' own objects. Through slow-to-arrive "aha" moments that include close observation, written reflections, and presentations, students see for themselves the way they apply stereotypical gendered assumptions across spaces and objects. This opens space for deeper investigation into gender as social construction.

We use the "slow start" within and across units as we move through increasingly complex gender-related content. We hold space for students to explore new information first on their own, then in groups, and then as a full class. We center individual experiences, ideas, assumptions, and reactions through both in-class writing and dialogue and out-of-class writing prior to engaging new content. Through reading-response journals, iterative draft development, and peer review, students complete larger writing assignments that engage their analysis of gender while developing their written scholarly voice in a scaffolded, supportive community.

We find this approach to be remarkably successful. Early introductory essays reveal most of our students believed gender was binary and played little role in their life. They also described themselves as weak writers. Throughout the quarter, students *productively* engage with (and resist) texts and ideas. Their closing essays reveal a newfound attention to power and privilege, the limits of stereotyping and binaries, and a belief in the value of their scholarly voice. Most of them cite learning to communicate across difference as a critical course take-away.

UNDERSTANDING OUR ECOLOGY AS WE DEBATE NEUTRALITY

Practicing a nuanced non-neutrality in the writing classroom starts with a clear commitment to our core values of social justice and equity. How we enact these values in the classroom is a product not only of our beliefs but also careful calculation of what we deem possible in our social and institutional context.

Too often discussions of pedagogy treat the classroom as a decontextualized space outside of a specific institutional context. We argue that reading our institutional locations is key to performances of (non)neutrality in the writing classroom. We start with ourselves and our students and then consider how our class is nested within a larger program, school, university, and region. The mission, objectives, and values adopted at each level of analysis impact our pedagogical decision-making in our classroom.

Our decision to enact such pedagogy was grounded in our ability to argue that our approach aligned with our institutional mission. This provides security for pursuing non-neutral educational approaches. Had we not been able to make that argument, or were we part of a unit that was actively hostile to social justice pedagogy, we might have modified our approach. Each professor must assess the risk of adopting non-neutral pedagogical approaches for him- or herself. We must consider our context and who is likely to resist or react negatively to our strategies: students, faculty, or administrators? This may vary, based on our identities, as well. For colleagues in hostile contexts or who face additional layers of marginality beyond those we occupy, conduct a close read of the campus context. Examine the risks associated with adopting overtly non-neutral pedagogical processes. Non-neutrality that expels us from important sites of resistance is not productive non-neutrality. For additional considerations related to context, see Holt's chapter 10 in this collection.

CONCLUSION

Through slow-start pedagogy we build a setting in which students are simultaneously in control of their narrative and are supported to engage in progressively more complex analyses of themselves and the world around them. This process encourages respectful non-neutrality from students and instructors. The slow-start process applied throughout the course leverages: writing as a site of personal reflection on complex social phenomena, identifying and working with one's own assumptions and mindsets, and sense-making and stand-taking.

We offer "slow start" pedagogy as one way to add nuance to the discussion of teacher neutrality in the writing classroom. While we firmly agree with Freire's stance that our duty as teachers is to reject neutrality, to do so successfully within a public university requires that we act to minimize unproductive resistance both from our students and from our institution. We argue that the slow start provides a nuanced approach to rejecting neutrality that can be adapted across educational settings.

REFERENCES

Aber, Mark S., Kenneth I. Maton, and Edward Seidman. 2010. *Empowering Settings and Voices for Social Change*. Oxford: Oxford University Press.

Arao, Brian, and Kristi Clemens. 2013. "From Safe Spaces to Brave Spaces." In *The Art of Effective Facilitation: Reflections from Social Justice Educators*, ed. Lisa M. Landreman, 135–150. Sterling, VA: Stylus Publishing.

Bronfenbrenner, Urie. 1979. *The Ecology of Human Development.* Cambridge, MA: Harvard University Press.

Chaiklin, Seth. 2003. "The Zone of Proximal Development in Vygotsky's Analysis of Learning and Instruction." In *Vygotsky's Educational Theory in Cultural Context,* ed. Alex Kozulin, Boris Gindis, Vladimir S. Ageyev, Suzanne M. Miller, 39–64. Cambridge: Cambridge University Press.

Crenshaw, Kimberlé. 1991. "Mapping the Margins: Intersectionality, Identity Politics, and Violence against Women of Color." *Stanford Law Review* 43 (6): 1241–1299.

Cullen, Maura. 2008. *35 Dumb Things Well-Intended People Say: Surprising Things We Say That Widen the Diversity Gap.* New York: Morgan James Publishing.

Durst, Russel K. 1999. *Collision Course: Conflict, Negotiation, and Learning in College Composition.* Urbana, IL: NCTE.

Elbow, Peter. 1973. *Writing without Teachers.* Oxford: Oxford University Press.

Fausto-Sterling, Anne. 2012. *Sex/Gender: Biology in a Social World.* New York: Routledge.

Freire, Paulo. 1970. *Pedagogy of the Oppressed.* New York: Continuum.

Harro, Bobbie. 2013. "The Cycle of Socialization." In *Readings for Diversity and Social Justice,* ed. Maurianne Adams, Warren J. Blumenfeld, Carmelita Rosie Castañeda, Heather W. Hackman, Madeline L. Peters, and Ximena Zúñiga. New York: Routledge.

hooks, bell. 1994. *Teaching to Transgress: Education as the Practice of Freedom.* New York: Routledge.

Horton, Myles, Paulo Freire, Brenda Bell, John Gaventa, and John Peters. 1990. *We Make the Road by Walking: Conversations on Education and Social Change.* Philadelphia, PA: Temple University Press.

Inoue, Asao B. 2015. *Antiracist Writing Assessment Ecologies: Teaching and Assessing Writing for a Socially Just Future.* Fort Collins, Colorado: WAC Clearinghouse; Anderson, SC: Parlor Press.

Israel, Barbara, Amy J. Schulz, Edith A. Parker, and Adam B. Baker.1998. "Review of Community-Based Research: Assessing Partnership Approaches to Improve Public Health." *Annual Review of Public Health* 19 (Spring): 173–202.

King, Alison. 1993. "From Sage on the Stage to Guide on the Side." *College Teaching* 41 (1): 30–35.

Kloos, Bret, Jean Hill, Elizabeth Thomas, Abraham Wandersman, and Maurice J. Elias. 2012. *Community Psychology: Linking Individuals and Communities.* Boston, MA: Cengage Learning.

Kopelson, Karen. 2003. "Rhetoric on the Edge of Cunning; Or, the Performance of Neutrality (Re)Considered as a Composition Pedagogy for Student Resistance." *College Composition and Communication* 55 (1): 115–146.

Lichty, Lauren F., and Eylin Palamaro-Munsell. 2017. "Pursuing an Ethical, Socially Just Classroom: Searching for Community Psychology Pedagogy." *American Journal of Community Psychology* 60 (3–4): 316–326.

Minkler, Meredith. 2005. "Community-Based Research Partnerships: Challenges and Opportunities." *Journal of Urban Health* 82 (2): ii3–ii12.

Norgaard, Rolf. 2006. *Composing Knowledge: Readings for College Writers,* 1st ed. Boston, MA: Bedford/St. Martin's.

Rose, Mike. 1997. "The Language of Exclusion: Writing Instruction at the University." In *Cross-Talk in Comp Theory: A Reader,* ed. Victor Villanueva. Urbana, IL: NCTE.

Rosenberg, Marshall B. 2003. *Nonviolent Communication: A Language of Life.* Encinitas, CA: Puddledancer Press.

Siebler, Kay. 2007. *Composing Feminisms: How Feminists Have Shaped Theories and Practices.* Cresskill, NJ: Hampton Press.

Six Word Memoirs. Accessed January 30, 2018. https://www.sixwordmemoirs.com.

University of Washington Bothell. "Fast Facts 2017–2018." Accessed January 29, 2018. https://www.uwb.edu/about/facts/fast-facts-2017.

University of Washington Bothell. "Mission Statement." Accessed January 30, 2018. https://www.uwb.edu/about/vision.

Watts, Roderick J., Derek M. Griffith, and Jaleel Abdul-Adil. 1999. "Sociopolitical Development as an Antidote for Oppression—Theory and Action." *American Journal of Community Psychology* 27 (2): 255–271.

Watts, Roderick J., Nat Chioke Williams, and Robert J. Jagers. 2003. "Sociopolitical Development." *American Journal of Community Psychology* 31 (1–2): 185–194.

9

TRANSPARENCY AS A DEFENSE-LESS ACT
Shining Light on Emerging Ideologies in an Activist Writing and Research Course

Heather Fester

WALKING OVER BROKEN GROUND

Activist Writing and Research Course Survey Question: What is political or religious ideology?[1]

"Political or religious ideology are the core values or ideas that one holds which subconsciously shape many decisions or thoughts formed by the individual." *female student, 18 years old,* "I am a white middle class female which has shaped my social standings."

"A belief system that controls many peoples lives." *male student, 18 years old,* "White straight male, in Greek life. Likes to go out to parties and make friends."

"A way each individual recognizes, understands and lives their lives." *male student, 19 years old,* "I am an upper class strait white male."

"A belief that drives the perspectives and morals of an individual. It can range from the golden rule in the bible to believing that everyone regardless of age, gender, or background can and should be treated equally." *female student, 18 years old,* "My identity as an African American female has made my perspective a little less known that that of the majority solely based off of demographic and some of my challenges just being in the way that I voice my perspective. I would also include being in the middle working class as a component because some people on campus are coming from a more secure financial background, thus making the things they think about in terms of affordability different than myself who has to consider the costs of things more often."

According to Wayne Booth (1974), from the beginning of our species, rhetoric has functioned to help us assert the primacy of one value or belief over another: "We produce a great flood of value-ridden rhetoric directed, as it were, against one another. We talk ceaselessly to each other—and quite evidently have done so from the beginning—trying

DOI: 10.7330/9781607329992.c009

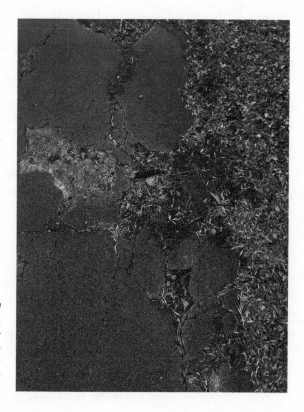

Figure 9.1. Fractured concrete sidewalk: a visual metaphor for our belief structures and the subconscious assumptions that protrude through them.

to show that *this* value is genuinely superior to *that.* And we all do so as if persuasion really mattered, and as if choices among values could be judged as really right or wrong" (125).

I went for a walk earlier to clear my head so I could write the current leg of this draft. As I was walking, I was studying the sidewalk and thinking about belief. For a long stretch of the sidewalk, I had to watch my step closely. The concrete ground was broken into jagged pieces beneath my feet. (See figure 9.1 for an image of the broken ground.) The roots pushing up through the broken surface made me think of the subconscious or latent content and assumptions or values that protrude through our belief structures.

But every so often, I also saw a landscaped yard where 'contraction joints' had been planned into whole swaths of concrete and other hard surfaces, as for a driveway. In these places, there was a "give" to the surface that allowed for the natural shifts underneath. (See figure 9.2 for contraction joints in concrete pavings.) There were many fewer cracks, many fewer places to trip.

Figure 9.2. Uncracked concrete pavings, scored by contraction joints: a visual metaphor for the resiliency of certain belief structures with natural "give."

***

I open this essay with a series of survey responses from students in an activist-themed writing and research class I taught at the University of Denver in the Spring 2017 quarter.[2] As I explore throughout this chapter the shifting ideological space of the classroom within the larger university geography, I will bring in voices of students from that class with their informed consent and permission. I will not be framing their replies or interpreting them as results from a formal qualitative study. Rather, I include their voices alongside my own to comment on and interrupt[3] my narrative of our shared classroom experience. Some of my survey questions, posed in the last third of the term, but not read until after grades had been submitted, asked them to "read" my ideology or identity to offer feedback about my own transparency and neutrality in the classroom.

I will let the voices of these students push up through the text without comment, and I'll let the reader decide if the concrete beneath our feet shifts naturally with the many voices moving through it or if it, too, becomes broken ground.

Changes since Karen Kopelson's 2003 article on rhetorical cunning, as this chapter asserts, can be understood as moving towards greater levels of inclusivity and rhetorical complexity around a range of possible views that can be expressed in the classroom, which includes the instructor's ability to be transparent about his/her/their own perspectives and social locations as these have shaped the curriculum and classroom environment. Admittedly, as other authors in the present volume have also pointed out, the ability to espouse *transparent* pedagogies can be correlated with privilege or else are "fraught performances" as an "emerging imperative" (Thomas and Rowland, chapter 16, this volume), while *neutrality* may be a lived necessity for those with marginalized bodies and social locations within institutions of higher education (in this volume see Brewer, chapter 1; Samuels, chapter 4; García and Hinojosa, chapter 13; Johnson and LeBouef Tullia, chapter 14).

Still, other authors in this volume, recognizing these likely correlations, maintain a complex view of both "transparency" and "neutrality" as signifiers that sometimes slip and should be understood internally more than dialectically (Stubblefield and Chisholm, chapter 15) or should be refigured with a both/and logic (Johnson and LeBouef Tullia, chapter 14), potentially leading to something like a "slow-start pedagogy" (Lichty and Rosenberg, chapter 8) or "translucent pedagogy" (Thomas and Rowland, chapter 16) or to perform respectability within assessment (Abbott, chapter 11). The word *ambiguity*, too, used to refer to a teacher's stance, is both lauded (Holt, chapter 10) and problematized (Johnson and LeBouef Tullia, chapter 14) within this volume. *Pluralism* is discussed for its seeming dangers as well. For instance, Mara Holt (chapter 10), in turns critical and reflective about her own positionality in relation to the diversity debates in Texas in the 1990s, claims that embracing multiple perspectives on an equal playing field assumes neutrality by avoiding issues of power. In other chapters, however, a "strategic" or situated neutrality (García and Hinojosa, chapter 13) is defended for the way it can help move students beyond the resistance that they might feel toward a specific teacher's perceived social location or political stance.

The relevance, urgency, and nuances of any such shifts need to be highlighted more reflectively and intentionally in the field's discourse because of the political, institutional, cultural, and technological changes that are advancing upon us rapidly and in interconnected ways. What needs to be reconceived, I would argue in relationship to other contributions to this volume, is a method of holding complexity in the classroom around multiple, viable perspectives on topics associated with ideologies, whether these be of a political, religious, or philosophical nature. I am not advocating for classroom pluralism or transcending difficulty. And not all perspectives are equally valid. Some are, in fact, potentially dangerous. However, holding *complexity*, as I discuss it in relationship to classroom conversations and assignments, means recognizing teacher positionality and the potential of student difference at the same time, in a way that doesn't dismiss possible tensions in the space between. It means holding a "brave space" (Arao and Clemens 2013), practicing what Wayne Booth has called "listening rhetoric" (2004, 10), or engaging compassion as García and Hinojosa (chapter 13) suggest. Not everything "must" be shared by the newly transparent instructor whose social location may make him/her/them exceedingly vulnerable; rather, complexity recognizes that the instructor's beliefs are always already a visible part of our shared curricular ground. Furthermore, the way we interact with student ideologies needs to be capacious and more open than it has been in the past as well.

A WAY OF SHINING LIGHT THROUGH: WHAT IS IDEOLOGICAL TRANSPARENCY?

Survey Question: What does ideological transparency mean to you?

"Ideological transparency means that those have a core ideology, however, they are open to understanding and accepting other ideologies." *female student, 18 years old,* "I am a white middle class female."

"I think anything that has to do with transparency means being open and exposed in all regards. Ideological transparency means that a group or person in a group is open to talking about their group and their beliefs. They don't shy away from conversations about what they believe in, even if their group is frowned upon by others or society." *female student, 19 years old,* "I am a white female. I come from a wealthy, middle-upper class family. I have spoken English my whole life."

"Ideological transparency is being open and forthcoming with where I stand." *male student, 23 years old,* "Human."

"Encouraging a plethora of ideologies and discussing them equally without a bias towards any specific kind of viewpoint." *female student, 18 years old,* "My identity as an African American female has made my perspective a little less known that that of the majority."

Rhetoric is a tradition offering a set of tools that allow us to "shine light through" and see multiple perspectives on ideas or issues at once. However, the space of a classroom needs to be *prepared*, similar to how Lichty and Rosenberg (chapter 8, this volume) discuss doing as a component of a "slow-start pedagogy," to allow for the interplay of the many possible perspectives, something I will discuss further in the "Holding Critical Complexity" section that follows.

Students already rhetorically analyze the teacher's self-presentation rhetoric, the readings and curriculum that the individual teacher (or in some cases, that the program) has designed, the assignments given (and the ways they are given), and other components of the classroom environment, such as views of classmates or the openness of the teacher to a range of perspectives or beliefs. They read these parts of the ideological ground of the class differently than we might, yet they do make inferences about them. This is particularly true for students who hold views or a social location or identity that is underrepresented in the landscape of the institution itself. And, when I refer to underrepresented views or identities, I mean both those that are marginalized in terms of power and those that may be found in the political mainstream, but which may be marginalized amongst viable academic ideologies explored in the classroom today, such as we find with the attention increasingly paid by administrators to far-right views on campus that shows up, for example, institutionally as revisions to existing campus free-speech policies.[4]

Holding Critical Complexity

Critical educators, such as David Seitz and Chris Gallagher, have looked at "gaps and traps" in first-generation approaches to critical teaching (Seitz 2002, 512), offering critiques of the ways that student learning can sometimes become secondary to rigidified notions about how or what we should be teaching as critical educators. Gallagher goes as far as to distinguish between *pedagogy* and *critical pedagogy*, claiming that in some cases, "critical pedagogy has become another academic regime of truth" (2002, 85). Too often, Gallagher claims, the critical teacher as transformative intellectual becomes "the academy's moral conscience—the lone voice of the dreamer who is fundamentally opposed to the senseless but indomitable forces of the institution" (79). Pedagogy, on the other hand, Gallagher says, is a type of situated knowledge production that "could not, by definition, be complete or static" (125), and because of this, it responds to the institutional or educational context instead of merely resisting perceived hegemonic or unreflexive values in the classroom or institution.

In a similar vein to Gallagher, David Seitz (2002) has questioned whether teaching "resistance to cultural reproduction must be an *a priori* goal of the course" (507), and has studied the various authentic motives students bring to the classroom, including those that are more instrumental in nature. He claims that "in terms of internally persuasive authority, my research has shown that most students do not see cultural criticism as a positive end in itself. Indeed, they may see it as just another part of the academic game" (506). Seitz favors, instead, the approach Bruce McComiskey (2000) relies on in *Teaching Composition as a Social Process*, which rejects the dichotomy between teaching *composition* and teaching *resistance* and, in Seitz's words, sees that "both approaches are necessary to nurture critical thinkers as doers in the world" (Seitz 2002, 506). Seitz also advocates that teachers give up their faith in converting students to a critical agenda, instead favoring "mutuality in course architecture" and nurturing what "Wallace and Ewald call interpretive agency," which means the "bringing of one's prior theory to bear in the creation of passing theory with others" (Wallace and Ewald, quoted in Seitz 2002, 507–508).

Both Gallagher and Seitz take what Robert Brooke (1987) has termed the "underlife" of students seriously in their reconsiderations of critical teaching in composition, including "students' anxieties over future employment" (Seitz 2002, 510). And, Seitz emphasizes Russel Durst's (1999) *Collision Course* to model some of the ways student ideologies, examined or not, can structure the classroom and challenge the curriculum. Seitz cites Durst's "reflective instrumentalism" as one example of an approach that "begins with most students' pragmatic motives for attending college, but seeks to cultivate critical analysis within a framework of students' examining school and career issues through textual and field research" (Seitz 2002, 511).

Further, Gallagher and Seitz, and perhaps also those who have influenced their approaches, demonstrate ways of "holding complexity" in the composition classroom: recognizing a multitude of perspectives as legitimate, or at least acknowledging they are present; using mutuality to negotiate the classroom agenda; teaching "reflexive instrumentalism"; and looking self-critically at what we value, why, and how we present it to students. The ability to communicate transparently about all of these is a *complex* process.

The complex critical educator would not begin with a predefined agenda or a set identity and present it to students—which further exemplifies a type of institutional rhetoric that we want students to become aware of and critique—but would be responsive to student feedback and emphasize points of contact between differing viewpoints. And, *complex criticality* means also being transparent about gaps created by inclusion or exclusion of the educator's own perspective as part of the negotiation. With such transparent complexity, relinquishing the constructive or interpretive authority or even the performed neutrality of a teacherly stance could never be total. It would, instead, be enacted complexly as part of the dialogic space of the evolving classroom. It would be part of the forces that can be made more apparent *between* student and teacher or *between* institution or governing body and curriculum.

Negotiating Power as Authentic Vulnerability

As Lisa Delpit (1988) writes, cultural power is something we trade, and "those with power are frequently least aware of—or least willing to acknowledge—its existence. Those with less power are often most aware of its existence" (282). If a critical education curriculum is meant, at least in part, to have students rethink institutional inequalities and possible responses, then it may seem politically regressive to teach "reflexive instrumentalism" or to view pedagogical knowledge as situated and complex. However, Delpit, herself a female African American researcher, seemed to advocate for a complex view. She says:

> As a result of careful listening to alternative points of view, I have myself come to a viable synthesis of perspectives. Both sides do need to be able to listen, and I contend that it is those with the most power, those in the majority, who must take the greater responsibility for initiating the process.
>
> To do so takes a very special kind of listening, listening that requires not only eyes and ears, but open hearts and minds. We do not really see through our eyes or hear through our ears, but through our beliefs. To put our beliefs on hold is to cease to exist as ourselves for a moment—and that is not easy . . . It is not easy, but it is the only way to learn what it might feel like to be someone else and the only way to start the dialogue . . .
>
> We must keep the perspective that people are experts on their own lives . . . We must not be too quick to deny their interpretations or accuse them of "false consciousness." We must believe that people are rational beings . . . And finally, we must learn to be vulnerable enough to allow our world to turn upside down in order to allow the realities of others to edge themselves into our consciousness. In other words, we must become ethnographers in the true sense. (Delpit 1988, 297)

Delpit has exemplified complex transparency in the passage above, much in the way I use it in this essay as well. She points to the need for allowing multiple viewpoints, even those we want to deny, and letting those make us vulnerable as well. She asks us to open our hearts and minds and recognize the way that we see "through our beliefs" (297).

When instructors *can* be transparent—and present the complexity in ideology and the reality of moral emotions about injustice—then we are not alienating students against their own authentic motives. In fact, we are inviting them to consider deeply how their views were formed (see Brown, chapter 7, in this volume). Also, there's some give in the discussion or lesson plan. Students are invited to change based on arguments that respect their autonomy and agency. Such models move toward what William G. Perry (1970) called the position of commitment in relativism or pluralism from his famous study of the intellectual and ethical values of college students.

Furthermore, Chris Gallagher, Peter M. Gray, and Shari Stenberg enact a post-dialectical logic in their work with the term *con/fusion*, another way of holding complexity for teachers, administrators (and maybe also students) that embraces the tension of different perspectives held simultaneously. They say *con/fusion* is "the coexistence of fusion as an end-in-view and confusion as a positive condition that we should embrace" (Gallagher, Gray, and Stenberg 2009, 22). Holding this tension does not require adopting a relativistic stance, and it can also happen simultaneously with an intellectual or ethical commitment.

Wayne Booth also articulated the practice of "listening rhetoric," by which he meant "the whole range of communicative arts for reducing misunderstanding by paying full attention to opposing views" (2004, 10). The listening rhetor thinks, "I am not just seeking a truce; I want to pursue the truth behind our differences." A recent popular example of such a practice was referenced in Theo E. J. Wilson's TEDx Denver talk, "A Black Man Goes Undercover in the Alt-Right." Wilson refers to "courageous conversation . . . with people who do not see the world in the same way" (2017, 13:42) as a key to change.

Along these lines, a complex classroom space I have offered and enacted in the last couple of years is the "brave space" (Arao and Clemens 2013). Such a space operates on a set of agreements, five "common rules" that can be negotiated with students: agree to disagree, don't take things personally, challenge by choice, be respectful, and no attacks.

Metacognitive Complexity: Holding Multiple Perspectives and an Integral View

It is possible to view what is at stake in the critique of critical pedagogy through the lens of integral philosophy as well. Integral thought and practice were first articulated in the mid-twentieth century by such figures as Indian freedom fighter, poet, and sage Sri Aurobindo Ghose (1914) and postwar German philosopher and poet Jean Gebser (1985). However, integral thought has been given its most cogent contemporary form by philosopher Ken Wilber (1995).[5] All of these versions of *integral* have, I believe, something useful to offer the composition instructor and the field of rhetoric and composition today. That contribution may take the form of a compelling archaeology of perspectives on issues in our field and a narrative of how these have been shaped by historical forces. Or not. But, because integral thought is where I get some of my phrases above, like "holding the complexity" of ideologies and taking multiple perspectives on an idea, I share this information to show how it has influenced my thinking—a type of potentially "risky" ideological transparency for me as a researcher.[6]

With the integral structure of consciousness,[7] there is a capacity to see perspectives taken on reality from earlier levels of cognitive complexity or psychospiritual development with greater objectivity, while including them in one's understanding as valid but partial views. Integral thought can be described as a type of post-postmodern ideology or philosophy.[8] In perspective theory from integral thought, an important shift takes place that is described as taking a fourth-person perspective (or dimension of depth) on an issue being discussed or studied in the classroom. Postformal development researcher Suzanne Cook-Greuter (2013) defines "fourth-person perspective" as representing "a major watershed . . . as [a stage] it signifies the move from conventional to postconventional meaning making . . . Overall, each new stage represents a new reality for the subject, a new way of identifying as a self and of understanding and relating to the world" (53). Significantly, she says, "The 4th person perspective allows individuals to stand outside the system they grew up in and observe themselves and their cultural surroundings . . . One can look at the familiar (status quo) through a new lens and query many of its tacit assumptions, values, and beliefs" (53).

An instructor's identity or ideology, accessed from a fourth-person perspective, would become an object in their awareness to take a perspective on. As an *object of awareness*, the ideology is not alienated from the person's subjective experience or disembodied from socially located and embodied realities; the term is used in much the same way as in object-relations theory. Rather, in the words of postformal psychologist Robert Kegan (1998), in undergoing the move from subject to object, there is a shift that happens so that the ideology doesn't "have" one (in its grip via means of one's subconscious commitment to it), but where a person "has the theory" (in conscious awareness).[9] In Wilber's (1995) terms, this looks like *transcending* and *including* an old perspective or belief tied to an earlier structure of consciousness that one is no longer operating out of exclusively or unquestioningly. When even identity politics are *transcended and included* in the classroom, they can be valued, discussed from multiple perspectives, and the complex underpinnings that support them can be made more apparent, or *trans*parent, all in a way that preserves the complexity at the heart of the issues.[10]

COURSE DESIGN: WHAT DOES IT MEAN TO HOLD COGNITIVE COMPLEXITY IN THE CLASSROOM?[11]

Survey Question: Is the professor of this course transparent about his/her/their ideology or beliefs and identity? How do you know? (Feel free to share a story or example.)

"I feel if I were to ask my professor her beliefs on any topic, I would receive an honest and whole answer." *male student, 19 years old,* "I am a lower-middle class white male from Southern Louisiana. I have a different cultural upbringing than most students at DU."

"I wouldn't say Professor Fester is very transparent about anything, which I think is a beneficial thing. I think too much demonstration and bias about beliefs would inhibit learning for the class and possible make some people feel like they shouldn't speak." *female student, 19 years old,* "white female from a wealthy, middle-upper class family."

"No. There is more of a focus on critical thinking as opposed to expression of ideology." *male student, 23 years old,* "Human."

"I think so. She never favors one ideology more than the other and creates an environment where no viewpoint is treated differently than the others even if some ideologies are favored as a majority. There's no persuasion to discuss a specific kind of ideology." *female student, 18 years old,* "My identity as an African American female has made my perspective a little less known that that of the majority."

When I started teaching a course themed around activist writing and research at the University of Denver (DU) in the spring quarter of 2017, as I mentioned in the introduction, I anticipated some pushback from at least a few students about the political nature of the content. The advertised theme (which was posted prior to their enrollment selections) was as follows:

Activist Writing and Research—If there is a spectrum of attitudes between indifference and the call to activism, then X can stand in as a medium for movement between these extremes. It can be a third thing. Let X stand for whatever that might be to you: community, culture, research, imagination, your own voice, innovation, change. Let it be a sign of the times. Let it be your own signature, when as James Wright says "we have experienced more than we know how to express." In this class, we will read widely and research the difficult, the [alienated], the inexpressible, and

ways of making a difference in contexts where we live and find our meaning. There will be a mini-ethnography component and two main research
papers engaging textual and qualitative research techniques. (University
of Denver Writing Program 2017)

I expected that the nudge toward activism—selected kairotically in the
face of tumultuous feelings (mine, and as I anticipated, my students')
following the 2016 presidential election—would bump up against some
student resistance, inflame some long-held family beliefs in at least a few
of the students in the section, enrolled to the maximum with sixteen at
the start of the term. Not everyone reads the course descriptions carefully before enrolling, after all. Some choose to sign up for a specific
themed section because of time preferences or for another reason that
has nothing to do with the focus of the course. I took inventory at the
beginning to get a sense of why students were there and whether their
choices were theme-related. I also had the students develop a theory
of activism and share their past experiences with activist work or ideas
as part of their first informal two-page writing activity. (See the full sequence of assignments in table 9.1.) As a follow-up to that activity, I asked
students to reflect on distinctions between activism and research in a
class discussion, playing up each in their more traditional expressions to
accentuate perceived differences. This helped prepare them to explore
the values of activism and research in their first longer writing activity,
which I designed as a mini-ethnography and write-up.

As the course progressed and rolled into week two, one student
dropped, and when the add/drop date had passed, I considered the
students to be relatively well-informed about the value-laden foundation
of the coursework and my own motives as a teacher.

I had also built in a component in which students would give a presentation on an activist organization or cause to their peers, with the
support of a visual aid for 12–15 minutes. I considered this to be a formal presentation in the course, and students were also given a rubric by
which they would be evaluated in advance.

About halfway through the course, I assigned an informal ideology
inventory journal response to be submitted via the discussion forum in
our learning management system (LMS), and at that time we were also
exploring together the meaning of the term *ideology* and looking at the
contexts in which the term is used. The students interpreted *ideology*,
even following our brief discussion, more broadly than I did. Many of
them included things like general outlook on the world or basic values
(like the "golden rule") in their inventories and less often listed official
movements as examples (like "feminism").

Table 9.1. Sequence of assignments

Assignment	Course Timeline
1. Informal short write: Theory of activism	Weeks 1 and 2
2. Anonymous feedback forms introduced and discussed	
3. Mini-ethnography and write up	Week 3
4. Formal presentations on an activist or organization	Throughout course
5. Informal ideology inventory (journal response)	Half-way through the spring quarter
6. Ideological transparency survey	In week 8 (two weeks before the end of the spring quarter)

The two longer formal essay assignments are not included in this timeline or course-design description, but these explored, first, qualitative and, then, text-based research approaches to activist-themed topics. At the end of the course, students transformed one of their essay projects into a multimodal activist argument and presented it to each other.

As another part of my intentional strategy to be transparent and to hold ideological complexity, I frequently made references to the possibility that we could take multiple perspectives on any issue, and when students asked for my view on topics we explored together—something they did not often do—I offered it, with the disclaimer that it was my view, and other viewpoints were certainly possible and encouraged. For instance, one student asked me how I might explain "anti-racism" as an idea to those who didn't believe racism continued to be a problem in our country. I offered my perspective and then asked the class to offer their views as well.

This way of handling a range of perspectives on a course topic that might have been presumed as liberal-leaning in nature was the one I decided to adopt so students would feel comfort engaging in debate openly instead of worrying that any oppositional stances might hurt their grade or automatically be perceived as prejudice. The students had a range of different trainings around using the language of social location or power, but I modeled those usages and often told them that was what I was doing at the time. In doing my own work of recognizing my White privilege in the preceding two years, with the support of two semester-long book groups and an activist organization, I had discovered that we often begin in ignorance about our own unearned privilege and exclusionary uses of power before authentic awareness dawns or lifestyle changes become necessary to accommodate the transformed/-ing perspective. In a racial microaggressions workshop I attended, Nathaniel

Granger, president of the Society for Humanistic Psychology, likened learning to recognize oppressive practices in ourselves or around us to learning to dance. Sometimes we might step on our partner's toes or feel clumsy, but if we stay on the dance floor, it will get easier. And, perhaps the discomfort is also part of the transformative work as well. So, I wanted those edgier places where real growth can take place to be part of the classroom without making them the central objective of the course. I wanted this to be a "brave space" in the course.

I chose to invite the students' feedback on all aspects of the course very early on in the form of anonymous feedback forms. From the anonymous feedback forms, I then generated a list of their suggestions on the board, and we discussed and voted on the suggestions we wanted to keep, quit, or start doing as a class.

I also built an anonymously submitted, online, late-term survey into our class time, and I announced that I would not read it until the course was over and grades had been submitted. Even though I wouldn't see their responses to survey questions until it was too late to modify the course content, I designed the questions to promote their reflexive awareness of the classroom ideological space that I saw all of us responsible for creating and maintaining. The questions were chosen, therefore, not only to get feedback to inform future sections I might teach or the exploratory research question I was holding for this project, but also to help heighten their awareness of my intentions, views, choices, and process as a teacher, if those had been invisible to them previously. I was making apparent some of the decisions I had made and had been making throughout.

Being more intentional about opening the space to a range of viewpoints allowed me to consider my own assumptions carefully as well. I had long taught from a seemingly neutral ideological position, following Gerald Graff's (1993) advice in *Beyond the Culture Wars* to teach the conflicts. In previous semesters and at other institutions, when I encountered bias or prejudice in a student's essay or responses in class, I had learned to call attention to audience awareness, biased language, counterarguments, and logical fallacies when needed, like many other composition teachers. My decision to share my beliefs in the classroom while inviting deeper discussion of a broader range of viewpoints coming from the students as well was therefore a new risk for me.

The students responded well to the risk, however. On their informal surveys, six of the eight students who responded indicated that they were comfortable or very comfortable with the way political views were expressed in class, and the other two respondents said they were moderately comfortable with it. When asked if they would be comfortable expressing a view that had not already been expressed in class, seven out of eight students indicated they would be comfortable or very comfortable doing so. And, based on their experience of the first eight weeks of the quarter, four of the students who responded to the survey indicated they had a *theory* about what my political beliefs were, two indicated they thought they knew what my beliefs were, and two said they didn't think about it.

POST-DIALECTICAL TENSIONS: WHOSE IDEOLOGY? WHOSE VOICE?[12]

Survey Question: Based on your response above, how do you feel about your WRIT 1133 professor's perceived level of transparency about her/his/their ideology, beliefs, and/or identity? Should this change? If so, how? If not, what should stay the same?

"I think transparency has its time and place. I think to maintain a professional relationship between student and professor, neither party should be too transparent about any one thing." *female student, 19 years old,* "I am a white female. I come from a wealthy, middle-upper class family"

"I think the focus isn't on our professor's ideology so much as learning about what makes up ours and learning rhetorical language to think critically about what we see and hear every day in this information age." *male student, 23 years old,* "Human."

"I think that my professor does an adequate job at her level of transparency. She appears to be open to new opinions and have an understanding to support her own as well as others ideological beliefs." *female student, 18 years old,* "I am a white middle class female."

"Not sure." *male student, 19 years old,* "I am an upper class straight white male."

One premise of this argument, meant to inspire similar approaches or to act as a lens for curriculum planning by other instructors, is that our interpretation of cultural practices that we offer students is powerful, influential, and mostly invisible as we typically model it. Teacherly interpretive acts often *pass* as invisible in the classroom. When a teacher also *performs* a simple form of neutrality in the classroom, the ideologies informing the curriculum and assignments can become invisible too. For instance, as instructors approve an essay topic proposal or reject a possible topic that disrupts a dominant reading of the assignment, we practice interpretation based on implicit value assumptions (often, the value being that we want the student to do well on the assignment). Furthermore, the questions instructors ask students in relationship to course readings or the writing they turn in also refigure student readings of texts (or silences) as forms of meaning-making that we can choose to acknowledge, privilege, disrupt, or ignore. How do institutional statements about freedom of expression further complicate the way we read the ideological space of the classroom or a student text?

As a result of the explorations described above, my own understanding of ideological transparency in the classroom grew to include awareness of three different components: (1) students should be made aware of transparency and neutrality with careful context-setting discussions (see "translucent pedagogy" in Thomas and Rowland, chapter 16 in this volume, or "slow-start pedagogy" in Lichty and Rosenberg, chapter 8, also in this volume); (2) teachers can't negate the authentic values (short of dangerous or hateful ideologies) students bring into a class in an *a priori* way if something like this is going to work; and (3) to do these things, it is essential for the teacher, also, to be actively responsive and vulnerable in the mutually negotiated, *brave* space of the classroom.

Until our critical pedagogies are willing to examine more closely and in a sustained way the viability of a range of student values and the way their resistance can be seen as a type of authorship, introducing student voices alongside ours allows us to find areas of complexity, tension, and surprise—the last of these being possibly the most valuable gift of ideological transparency overall.

NOTES

1. These survey responses were used throughout the chapter "interruptively" (see note 3). Furthermore, all gender identifications listed after the quotes were voluntarily self-disclosed via an in-class survey students completed in the spring 2017 course they took with me. The material in quotation marks following demographic information is each student's voluntarily self-disclosed social location. I have chosen to leave grammar and usage as it was submitted for these responses, but I ask readers to keep in mind that the students approached the survey as an informal writing opportunity.

2. Only eight of the fourteen students who completed this section of the course chose to respond to the optional, anonymous survey, given in class on May 8, 2017. Three students were absent on that day and were reminded by email that they could participate in this voluntary, anonymous survey.

3. I use *interrupt* here in a way that was inspired, however loosely, by Gallagher, Gray, and Stenberg (2002). I have tried to stay true to some of their intent in using the term to describe their model of collegiality and the role of voices in negotiating or interpreting power relationships.

4. "Increasingly," here, refers to the time right before and following the 2016 presidential election, around the time when the Southern Poverty Law Center (2017) released a guide about working with the alt-right on campus. However, this is not a new issue, and visits from controversial political speakers has been part of campus

discourse and politics for decades. Since the election, however, the University of Denver Ad Hoc Committee on Freedom of Expression revised and released a freedom of expression policy to the whole campus (2017).

5.   Other notable integral thinkers include Hungarian philosopher of science and systems theorist Ervin László, social philosopher and cultural critic William Irwin Thompson, and philosopher and psychologist James Mark Baldwin.

6.   See note 8.

7.   One way to define a *structure of consciousness* is as "the way in which an individual or group of people make sense of the world as a result of operating at a specified stage of cognitive development and operating out of a particular logic. For example, modernity operates out of formal operations and rational logic while a participatory worldview operates out of postformal operations and a dialectical logic" (Wang 2014, 124).

8.   Notable post-postmodern thinkers include *fictional* Metamodernist philosopher Hanzi Freinacht (2017) created by Danish writers Emil Ejner Friis and Daniel Görtz, controversial German cultural critic Peter Sloterdijk (1987), postformal Australian educator Jennifer Gidley (2017), controversial Canadian psychology professor Jordan Peterson (2018), and SUNY Series in Constructive Postmodernism original series editor (and author) David Ray Griffin (1988). Freinacht and Gidley are two who have been part of the integral theory dialogue, but not Griffin, Peterson, or Sloterdijk, to my knowledge.

9.   Ownership or possession is not implied by the use of the word *having* here from Kegan's (1998) terminology.

10. What integral theory and contemplative pedagogy hold in hopeful ways for rhetoric and composition, in my opinion, is modeling of metacognition and application of *transcending and including*, a process that leads to greater understanding (or tolerance) of multiple perspectives, seeing them as partial. Such perspectives can still be dismantled or evaluated by this logic. This does not mean all viewpoints are equal or valid. Integral thought has both a reconstructive and deconstructive aspect, according to some theorists (Hampson 2007).

11. I share my curriculum for this themed course as one sample approach to achieve greater ideological transparency in the classroom while holding complexity and using a critical pedagogy approach. The practices I used in Spring 2017 are still being tested, refined, and explored, and I welcome feedback on them as well.

12. Another feature that characterizes the integral structure of thought, this time coming from Jean Gebser's writings (1985), is *aperspectivity*. Aperspectival awareness, captured here in the term *post-dialectical*, operates by a different logical system than dialectical tension (Hegel) or dialectical materialism (Marx), both of which fall within the logic(s) of the mental-rational structure of consciousness and favor a version of progress over paradox.

REFERENCES

Copies of assignments mentioned above, student survey instrument, and informed consent available upon request (hfester@uccs.edu).

Arao, Brian, and Kristi Clemens. 2013. "From Safe Spaces to Brave Spaces: A New Way to Frame Dialogue around Diversity and Social Justice." In *The Art of Effective Facilitation: Reflections from Social Justice Educators*, ed. Lisa M. Landreman, 135–150. Sterling, VA: Stylus Publishing:

Aurobindo Ghose, Sri. 1916. *The Human Cycle: The Psychology of Social Development*. Pondicherry, India: Lotus Light.

Booth, Wayne. 1974. *Modern Dogma and the Rhetoric of Assent.* Ward-Phillips Lectures in English Language and Literature, 5. Chicago, IL: University of Chicago Press.

Booth, Wayne. 2004. *The Rhetoric of Rhetoric: The Quest for Effective Communication.* Blackwell Manifestos. Malden, MA: Blackwell Publishing.

Brooke, Robert. 1987. "Underlife and Writing Instruction." *College Composition and Communication* 38 (2): 141–153.

Cook-Greuter, Suzanne. 2013. "Nine Levels of Increasing Embrace in Ego Development: A Full-Spectrum Theory of Vertical Growth and Meaning Making." http://www.cook-greuter.com, Accessed 18 February 2018.

Delpit, Lisa. 1988. "The Silenced Dialogue: Power and Pedagogy in Educating Other People's Children." *Harvard Educational Review* 58 (3): 280–298.

Durst, Russel. 1999. *Collision Course: Conflict, Negotiation, and Learning in College Composition.* Urbana, IL: NCTE.

Freinacht, Hanzi. 2017. *The Listening Society: A Metamodern Guide to Politics, Book One.* Metamodern Guides 1. Jaegerspris, Denmark: Metamoderna ApS.

Gallagher, Chris. 2002. *Radical Departures: Composition and Progressive Pedagogy.* Urbana, IL: NCTE.

Gallagher, Chris, Peter M. Gray, Shari Stenberg. 2002. "Teacher Narratives as Interruptive: Toward Critical Colleagueship." *Symploke* 10 (1–2): 32–51.

Gallagher, Chris, Peter M. Gray, Shari Stenberg. 2009. "Making Trouble Elsewhere: Second Generation Con/fusion." *Transforming English Studies: New Voices in an Emerging Genre,* ed. Jeff Ludwig, Jim Nugent, and Lori Ostergaard. Anderson, SC: Parlor Press.

Gebser, Jean. 1985. (1949/1953.) *The Ever-Present Origin.* Translated by Noel Barstad with Algis Mickunas. Athens, OH: Ohio University Press.

Ghose, Sri Aurobindo. 1914. *The Life Divine.* (First published in the monthly review *Arya* from 1914–1920).

Gidley, Jennifer. 2017. *Postformal Education: A Philosophy for Complex Futures.* Critical Studies of Education, 3. New York: Springer.

Graff, Gerald. 1993. *Beyond the Culture Wars: How Teaching the Conflicts Can Revitalize American Higher Education.* New York: W. W. Norton.

Griffin, David Ray. 1988. *God and Religion in the Postmodern World.* SUNY Series in Constructive Postmodern Thought, 3. Albany, NY: SUNY Press.

Hampson, Gary P. 2007. "Integral Re-Views Postmodernism: The Way Out Is Through." *Integral Review* 4: 108–173.

Kegan, Robert. 1998. *In Over Our Heads: The Mental Demands of Modern Life.* Cambridge, MA: Harvard University Press.

Kopelson, Karen. 2003. "Rhetoric on the Edge of Cunning; Or, The Performance of Neutrality (Re)Considered as a Composition Pedagogy for Student Resistance." *CCC* 55 (1): 115–146.

McComiskey, Bruce. 2000. *Teaching Composition as a Social Process.* Logan: Utah State University Press.

Perry, William G., Jr. 1970. *Forms of Intellectual and Ethical Development in the College Years: A Scheme.* New York: Holt, Rinehart, and Winston.

Peterson, Jordan. 2018. *Twelve Rules for Life: An Antidote to Chaos.* Toronto: Random House Canada.

Seitz, David. 2002. "Review: Hard Lessons Learned since the First Generation of Critical Pedagogy." *College English* 64 (4): 503–512.

Sloterdijk, Peter. 1987. *Critique of Cynical Reason.* Theory and History of Literature, 40. Translated by Michael Eldred. Minneapolis: University of Minnesota Press.

Southern Poverty Law Center. 2017. "The Alt-Right on Campus: What Students Need to Know." https://www.splcenter.org/sites/default/files/soc_alt-right_campus_guide_2017_web.pdf, Accessed 18 February 2018.

University of Denver Ad Hoc Committee on Freedom of Expression. "University of Denver Statement of Policy and Principles on Freedom of Expression." Prepared April 27, 2017. https://www.du.edu/media/documents/statement-policy-principles -foe-4–27-rev1.pdf, Accessed 18 February 2018.

University of Denver Writing Program. "Spring 2017 Course Descriptions." University of Denver. https://www.du.edu/writing/, Accessed January 2017.

Wang, Victor C. X. 2014. *Handbook of Research on Scholarly Publishing and Research Methods.* Hershey, PA: IGI Global.

Wilber, Ken. 1995. *Sex, Ecology, Spirituality: The Spirit of Evolution.* Boston, MA: Shambhala.

Wilson, Theo E. J. 2017. "A Black Man Goes Undercover in the Alt-Right." *TED.com.* https://www.ted.com/talks/theo_e_j_wilson_a_black_man_goes_undercover_in_the _alt_right, Accessed November 2018.

10

IT DEPENDS ON THE CONTEXT
Cultural Competencies in First-Year English

Mara Holt

I write as a director of composition in the mid-stages of a project in which I am integrating cultural competencies, or racial and other literacies, into first-year composition (FYC). This work started in Spring 2016 when Black Lives Action Coalition (BLAC) was formed at Ohio University after racist graffiti appeared on a prominent concrete-block abutment just west of the student center. An image of a lynching was among the racist comments, and this led to a protest of about thirty White and Black students in the student center. A few students who were left at the end of the protest received racist threats from students walking by. In response, they formed BLAC, and they requested that the university create a required course in what they called "Cultural Competencies." Local social media such as Yik Yak had erupted with ugly racist comments. BLAC wanted the student population to be educated, and they hoped that a course dedicated to addressing racism could do that. Faculty and administrators were sympathetic, but they cautioned that a dedicated course was not realistic in the short term.

Doctoral student Madeline ffitch brought BLAC to the English department for help. I affirmed the caution about a dedicated course, but I opened the door to cultural competencies in first-year composition. Soon we had stakeholders from the Multicultural Center, the LGBTQ Center, the Academic Advising Center, African American Studies, English Studies, and Psychology. I sought counsel from the WPA and was advised to conduct a pilot study in Spring 2017. That fall, new TAs taught first-year English from a syllabus integrated with cultural competency goals and materials.

I will discuss how we got from A to B, but first I address the path that brought me to this decision. Occasionally, I ask myself if I have the right to do this. What are the consequences of integrating cultural competencies into a first-year curriculum with new TAs? What are the

DOI: 10.7330/9781607329992.c010

consequences of not doing it? I've been asking myself these questions in one form or another at specific points in the last twenty-five years. I will explore these questions by framing them within previous such discussions in the field. The pertinent events cluster into three historical moments: 1991–1992, 2002–2003, and 2016–2017. Before I begin my historical narrative, I will briefly review relevant scholarship on teacher neutrality. To clarify, in this chapter I am addressing teacher neutrality at the level of the curriculum, not at the level of the individual classroom.

From three different perspectives, Deirdre M. Kelly and Gabriella Minnes Brandes, Jessica Heybach, and Paula Martin share a skepticism of teacher neutrality. In "Shifting Out of 'Neutral'" (2001), Kelly and Brandes dismiss neutrality options such as obedience to the state and multiculturalism. Instead they argue for a notion of good citizenship that embraces the conflict of social struggles and engages the students in social action. The purpose of education for them is "learning how to discuss and debate these emotionally charged and messy issues" towards the goal of "working with others to solve collective problems" (437–438). If, for Kelly and Brandes, the problem with teacher neutrality is subjection to the state or the empty equivalence of multiculturalism, for Jessica Heybach in "Troubling Neutrality" (2014), the problem is that it is a "dangerous, often ignored, creeping practice perpetually in vogue" and common in authoritarian states (43). Heybach draws on Simone de Beauvoir to argue for teacher "ambiguity," or the responsibility of teachers to wake up to their own freedom, responsibility, and ability to make choices in the moment, rather than be guided by a rigid notion of what ought to be done in a standardized way. Ambiguity requires the teacher to be alert and improvisational, adapting to changing circumstances (54). Heybach's notion of the skills required in the role of teacher ambiguity supplement Kelly and Brandes's educational goal of students grappling with difficult issues towards collective action.

Paula Martin in "I'm White, Now What?" (2008) focuses specifically on racial injustice, defining teacher neutrality as White. Just as those who are unconscious of White privilege see whiteness as the natural order of things, Martin says, neutrality is a construction that assumes White is the only unbiased perspective. The needs of minority students are ignored, erasing their identities and possibilities. Antiracist education challenges White supremacy and its structural impact on education (163). To make this shift in thinking, she believes, teachers need intensive training involving "tenacity challenges," one of which is to immerse oneself into a community in which one is a minority. White people gain a positive role from this exercise, she maintains (166).

Kelly and Brandes, Heybach, and Martin together posit neutrality as problematic, and they support a flexible teacher role that negotiates particular contexts. Their stances have their own histories to guide them, each demonstrating de Beauvoir's model of reflective improvisation, always situated in particular circumstances. I argue that no one stance can work with every circumstance, but instead there must be an openness to testing out various options, a self-awareness, an understanding and commitment to one's core values, concern about the people impacted, and a willingness to tolerate the discomfort of uncertainty. I will begin my historical narrative with that argument as a focal point.

FIRST FLASHPOINT: 1991–1992

My first opportunity to consciously address teacher neutrality came in 1991. Linda Brodkey had been hired to become writing program director at the University of Texas in 1990, and she adopted a textbook that was a collection of court cases, titled *Racism and Sexism* (1988), edited by Paula S. Rothenberg. A right-wing group called Accuracy in Academia, whose members sat in random classes to evaluate liberal content, protested the book adoption. They were joined by conservative members of the English department, and several articles (Gribben 1990; Mangan 1990, 1991) covering the controversy were published in the *Chronicle of Higher Education*. The textbook was dropped. Then a recent University of Texas (UT) graduate, I was in a tenure-track job at Ohio University. Although I wasn't strictly a WPA, I was responsible for the curriculum, the textbook, and TA training. I had also been an assistant WPA at UT and had been a member of the composition committee.

During the controversy over the Rothenberg textbook, John Trimbur and Patricia Bizzell drew up a petition to protest the dropping of the *Racism and Sexism* textbook (Trimbur 1993, 248), and Trimbur asked me to sign it. I chose not to. Although my pedagogical politics were aligned with the signers, my recent experience at Texas had given me a different angle on the situation. I believed that Linda Brodkey had jumped the gun, moving from a standard rhetoric to a textbook of court cases without an interim step. Our ideals were similar, but our rhetorical situations were different. Trimbur and Bizzell were teaching at private schools in the Northeast. They were justified in objecting to right-wing tactics to threaten academic freedom. It wasn't neutrality I was supporting, but rather a slower strategy, in line with what Laura Micciche in 2011 would call *slow agency*, or "less visible but no less important forms of agency like thinking, being still, and processing" (73). I believed that the most effective way to approach Brodkey's goal would have been an administrative version of what Lauren F. Lichty and Karen Rosenberg (chapter 8 in this volume) describe as *slow-start pedagogy*: "we make our decisions about ideological transparency and nuanced non-neutrality based on our read of our own institutional context" (128). I wasn't necessarily right; the signers of the petition weren't necessarily wrong. We were speaking with self-awareness from our specific circumstances and addressing the situation in line with our shared core values, but from slightly different perspectives, revealing the complexity of a community with room for dissent.

Two years later, I was in a similar position. Maxine Hairston's article "Diversity, Ideology, and Teaching of Writing" was published in *CCC* in 1992. "Everywhere I turn," Hairston said, "I find composition faculty—both leaders in the profession and new voices—asserting that they have not only the right, but the duty to put ideology and radical politics at the center of their teaching" (Hairston 1992, 180). She called out James Berlin, Patricia Bizzell, John Trimbur, and her colleague Lester Faigley, among others (181), arguing that an ideological focus in required writing courses keeps students and TAs from drawing on their strengths (186) and appropriates writing courses for political purposes (192). An acknowledged liberal (Trimbur describes her perfectly in his interview with Daniel P. Richards in chapter 5 in this volume), Hairston believed in the importance of diversity, but she believed that diverse students would bring their experiences to the classroom (191).

In *CCC's* "Counterstatement," several scholars pushed back against Hairston, beginning with John Trimbur (see chapter 5 of this collection for more insight into how Trimbur's thoughts on the matter have changed). He read Hairston's ideal first-year English course as "actually a retreat from rhetoric toward what I would call 'sharing time in the metropolis,' a pedagogy that appears to celebrate diversity in the classroom but refuses to ask students where their differences come from, what consequences their differences might have, and whether they can imagine ways to live and work together with these differences" (Trimbur 1993, 248). I agreed with Trimbur. Ten years before, we had worked together as writing center directors in Kenneth Bruffee's Brooklyn College Institute. At Texas, Lester Faigley had been my dissertation director, and I had taken a class with James Berlin. I was allied with the group Hairston was criticizing in that piece. Yet I knew how complicated departmental politics were at Texas and how her history with the department had influenced her stance. As the lone rhetorician in the department for decades, Hairston had been marginalized for her views that students' writing was important in itself and not just in the service of literature. When she began to be marginalized by rhetoricians who wanted students' writing to be in service of cultural critique, it must have been like reliving a nightmare.

I agreed with those who differed with her in the "Counterstatement" section of *CCC*, but I didn't join them, and I cringed at the intensity of their critique. I knew that in some ways they had misunderstood her, that there may have been more common ground than they realized. I saw them as possibly afraid of different things. She was afraid that writing instruction would disappear in courses that focused on culture, and they might have been afraid that social justice, from which the new field of composition and rhetoric had emerged, would be lost to the pretense of neutrality that masquerades as "writing skills." Hairston's version of teacher neutrality, however, made her complicit in assuming an equal playing field.

I would not have wanted Hairston to go unchallenged. It was important for the readers of *CCC* to understand the stakes of her argument. It is not the outcome, but rather the process that interests me. Why shouldn't our scholarship, as well as our teaching, be attuned to context? The debate itself was not contextualized in terms of place. As scholars we often show a lack of awareness of our own and others' institutional contexts when we challenge others' assumptions. It is not just a matter of empathy. We miss out on intellectual substance when we fail to take context into account.

SECOND FLASHPOINT: 2002–2003

In 2002, I was director of composition, making a decision about a textbook. The choice was whether or not to go with readings I was ideologically in favor of or with a standard rhetoric. One choice was *Writing as Reflective Action* (2002) coedited by Duncan Carter and my colleague Sherrie Gradin. Sherrie wanted me to use it, and it would have been politic to do so, but I couldn't bring myself to impose on new TAs a book with controversial readings and not much pedagogical apparatus. bell hooks's "Killing Rage" was in the text, and I knew that TAs were having trouble teaching it. I had taught it once without fully understanding it, and had sown confusion in the class at the expense of a student of color. I wasn't sure I was up to the task of helping TAs negotiate the complexities of the readings. As a culture, we were not that far away from the politically motivated attacks on the World Trade Center in 2001 and the Islamophobia that followed. I was worried about the impact on TAs of teaching such controversial materials in that environment.

There were other influences on me as well. Kristine Hansen, in "Second Thoughts on 'Diversity, Ideology, and Teaching Writing'" (2002), reflected on Hairston's article after years of mentoring TAs. As a Texas graduate student, she had disagreed with Hairston, but as a WPA at Brigham Young, her context had changed. The progressive readings she assigned TAs to teach in first-year English caused conflicts with students and their parents. She had more sympathy with Hairston's stance when she saw TAs struggling with their own writing and with class-management skills. Mastering unfamiliar readings and concepts for themselves was a challenge, let alone teaching those readings (241). Hansen's article was timely for me. It affirmed my instinct that I was not ready to adopt Duncan Carter and Sherrie Gradin's (2001) *Writing as Reflective Action*. I had heard undergraduate students' dismissive remarks about the progressive readings they were required to read in many of their classes beyond English. Their teachers' intentions were not bearing fruit. Although Carter and Gradin wanted students to reflect on their *own* beliefs, not take on teachers' values, I wasn't far enough in my thinking and experience then to understand how to teach TAs to do that.

It was during that time that I read Catherine Fox's article "The Race to Truth" (2002). Fox questions the efficacy of our privileging liberal ideology in the writing classroom, perhaps unconsciously. Using her own tendencies as an example, she cautions progressive teachers against reifying critical thinking into the practice of merely adopting viewpoints critical of the status quo. Remembering previous comments she wrote on student papers, she asked herself whether she was unconsciously affirming some beliefs and questioning others (203). She quoted Wallace and Ewald's pithy statement that "privileging resistance can itself become an expression of a teacher's absolute authority" (200). This rang true, given some of the conversations I had witnessed among undergraduate students.

When one of my students brought me a copy of Karen Kopelson's "Rhetoric on the Edge of Cunning" (2003), I was up for a consideration of strategic neutrality. Kopelson suggested we put *ourselves* aside for a minute to allow our students the illusion of objectivity that it is nearly impossible to wrest from them anyway. Kopelson's premise is similar to Fox's in that they both perceived a certain type of teacher role as an obstacle to students' learning. They differed slightly in their perceptions of what kind of teacher role was more effective at the time. Fox frames her stance as humility, a practice of listening to students, and her insurance against pluralism is that they address the consequences of their opinions. Kopelson's frame is strategic performance, or "craftiness," with the hope of disarming students' resistance. In the particular cultural environment from which she was speaking, Kopelson was concerned that directness might not only fail, but could "fuel the fire of conservative counterattacks" (142). She reminds teachers of the importance of attending to context when making choices about teacher roles. She ends the article with the following question: *"How* might we speak, *as whom* might we speak, *so that students listen?"* (141). The models of Kopelson, Fox, and Hansen embody my argument that there is no one right stance in the debate over teacher neutrality. Each of them recounts a process of self-awareness, considering various options, attempting to choose a stance both consonant with their values and cognizant of the historical situation in which they are embedded.

The particular historical moment for Kopelson's urgency in her 2003 article was the aftermath of 9/11 when the fear of Muslims and the lash of racism was at a high peak. We are living another historical moment in 2020, when a backlash against Barack Obama's vision of the United States has amplified White supremacy, and the current president is supporting White nationalism. I did not choose Carter and Gradin's book in 2002, but I did choose to bring antiracist readings to the first-year curriculum in Fall 2017, and so I have to ask myself why. What was different this time?

Some of it has to do with what happened in the country between then and now and how it influenced me. I eventually came to the conclusion that the comfort of the TAs was less important to me than the comfort of the undergraduates who were enduring racism. Lee Mun Wah's documentary *The Color of Fear* (1994) made it clear to me that it was up to White people to educate other White people about racism. Several national events were factors in my change of heart, along with a series of local events that culminated in a request, one I was ready for this time. Just as my experiences had converged to decline the Carter and Gradin textbook in 2002, events began a slow convergence that led to a different decision in 2017.

Black Lives Shattered

Hurricane Katrina hit New Orleans in 2005. Back from a sabbatical year in Austin, I watched the TV screen in horror, Black people neglected and suffering and dying before my eyes, while people around me turned off their TVs and went on with their lives, markedly differently than they had done on 9/11. Invited to a TA orientation lunch, I found the single Black student who had been accepted into our program that year, and we bonded over the anguish of Black bodies in New Orleans. In 2012, when Trayvon Martin died, I was again fixated on the television screen during the long trial of George Zimmerman. I watched the unspeakable treatment of Black bodies being refused, treated as refuse, while the White body of George Zimmerman was protected by the defense lawyer who was better at his job than the prosecutor. I had lived in Daytona Beach, not far from Sanford, Florida, where Trayvon was shot to death. Interviewed by Anderson Cooper after the trial, a White juror spoke about Zimmerman almost affectionately, calling him George. I tried to imagine the racial reverse of that situation, but couldn't. When the verdict came in, I joined a quiet group of people gathered outside a campus building to honor him. We wore hoodies.

When Michael Brown was killed in 2014, I was teaching an advanced composition class focused on engaging difference. I screened *Fruitvale Station*, about Oscar Grant, who was killed by police in a subway station. When Michael Brown was killed, we walked to the protest as a class and listened to community activists. In class, we watched the video of Eric Garner who kept saying "I can't breathe" while he was dying, his neck pressed on the ground by police officers, for (past incidents of) selling cigarettes outside shop doors. I joined a protest that night and chanted "I can't breathe" and walked through town and across campus, and participated in a "die-in." When Tamir Rice was killed in in a park in Cleveland because the police gave themselves three seconds to decide that his toy gun was real, the students and I watched that video together in class. My history with the issues at stake in racial literacy was compounding, leading up to the moment in which I would be asked to do something.

THIRD FLASHPOINT: 2015–2017

In Fall 2016 I taught a graduate course on the history of racial injustice and the identity of composition studies. Three students of color and four White students were in the class. Three of the four White students resisted seeing themselves as having been influenced by structural racism. Antiracist educator Robin DiAngelo defines Whiteness as a pervasive structural force grounded in institutions and cultural practices, rather than simply skin color (DiAngelo 2011, 56). White Americans, living in the bubble that Ta-Nehisi Coates calls "the Dream," are protected from the kind of racial stress that people of color experience daily. Because White Americans haven't developed a tolerance for what DiAngelo calls "racial disequilibrium," even a minimum amount of racial stress becomes intolerable, triggering a range of "defensive moves" (54). She calls this "white fragility." This accurately describes my experience with White students in the graduate class.

Early in the course, I created a group exercise in which White students were in one group, and students of color in another. I encouraged the students of color to leave the room and go find some privacy. The White students protested, as if I were being racist. I had brought attention to the racial division in the class, implying that if the people of color were "raced," so were the White people, a threat to individualism, according to DiAngelo (57). They didn't want to be in a group with Whites only, they said, apparently not realizing that the people of color might have things to say to each other that they wouldn't feel comfortable saying in front of their White peers. In another exercise, I asked students to freewrite about when they first realized they were of a particular race. One of the White students refused to do it, saying that he resented the position I was putting him in, and there was no way he could come out as a "good guy" in such an exercise. This student may have felt that this was a game with an uneven playing field, one in which he was at a disadvantage, not a feeling he was accustomed to.

When we read Yawo Brown's "The Subtle Linguistics of Polite White Supremacy" (2015), a White student offered a defense of White fragility. I struggled with this. Having taught at an HBCU in Alabama, I was well aware of White racial discomfort and how, when I was teaching there, my only space of racial disequilibrium was the university, whereas my students' only spaces *without* racial stress were the university and their neighborhoods. Though Alabama State's campus is in the middle of town, none of my White friends knew where it was. I have no patience for White racial discomfort.

Amy Winan's work is an example of taking White fragility seriously. Drawing from Jennifer Seibel Trainer's work, Winans explains that an obstacle to students' acceptance of their own White privilege is an oversimplification of the White experience. Scholars "construct a generic, middle-class white student who needs to learn about [his or her] own racism but who is unable or unwilling to do so" (Winans 2005, 256). Winans turns students into researchers of their own history and its relationship to larger structures. Although Winans' article was on the reading list for that graduate class, I didn't use her strategies. I challenged the students' need for comfort, since people of color don't get that choice. Looking back, I would go deeper than that, with Winans as a guide, for the sake of both the White students and the students of color, who didn't want my hot light on the White students to reflect on them.

While I was teaching this class, Madeline and Jazzmine from BLAC came to the English department. I was given an opportunity to integrate racial literacies into the first-year curriculum, and I took it. I want to be clear about my motives. I pursued this project because it felt more urgent than controversial. The perhaps unconscious racism, starting with Katrina and continuing with Puerto Rico, had become too painful to watch without doing something. I think of small reparations, of doing what's in front of me, what I can do from where I am located at the moment.

The Study

Doctoral student David Johnson and I were co-investigators on a pilot study on five experimental classes. We interviewed teachers and students, observed classes, and collected writing. Jazzmine and Jolana of BLAC were research assistants. Assuming that racist comments on the graffiti wall, on Yik Yak, and on the streets were in part spawned by ignorance, we wanted to give first-year students a chance to read and engage in productive conversations that might prepare them for the environment they were entering. New cultural competency outcomes supplemented the standard ones recommended by the WPA. They involved knowing the contexts of cultural beliefs, reflecting on the impact of privilege, and exploring options to balance the playing field.

In teacher interviews, I learned that no one felt comfortable teaching when the topic was race—neither White teachers nor teachers of color. In student interviews, I learned that two students felt that their teacher of color was more knowledgeable than a White teacher would be. Nearly all the students I interviewed said that exposure to cultural competencies was important in a first-year English class. It's needed, they said, even those who volunteered that they had voted for Donald Trump.

Implementation: Fall 2017

In Fall 2017, I began the new curriculum. I made mistakes. I did not announce during orientation that the curriculum was created partly to satisfy a university need for cultural competencies for all new students, given the heightened racist acts and attitudes on campus that we had been experiencing over the past couple of years. My lack of clarity was a choice, a decision partly based on my desire to normalize such a curriculum. Another factor was my fear that hypothetical conservative TAs might react against the activist origin of the project before even attempting the curriculum. And finally, I had developed an analytical method for teaching the materials that I believed allowed for neutrality. The first step in the method was to suspend judgment. It was not about students' opinions, I told myself. It was about close reading. My tactic was in line with what a graduate instructor in Meaghan Brewer's chapter 1 in this volume, "The Limits of Neutrality," called *text-based*: "If you can keep it 'text-based,' . . . you can talk about almost anything" (32). Using a textbook that taught students not to argue but to analyze, I sought to use close reading as a tactic to defer or displace conflict for the new TAs.

Looking back, I realize that I had seen neutrality as safety, not as the "dangerous, often ignored, creeping practice" that Heybach warns about (2014, 43). I had created a space in my mind in which we could all be neutral except for the voices in the print and visual texts. I had left it up to Victor Villanueva and Gloria Anzaldúa and Alicia Garza and Tim Wise to teach the students how to engage in difficult conversations about race and difference. I thought I could make this work without coming out as an antiracist educator, because I was afraid of a conservative backlash. I was a ramshackle version of Kopelson, but without the cunning.

I knew we were not as prepared as we should be. Paula Martin's (2008) "tenacity challenge" is what the TAs needed, a training that requires of new teachers an immersion in a non-White environment long enough to understand what White supremacy means. To do this right, the teachers need a perspective shift, and then they'll know that there are no right answers, just stumbling in the dark—and that that is enough. That's life without White privilege. I decided to go through with it anyway, with trepidation, because I knew that in this case something was better than nothing. I was concerned that if I waited for a better time, for more resources, the moment would be gone, and nothing would happen. The students from BLAC had tirelessly sought the creation of a dedicated, required course on cultural competencies, and they had been turned down at every juncture by administrators and faculty members who understood the difficulty of making that happen within the current university structure. A few supportive faculty members across the university who were aware of the unconscious racism that students of color experienced routinely helped reassure me that something was better than nothing.

As I look back, I think my unconscious attempt to use neutrality as an escape hatch was understandable. I knew that moving on without the best possible conditions was risky, and it would likely lead to racial disequilibrium for White TAs and their students. Nevertheless, students would learn something about dealing with race on campus, because they would have immersed themselves in texts that taught them a history of the situation we were facing on campus and nationally. The deferral of opinion that the instruction to "suspend judgment" provided was good for students' intellectual development and made it easier for teachers to approach controversial material. And perhaps not surprisingly, student evaluations demonstrated that most of them welcomed the approach to writing and the texts that taught them so much they hadn't known. TAs were uncomfortable, but for the most part students were not.

In her excellent paper at the National Women's Studies Association (NWSA) conference, Madeline ffitch (2017) addresses the issue of who has the right to act by framing it in discussions of ally/accomplice activism. In the *ally* model, she says, the momentum should come from the people of color. So perhaps when some members of BLAC graduated and the project was left to a mostly White group of TAs, the project should have stopped. But the ally model is flawed, she continues, in that this gives White people an excuse to be little more than bystanders. An *accomplice* model, on the other hand, gives White people the responsibility to make things happen. And in making things happen, we have conflict, we don't satisfy everyone, we make mistakes. ffitch notes that our attempts to be accomplices in antiracist activism are full of gaps and conflicts, but she says that this kind of antiracist accomplice work must continue beyond the need for perfection. "I'm learning," she says, "that . . . this work will be about being willing to abandon expectations of perfection in favor of a process that more honestly reflects both the magnitude of the mess that we are in and the urgency of fighting back" (6).

For the following year we revised our custom reader, *Readings on Writing* (Holt, Ryerson, and Bossiere 2018), to cover a broader range of issues, including more readings on sexuality, Appalachian culture, and Islamophobia. At TA orientation, we announced the cultural competencies objectives of the course and gave a slide show depicting the racism on campus that had led to these objectives. We have moved to a rhetoric in which there is more attention to argument, as well as analysis.

Through the long slog of this reflection, I have become convinced that the stances I have taken at different points in the field were the right decisions to make at the time. I think an attention to context includes not just what is happening in the culture or the immediate environment, but also what is happening inside you, how ready you feel for it, how well you understand it intellectually, and whether your fear is cautionary or a normal part of taking a risk.

My first opportunity to examine my stances towards teacher neutrality in 1992 involved choosing not to sign a petition in support of curricular change at Texas and not to publicly support those whom Hairston attacked. My second opportunity came in 2002 over choosing a textbook for training new TAs at my own institution between the 9/11 attacks and the Iraq War. My third opportunity involved changing the first-year curriculum in 2016, in the wake of publicized police shootings of African Americans, the election of Trump, and the Muslim Ban. At each opportunity, I responded to the context surrounding the issue, reflected on my motives and the possible consequences, and took a risk. I will not know all the possible outcomes, which may include hardening students' resistance to perspectives other than their own.

Whatever the outcomes that I have no control over, I believe that the stakes are higher than they have ever been in the length of my career. I have grown more certain of the dangers of what we call White privilege. Tolerating racial stress develops empathy for others who are not the focus in our White privileged world, and it develops a tough skin that we will need to survive the changing demographics. We need to peek out from under the Dream that Ta-Nehesi Coates describes to inhabit a place that has always been risky, that was always uncomfortable for everyone who wasn't allowed the illusion of an equal playing field. Coates's Dream, he says, "thrives on generalization, on limiting the number of possible questions, on privileging immediate answers" (2015, 50). Neutrality is Coates's Dream: It's a place that exists only in our minds, and it doesn't serve us. Waking up is to our benefit.

REFERENCES

Brown, Yawo. 2015. "The Subtle Linguistics of Polite White Supremacy." The Magical Negro.net. https://medium.com/@YawoBrown/the-subtle-linguistics-of-polite-white-supremacy-3f83c907ffff.

Carter, Duncan, and Sherrie Gradin. (2001). *Writing as Reflective Action*. Boston, MA: Addison Wesley Longman.

Coates, Ta-Nehesi. 2015. *Between the World and Me*. New York: Random House.

The Color of Fear. 1994. Directed by Lee Mun Wah. Ukiah, CA: StirFry Seminars.

DiAngelo, Robin. 2011. "White Fragility." *International Journal of Critical Pedagogy* 3 (3): 54–70.

ffitch, Madeline. 2017. "Ally or Accomplice? Weaponizing Privilege and Building Relationships Beyond the Ally Badge." National Women's Studies Association, Baltimore, MD.

Fox, Catherine. 2002. "The Race to Truth: Disarticulating Critical Thinking from Whiteliness." *Pedagogy* 2 (2): 197–212.

Fruitvale Station. 2013. Directed by Ryan Coogler. Oakland, CA: Forest Whitaker's Significant Productions.

Gribben, Alan. 1990. "Textbook Led to Dispute Over U. of Texas Course." Letter to the editor. *Chronicle of Higher Education*, December 12.

Hairston, Maxine. 1992. "Diversity, Ideology, and Teaching Writing." *College Composition and Communication* 43 (2): 179–193.

Hansen, Kristine. 2002. "Second Thoughts on 'Diversity, Ideology, and Teaching Writing.'" In *Against the Grain: A Volume in Honor of Maxine Hairston*, ed. David Jolliffe, Michael Keene, Mary Trachsel, and Ralph Voss, 227–247. Cresskill, NJ: Hampton Press.

Heybach, Jessica A. 2014. "Troubling Neutrality: Toward a Philosophy of Teacher Ambiguity." *Philosophical Studies in Education* 45: 43–54.

Holt, Mara, Rachael Ryerson, and Zoe Bossiere, eds. 2018. *Readings on Writing*, 4th ed. Cincinnati, OH: Van Griner Press.

Kelly, Deirdre M., and Gabriella Minnes Brandes. 2001. "Shifting Out of 'Neutral': Beginning Teachers' Struggles with Teaching for Social Justice." *Canadian Journal of Education* 26 (4): 437–454.

Mangan, Katherine S. 1990. "Battle Rages over Plan to Focus on Race and Gender in U. of Texas Course." *Chronicle of Higher Education*, November 21.

Mangan, Katherine S. 1991. "U. of Texas Postpones Writing Course, Kindles Debate over Role of Outsiders in Academic Policy." *Chronicle of Higher Education*, February 20.

Martin, Paula S. 2008. "'I'm White, Now What?': Setting a Context for Change in Teachers' Pedagogy." In *Ideologies of Education: Unmasking the Trap of Teacher Neutrality*, ed. Lilia Bartolomae, 161–179. New York: Peter Lang.

Micciche, Laura R. 2011. "For Slow Agency." *Writing Program Administration* 35 (1): 73–90.

Kopelson, Karen. 2003. "Rhetoric on the Edge of Cunning; or, The Performance of Neutrality (Re)Considered as a Composition Pedagogy for Student Resistance." *College Composition and Communication* 55 (1): 115–146.

Rothenberg, Paula S. 1988. *Racism and Sexism: An Integrated Study*. Boston, MA: St. Martin's Press.

Trimbur, John. 1993. "Responses to Maxine Hairston, 'Diversity, Ideology, and Teaching Writing,' and Reply." *College Composition and Communication* 44 (2): 248–249.

Winans, Amy. 2005. "Local Pedagogies and Race: Interrogating White Safety in the Rural College Classroom." *College English* 67 (3): 253–273.

11

THE MÊTIS OF RELIABILITY
Using the Framework for Success *to Aid the Performance of Neutrality Within Writing Assessment*

Tristan Abbott

In "Rhetoric on the Edge of Cunning" (2003), Karen Kopelson theorizes the bodily performance of neutrality as a means of securing instructional authority within the composition classroom. By masking their identifiers, effectively "performing neutrality," instructors may achieve the authority inherent in objectivity—a sense of distance, or bodily removal from abstract subjects. As Kopelson describes it, "the performance of neutrality, or of *greater teacher distance*, may help to increase students' critical involvement with difficult issues by decreasing their preoccupation with the teachers' identity positions" (126, emphasis added). In this sense, the performance of neutrality can be considered "subversive savvy" (138), as it allows instructors to question, and potentially disrupt, the standards of authority they are mimicking.

In this chapter, I use Kopelson's observations as grounding for an ethical approach toward the assessment of writing. I argue that objective-seeming and/or test-based assessment practices are more widely respected than overtly contextual or subjective-seeming assessment, even when these practices run counter to established best practices in composition (Broad 2003; Elbow 1993; Elbow and Belanoff 1986; Gallagher 2007; Gallagher 2011; Huot 2002; National Council of Teachers of English 2009; White 1994; Yancey 2012a). I argue that pedagogically effective assessment practices must in effect "perform neutrality," signaling objectivity in an outward sense as a means of influencing the conceptual negotiations between *neutrality* and *immersion*—concepts that are rhetorically defined through contradistinction with one another. I then demonstrate that such a politically minded and essentially rhetorical understanding of assessment has long influenced the development of writing-assessment practices within composition studies. I end by discussing specifically how assessment practitioners can utilize the "habits

DOI: 10.7330/9781607329992.c011

of mind," taken from the *Framework for Success in Postsecondary Writing* (CWPA 2011), to enact assessment practices that appear neutral but nonetheless allow for the embedded subjectivity that is crucial to sound writing pedagogy.

Kopelson's pedagogy can be held in distinction to what Virginia Anderson (1997) criticizes as "confrontational teaching." Anderson stresses that while socially conscious pedagogy is vital, overt confrontation overlooks persuasion—in other words, it does not recognize the inherent rhetoricity of moral and ethical concerns. Drawing on Burke, Anderson calls for the adoption of a pedagogical/rhetorical strategy built upon identification and unification, noting that "the pressure to transcend opposition and division is so fierce that the trope of unification underlies many of our art forms as well as our persuasive appeals" (203). Furthermore, "traditional appeals like myths and even traditional commonplaces should not be rejected as contaminated because of [the] negative associations" they have with what we would consider culturally conservative tropes (205). Composition instructors stand to gain little through the wholesale rejection of popular systems of validation and adjudication, even if, as Anthony Petruzzi (2008) notes, rhetoric's "appeals to practical reasoning, [serve as] a sufficient way to adjudicate truth claims" in and of themselves, within our own field (221). Composition teachers and administrators need to operate within the bounds of the discourses that surround our classrooms and our institutions.

I suggest thinking of the effect of rhetorical neutrality as a sort of distancing mechanism—in Kopelson's words, it can create a sense "of greater teacher distance" within a classroom (126). Key here is the removal of a sense of physical presence from the pedagogical actions that are taking place: "the refusal to represent oneself" allows teacher-subjects to avoid being conceptualized reductively and opens up space to enact more effective practice (140).

To Kopelson's (dis)embodied instructor, the creation of distance allows an opportunity to co-opt the authority typically afforded to those who embody dominant identity signifiers. As applied to the assessment of writing, the authority being subverted has more to do with a foundational distrust of embodied or subjective acts of assessment. As I will discuss, the assessment mechanisms with the most political and institutional clout tend to be those that best signal disembodied objectivity—those that, in other words, create a salient sense of distance between the things being measured and the embodied subjectivities of those who design and enact the measurements. I finish my overview of assessment practices by arguing that the landmark CWPA/NCTE/NWP *Framework for Success in Postsecondary Writing* (CWPA 2011) is most productively interpreted in this manner, as a means of generating a sense of distance between the subjectivity of assessors and the assessments they produce.

DISTANCE AND NEUTRALITY WITHIN ASSESSMENT

Neutrality's immense rhetorical weight, the tendency of "the neutral" to be regarded as *de facto* removed and therefore authoritative, has clear implications for the practice of writing assessment. In a moment, I will discuss composition studies' preference for openly subjective and contextualized assessment, and analyze some trends in writing assessment to highlight how that preference has been actualized by making rhetorical concessions toward neutrality. First, I would like to discuss some germane observations from Avital Ronnell's *The Test Drive* (2007) regarding the power of objective-seeming assessment ("the test" or "the experiment") in the discoursal construction of "truth."

The key function of *the test* within discourses is its ability to generate "a vocabulary of doubt" (Ronell 2007, 66), which paradoxically strengthens statements by putting them through some routinized means of questioning. This function is most immediately visible within the formal discourses involving experimentations and scientific method. Drawing from a large number of Enlightenment philosophers, Ronell notes that "contemporary science is rooted in the kind of guesswork described by Bacon, consisting of 'anticipations, rash and premature,' and of 'prejudices.' . . . Both Bacon and Popper prepare scientific thought with purges and cleansing activities so that work to come can attain an ascertainable level of purity. For Bacon, the mind has to be purged of anticipations, idols, and prejudices before it can apply itself to an untainted reading of nature" (38–39). Ronell demonstrates the ability of scientific discourse to act as a purification ritual, in which a writer's perspective is demonstrated to be drawn from observation-in-isolate, free of unaccountable variables. "Though consistently attracted to leakage from the presumed outside" she notes, "the lab [that is, the site of the test] must evacuate 'Nature' from its premises" (48). There exists a pressing need for the purity of removal.

These observations do not apply only to rigid methodologies; indeed, we can find testing functions operating even in relatively informal discourses. In most discourses, there exists a widespread conflation between the *neutral* (as it is perceived or signaled as a rhetorical object) and the *objective*. "Testing," broadly understood, is the process through which neutrality is summoned and demonstrated. Testing "consists of two significant axioms, the first of which involves an internal control apparatus; the second axiom postulates a community of verifications and double-checkers" (Ronell 2007, 64). Testing strengthens statements by subjecting them to doubt in a manner expected by members of a discourse community. Understood in this sense, testing can be said to be present in all overtly persuasive discourses, manifesting as a need to mute the embedded subjectivity of immediate understanding and to amplify observations drawn from the disembodied coldness of set methodologies. Even now, in this academic essay aimed toward progressive humanists, I feel pressure to temper my statements ("perhaps," "I argue that," "it appears that"), and to soften my own voice and observations by making as many citations as possible. Paradoxically, the hedging and references don't weaken my authority; if done well, they strengthen it. That's how testing works.

Here we find implications not just for the formal processes of writing assessment but for the manner in which writing assessment is conceptualized and discussed. These implications are especially pointed for humanistic-minded scholars in rhetoric and composition, as we tend to favor assessment practices that eschew claims of objectivity and, increasingly, compositionists have come to embrace an overtly activist approach to writing assessment (even if our institutional realities do not always allow us to actualize such practices).

A recent issue of *College English* was dedicated entirely to the politics of writing assessment. In their introduction to the issue, guest editors Mya Poe and Asao B. Inoue (2016) explain that "so much of the writing assessment work we [academics] do seems complicit in sustaining inequality. No wonder we are drawn to seemingly more democratic assessment methods like directed self-placement, portfolios, and contract grading" (119–120). This is perhaps an understatement. Composition's disciplinary history from about the late 1960s onward has been deeply concerned with the ethical and political ramifications of writing assessment practices, even when those concerns are not the overt focus of assessment scholarship. Throughout this period, however, the adoption of progressive assessment practices has involved continual concessions toward neutrality, masking our inherent subjectivity with language and processes that establish a sense of removal.

I would argue that the "ethical turn" in writing assessment began with, and was enabled by, the field's embrace of the conceptual split between reliability-focused and validity-focused assessment practices.

Understood initially as a turf war between indirect, objective-seeming assessment (such as grammar quizzes) and direct, subjective assessment (actual student writing), *validity* was defined as "the extent to which a test measures what it purports to measure—in this case, writing ability" while *reliability* was "the extent to which a test measures whatever it does measure consistently" (Cooper 1984, 1). While such a conceptual split seems obvious now, its first enunciations were revelatory, allowing for the development of non-standardized and therefore less-objective-seeming assessment practices.

According to Yancey (1999), most of the writing assessment that existed before focus turned toward validity-based concerns attempted to measure writing ability in an objective sense. Yancey notes that "'objective' tests, particularly multiple choice tests of usage, vocabulary and grammar, dominated practice" (485). The pedagogical rationale of these assessment practices came from concerns raised by educational psychologists in the late 1920s, whose study of writing assessment found very little consistency among essay graders, but near-universal consistency among those grading short-answer or multiple choice tests (Cooper 1984, 1–2). As this was considered problematic, many instructors were discouraged or even banned from assessing student writing ability by analyzing actual student writing. This baffling pedagogy came about due to a fear and rejection of the subjectivity found inherent in the creation and reception of writing, from the sense that a grader's embeddedness within the rhetorical act would render their judgment sullied or impure.

Things began to shift with the enunciation of the reliability-validity split. The earliest example I can find comes in 1966, when Godshalk, Swineford, and Coffman (1966) published a landmark white paper for the College Entrance Examination Board demonstrating that short-essay examinations could be administered in a manner that achieved a high degree of sampling reliability among raters. This helped spawn a large number of studies that sought to assess writing ability via holistic examinations, defined by Davida Charney (1984) as "quick, impressionistic qualitative procedures for sorting or ranking samples of writing" (67). These studies did not seek to assess "organic" writing, such as classroom assignments, as even trained readers did not tend to judge those in a uniform (reliable) manner. Instead, holistic exams were "set[s] of procedures for assigning a value to a writing sample according to previously established criteria" (67), usually by using *very* specific criteria and rigorously normed readers.

By the late 1970s, *validity* and *reliability* were considered important enough that in-depth definitions of the two terms were used as a framing device in the introduction of Cooper and Odell's (1977) edited collection, *Evaluating Writing*. Throughout this time, and continuing until quite recently, there was a gradual shift in the dominant narratives surrounding writing assessment. Whereas objective-seeming uniformity and replicability were once the prime directives of writing assessment, discourse has shifted and "*validity* associated with fairness [has become] the aim of assessment" (Elliot 2014, 680), both within and beyond writing studies. This was no accident. The embrace of validity over reliability has allowed for the development and implementation of assessment practices that, while imperfect, address many of the severe ethical and pedagogical concerns associated with a uniform or standardized approach to writing instruction. Throughout this slow shift, assessment scholars made concessions to validity concerns, and to the preferences for objectivity found therein, but the focus on validity concerns has shrunk gradually.

Here it will be instructive to look at some representative examples from various periods in the recent history of writing assessment, as well as some of the general rationales given for the adoption of different varieties of assessment mechanisms. As mentioned earlier, the first widely adopted forms of relatively direct assessment were holistic examinations. Understood broadly, holistic scoring attempted to "reflect a rater's general impression of the quality of writing" (Huot 1990, 238), rather than keep the rater beholden to judging a narrow set of traits that were thought to signify good writing. An outline of and justification for a typical holistic procedure is given by Miles Myers (1980), who explains that "the whole of a piece of writing is greater than the sum of its parts" (6), and therefore a student's writing should be graded via the normed scoring of an entire piece of actual writing, not by their simply demonstrating abstract knowledge that could potentially be applied to the writing process.

Myers's entire book is dedicated to detailing the methods that should be followed in selecting *prototypes*—"typical examples" of writing passages evincing various levels of competence (7)—and then training scorers to sort student writing passages according to the degree to which they resemble those prototypes. Such an exhaustive description made sense when understood in terms of the general expectations regarding testing at the time. The rigid, procedural nature of this norming process gave the exams a sense of objectivity, while the rhetorical evocations of holism kept them in line with the prevailing trends of composition theory. The result was a politically expedient form of assessment that allowed composition to move away from the pedagogical implications of indirect, objective-seeming assessment while still making concessions toward the concerns that made such assessment practices viable.

In hindsight, holistic examinations seem like an obvious compromise between cutting-edge pedagogy and non-pedagogical mandates for objectivity. Once the general preference had shifted to pedagogical impact over the uniformity of judgment, validity concerns began to seem outmoded. It was therefore perhaps inevitable that such assessment would become regarded as capitulatory. Progressive-thinking assessment theorists began to demand a more specifically pedagogical, student-centered approach to writing assessment.

What Yancey (1999) identifies as the third wave of composition assessment, starting in the early 1990s (and just recently transitioning over to the fourth [Yancey 2012b]), is typified by the portfolio-based Elbow-Belanoff model, which makes even fewer obvious moves toward removing an assessor's subjective judgment from the act of assessment. This model is centered on the belief that "proficiency examinations undermine good teaching by sending the wrong message about the writing process: that proficient writing means having a serious topic sprung on you . . . and writing one draft" (Elbow and Belanoff 1986, 336). Such an undermining of good teaching was chalked up to writing assessment's being too beholden to standards of reliability and therefore too disconnected from rhetorical acts, and the manner in which this was explained was often outright dismissive of validity concerns.

Through their individual and collaborative works, Elbow and Belanoff sought to make composition assessment more classroom-based, and therefore more reflective of the values internal to composition studies. They focus on the moral and practical inefficacy of reliability-based assessment, and claim that such inefficacy comes from the desire to rank students. Elbow (1993) notes that ranking necessarily involves judging student writing "along a single continuum" (191); if we want to rank students, we have to judge them all according to a one standard drawn from a single, static context. By necessity, this leads to an inorganic level of uniformity in reading and evaluation. When assessing student writing, holistic scorers "stop reading the way they normally read" (189) and instead judge students based on a set of criteria that do not apply to how readers actually consume texts, rendering the assessment invalid.

Once normed/standardized assessment had been cast as inorganic, it was possible to posit alternate values according to which assessment systems could be calibrated. Elbow and Belanoff's (1986) model called for the adoption of portfolio-based assessment criteria. The goal for such assessment practices was to demonstrate personal growth on a student-by-student basis. Such a model was necessitated, internally, through the dismissal of student ranking. Instead of ranking students against one another so as to declare some competent, others exemplary, and still others in need of remediation, "the portfolio process uses a very different model of evaluation—criterion-referenced or mastery-based or competence-based—which assumes that the ideal end product is a population of students who have *all* finally passed because they have all been given enough time and help to do what we ask of them" (337). I find the last part of that sentence especially remarkable. It is, at heart, a rather openly subjective take on assessment. Implicit within it is an argument against some of the most unseemly-yet-dominant threads of thought in higher education administration and in favor of a student-centered approach that is concerned with helping students become better writers, not with pitting them against one another. It took no small amount of discursive maneuvering to make a sentiment such as this seem acceptable within educational research. It also required a good deal of compromise; third-wave assessment methods still had to demonstrate replication of results in order to be considered reliable, and were still concerned with the generation of quantitative data. Here, however, these reliability-based concerns were regarded more as tertiary afterthoughts, things compositionists had to worry about to appease the concerns of those in other fields. Nonetheless, the bulk of the concerns discussed within wave-three assessment practices were internal to composition and reflective of the field's shared values; subjectivity was more conspicuously embraced, and neutrality was demonstrated only when necessary.

None of this means to suggest that portfolio assessment is perfect as either a pedagogical tool or a lens of composition scholarship. For example, there is no real agreement upon what even constitutes portfolio-based teaching, which can lead to severe problems when it comes to reporting widespread usage or the general effects of portfolios (Murphy and Yancey 2007). And even though portfolios are often presented as a means fostering critical reflection, *reflection* as a concept is generally undertheorized, and studies have shown that most students do not find any especial value in the act of creating a portfolio (Scott 2005). Still, compared to normed exams and multiple choice tests, the superiority of portfolios is effectively undisputed.

COMPOSITION ASSESSMENT REACTS TO
WIDESPREAD INSTITUTIONAL SHIFTS

The trouble is, this form of highly subjective and individualized assessment came about during a time when compositionists had a relatively large amount of autonomy in regard to the design of writing assessment. In the 1980s and 1990s, administrative and political factors weren't as pressing a concern as they are today—or, in the very least, they pressed differently. As Yancey (2012b) explains, "increasingly, we have seen the role of the federal government move from a benign disinterest [in writing assessment] to a focused effort to encourage a certain view of institutions and to influence their practices: encouraging an outcomes-based, standardized assessment model pointing toward comparability across institutions with no interest in local contexts or values" (186–187). This move has, I feel, put compositionists in a bit of a bind, as we struggle to maintain the hard-fought, ethically minded gains of our pedagogy in the face of newer and more intrusive demands for neutrality.

As Yancey (2012b) shows in the aforementioned quote, the political assessment regimes of the twenty-first century posit strong aversions to localized and/or subjective assessment. They do not demand objectivity *per se*—contemporary testing experts are careful to avoid charges of positivism—but, within alarmist discussions as wide ranging as the Spellings Report, No Child Left Behind, and *Academically Adrift* (Arum and Roksa 2011), we can discern clear calls for uniformity within educational assessment. Much work has been done to debunk all of these projects and works, which are each premised on false assumptions and offer up nostrums that are at best needless and at worst incredibly harmful.[1] I do not feel it necessary to further discredit them here, especially not on their own terms. I would instead encourage us to think of them not as a radical break from past assessment discourses but as a logical extension of demands for neutrality that can be traced back for at least the past several decades. Understood from this perspective, we can begin formulating approaches to assessment that are efficacious *and* ethical—approaches that continue our field's proud history of centering students via the co-optive performance of neutrality.

In his long-form review of then Secretary of Education Margaret Spellings's (US Department of Education 2006) "A Test of Leadership" report, Brian Huot (2007) makes several observations germane to this discussion. The most important is his explanation of the political impetus toward different approaches to education reform. Huot explains that the Republican-appointed Spellings Commission interprets legitimate concerns faced by higher education, such as a decrease in literacy rates among college graduates, through a lens of ideological conservatism. Huot criticizes the commission for not taking into account any demographic factors in their examination of this supposed drop in literacy. Doing so, he says, allowed them to make recommendations more in line with their ideology, leading them to suggest that universities adopt more uniform instruction and assessment practices. He explains that "writing centers and individual student conferences have been a liberal response to teaching the groups new to higher education. Testing and systems of accountability like those now present in American education can be conceived of as more of a conservative response" (514). This response seeks to redesign educational institutions so that they function more like businesses, with harsh performance metrics, a uniformity of focus, and a reverence for efficiency.

Huot (2007) finds the Spellings Commission's analysis explicable only on ideological grounds. He points out a key tautology: the commission believes that by taking a product-focused, goals-based approach to literacy students will score more highly on standardized assessment and therefore will be more literate. This, he says, presents a problem for portfolio-based assessment, "a practice that I and the majority of my colleagues in English would probably support, though such an approach is completely incongruous with the commission's recommendations for accountability" (520), which prefer uniform assessment mechanisms being given at regular intervals.

While I agree with Huot's diagnosis, simply ascribing this preference to *conservatism*, a rather nebulous term, does not fully explain its popularity. Chris Gallagher (2007) believes something more sinister is afoot, describing accountability-based assessment as an outright scam, something foisted upon an unwitting public by a generation's worth of conservative politicians who mean to undermine the humanistic foundations of public education. *Accountability* is a "byword of a coordinated, pernicious campaign that serves corporate interests at the expense of teachers, students, and communities" (19), he says. Such a campaign is intentionally meant to "disempower teachers' 'subjective' views vis-à-vis the more 'objective' views of technical experts," like standardized test manufacturers (Gallagher 2011, 459), and is empowered generally by the belief that "there is a negative correlation between primacy and *proximity to*, and direct involvement in, the work of teaching and learning" (463, emphasis added). This is an important observation. It may be true that some, or perhaps most, of those politicians who support a uniform approach to education are trying to actualize regressive ideological preferences—the desire to financially disempower instructors, or to further weaken a field they consider too closely associated with marginalized peoples, or to punish pedagogy that is considered too progressive. Then again, many, or perhaps most, supporters of uniform pedagogy and assessment are not especially regressive and may believe themselves to be working in the best interest of students. Tactically, this split matters little. What does matter is the fact that, within current educational discourse, embedded subjectivity is considered *a priori* flawed, and neutral-seeming practices are so unquestionably preferred they can be used as an ideological cudgel—even when they stem from poorly wrought government white papers, and even when they lead to unpopular and unappealing teaching practices. The people who can most convincingly claim the mantle of neutrality are those who will wield the most control over pedagogy, and neutrality is evoked by stressing a sense of distance within the act of assessment.

THE *FRAMEWORK* AS A DISTANCING MECHANISM

Here is where Kopelson's (2003) sense of mêtis might help composition-ists develop and embrace assessment practices that are pedagogically efficacious yet responsive to concerns outside of composition studies. While many of us may hesitate to adopt assessment practices that signal objectivity, we must remember that neutrality is a performance, and while its presence typically correlates with regressive ideology, it is not necessarily the cause, nor is it necessarily caused by, such ideology. To this end, I wish to briefly touch upon some of the most politically viable assessment scholarship produced in the last several years: the CWPA/NCTE/NWP *Framework for Success in Postsecondary Writing* (2011). This work provides us with the tools needed to package the values of compo-sition in terms that make them appear less obviously subjective without substantially altering pedagogy.

The *Framework* was developed by politically minded scholars whose work takes an activist bent. These authors all approach assessment politi-cally and seek to craft practices that will not only enable good pedagogy but also allow composition studies to define itself in an institutionally/politically acceptable manner, which requires masking our subjective embeddedness. This can, I feel, best be accomplished through use of a rubric-like artifact called the Habits of Mind, taken from *The Framework* (to echo the conversation had by Trimbur and Richards in chapter 5). This artifact allows for—and even embraces—a more fluid and subjec-tive approach to assessment, while nonetheless allowing assessors to dis-cuss and report assessment results in a manner that appears to remove their embedded presence from within the act of assessment.

In a preface to the *Framework* (CWPA 2011) in a special issue of *College English*, O'Neill et al. (2012) sum up popular attitudes toward assessment as consisting of "concerns about a perceived lack of consistent standards for high school graduation, the transition from high school to college, and the preparation of students for college and career" (521). In the early 2000s, these concerns spurred the adoption of Common Core State Standards, which were developed by politicians, absolutely without any input from composition scholars (522), and sought to define what skills K–12 students need to demonstrate to be considered "college ready." Seeking to remediate their being shut out of the conversation, composition scholars developed the problematically product-focused WPA Outcomes Statement, which sought to define the skills that students should ideally acquire in composition courses. The *Framework*, and especially the Habits of Mind, seek to replace the Outcomes Statement. While they may be utilized similar to a rubric, the Habits of Mind are nonetheless process-focused, acting as a guidepost for measuring the demonstration of habits that have shown to be conducive to successful writing (522).

This might seem like a minor shift in focus, but it is what makes the Habits of Mind so much more potent than the Outcomes Statement. While the Outcomes Statement gained political propriety by setting down measurable outcomes, those outcomes were static, rigid, and generalizable. By switching the point of measurement to the start and duration of a composition course, the *Framework* moves from a product focus to a process focus, which allows for much more fluid and locally defined points of assessment while still producing an artifact (the Habits) that can appear to be consulted in a uniform or objective sense.

The Habits include the following: Curiosity, Openness, Engagement, Creativity, Persistence, Responsibility, Flexibility, and Metacognition (527–529). Each habit is explicated with a handful of exemplary, but pointedly not specific, descriptions of what their successful demonstration might entail: *Persistence*, for example, might be the ability to "grapple with challenging ideas, texts, processes, or projects" (528), while *Flexibility* might mean that students "approach writing assignments in multiple ways, depending on the task and the writer's purpose and audience" (529). Engaging with these, an instructor-assessor might be struck by their squishiness or apparent un-measurability. This might be momentarily frustrating, but *it is the most important facet of the habits*. None of these can be defined or described in a manner that would fully befit writing contexts across various institutions, different sections within a single institution, or even separate papers written for a single assignment within a single classroom. It is instead up to each institution, department, instructor, and student to determine what constitutes an appropriate manifestation of each habit. The power of the Habits as an artifact is that they allow us to aggregate these wildly disparate manifestations into categories that perform the appearance of uniformity, to report the results of our classroom practices in a manner that disguises the fundamental embeddedness of each assessment act. The *Framework* allows assessors to co-opt the misguided valuation of superficial objectivity and to use it to strengthen a teacher's position within the classroom.

Of course, no assessment process is without flaws or critics, and any attempt toward adopting a field-wide standard poses the threat of homogenization. If relied upon without conscientiousness rigor, any rubric-like assessment artifact can result in mechanized, thoughtless assessment. But the *Framework* presents compositionists with a chance to apply Kopelson's insights to the wider discourses that surround our field and our institutions. Rather than rejecting neutral-seeming assessment practices out of hand, we should seek instead to co-opt the rhetorical power of neutrality, to pervert its typical intentions, to actualize pedagogy that is both sound and viable.

Like teaching, assessment is a balancing act. In both areas, expectations of stakeholders are not always—or even typically—aligned with the values and best practices developed within our field. As tempting as it may be to fully and forcefully actualize our carefully developed beliefs into practice, doing so without taking into account the ideologies and predispositions of those outside our field can lead to our own marginalization, ultimately harming ourselves and our students. Rhetorical awareness is key to the implementation of effective practice, and in today's academy that entails making key concessions to neutrality, even as we work to subvert political and ideological pillars that make neutrality so powerful. In order to embrace proximity, we feign removal.

NOTE

1.   The rebukes of No Child Left Behind are too numerous to list. For analyses specific to composition studies, Richard Haswell's (2012) terse response to Arum and Roksa's *Academically Adrift* (2011) is nothing short of devastating, and Brian Huot's (2007) "Consistently Inconsistent" demonstrates the effective incoherence of the concerns of the Spellings Report (US Department of Education 2006).

REFERENCES

Adler-Kassner, Linda. 2008. *The Activist WPA: Changing Stories About Writing and Writers.* Logan, UT: Utah State University Press.

Anderson, Virginia. 1997. "Confrontational Teaching and Rhetorical Practice," *College Composition and Communication* 48 (2, May): 197–214.

Arum, Richard, and Josipa Roksa. 2011. *Academically Adrift: Limited Learning on College Campuses*. Chicago, IL: University of Chicago University Press.

Broad, Bob. 2003 *What We Really Value: Beyond Rubrics in Teaching and Assessing Writing*. Logan, UT: Utah State University Press.

Charney, Davida. 1984. "The Validity of Using Holistic Scoring Evaluate Writing: A Critical Overview." *Research in the Teaching of English* 18 (1): 65–81.

Cooper, Charles R., and Lee Odell. 1977. *Evaluating Writing: Describing, Measuring, Judging*. Buffalo, NY: SUNY Buffalo University Press.

Cooper, Peter L. 1984. *The Assessment of Writing Ability: A Review of Research*. Princeton, NJ: Educational Testing Services.

Council of Writing Program Administrators (CWPA), National Council of Teachers of English (NCTE), and National Writing Project (NWP). 2011. *Framework for Success in Postsecondary Writing*. CWPA/NCTE/NWP. http://wpacouncil.org/aws/CWPA/asset _manager/get_file/350201?ver=2297.

Elbow, Peter. 1993. "Ranking, Evaluating, and Linking: Sorting Our Three Forms of Judgment." *College English* 55 (2): 187–206.

Elbow, Peter, and Pat Belanoff. 1986. "Portfolios as a Substitute for Proficiency Examinations." *College Composition and Communication* 37 (3): 336–339.

Elliot, Norbert. 2014. "Validation: The Pursuit." *College Composition and Communication* 66 (4): 668–687.

Gallagher, Chris W. 2007. *Reclaiming Assessment: A Better Alternative to the Accountability Agenda*. Portsmouth, NH: Heinemann Publishing.

Gallagher, Chris W. 2011. "Being There: (Re)making the Assessment Scene." *College Composition and Communication* 62 (3): 450–476.

Haswell, Richard. 2012. "Methodologically Adrift." *College Composition and Communication* 63 (3): 487–491.

Huot, Brian. 1990. "The Literature of Direct Writing Assessment: Major Concerns and Prevailing Trends." *Review of Education Research* 60 (2): 237–263.

Huot, Brian. 2002. *(Re)Articulating Writing Assessment for Teaching and Learning*. Logan, UT: Utah State University Press.

Huot, Brian. 2007. "Consistently Inconsistent: Business and the Spellings Commission Report on Higher Education." *College English* 69 (5): 512–525.

Kopelson, Karen. "Rhetoric on the Edge of Cunning; Or, The Performance of Neutrality (Re)Considered as a Composition Pedagogy for Student Resistance." *College Composition and Communication* 55 (1): 115–146.

Murphy, Sandra, and Kathleen Blake Yancey. 2007. "Construct and Consequence: Validity in Writing Assessment." In *A Handbook of Research on Writing: History, Society, School, Individual, Text*, ed. Charles Bazerman, 365–387. London: Routledge.

Myers, Miles. 1980. *A Procedure for Writing Assessment and Holistic Scoring*. Urbana, IL: NCTE.

National Council of Teachers of English. 2009. "NCTE-WPA White Paper on Writing Assessment in Colleges and Universities." http://wpacouncil.org/whitepaper.

O'Neill, Peggy, Linda Adler-Kassner, Cathy Fleischer, and Ann Marie Hall. 2012. "Creating the Framework for Success in Postsecondary Writing." *College English* 74 (6): 520–524.

Petruzzi, Anthony. 2008. "Articulating a Hermeneutic Theory of Writing Assessment." *Assessing Writing* 13: 219–242.

Poe, Mya, and Asao B. Inoue. 2016. "Toward Writing Assessment as Social Justice: An Idea Whose Time Has Come." *College English* 72 (10):119–126.

Ronell, Avital. 2005. *The Test Drive*. Urbana, IL: University of Illinois University Press.

Scott, Tony. 2005. "Creating the Subject of Portfolios: Reflective Writing and the Conveyance of Institutional Prerogatives." *Written Communication* 22: 3–35.

US Department of Education. 2006. *A Test of Leadership: Charting the Future of US Higher Education*. Report of the commission appointed by Secretary of Education Margaret Spellings. Washington, DC.

White, Edward. 1994. *Teaching Assessing and Writing*. San Francisco, CA: Josey Bass Publishing.

Yancey, Katherine Blake. 1999. "Looking Back as We Look Forward: Historicizing Writing Assessment." *College Composition and Communication* 50 (3): 483–503.

Yancey, Katherine Blake. 2012a. "The Rhetorical Situation of Writing Assessment: Exigence, Location, and the Making of Knowledge." In *Writing Assessment in the 21st Century: Essays in Honor of Edward M. White*, ed. Norbert Elliot and Les Perelman, 475–492. New York: Hampton Press Inc.

Yancey, Kathleen Blake. 2012b. "Writing Assessment in The Early Twenty-First Century: A Primer." In *Exploring Composition Studies: Sites, Issues, and Perspectives*, eds. Kelly Ritter and Paul Kei. Matsuda, 167-187. Logan, UT: Utah State University Press.

12

MASSIVE OPEN IDEOLOGY
Ideological Neutrality in Arizona State's Composition MOOCs

Adam Pacton

The relationship between ideology and higher education in America has been scrutinized by many for a century or more (depending on who's counting), but a cursory visit to nearly any media outlet will uncover a recent spike in attention to this relationship. Whether it is the University of Illinois's rescinding of Steven Salaita's job offer over tweets critical of Israel, debates on the limits of free speech on campus in the face of vitriolic campus speakers, or campus clashes over the material manifestations of opposing ideologies in the form of campus monuments: this ideological relationship is concrete and immediate, and requires critical exploration to ensure students' access to quality education rather than indoctrination.

But is this split between ideology and education a false dichotomy? In the case of college composition, most would answer "yes."

Some might argue that certain subject areas may be studied in higher education in ideologically neutral ways. *Neutrality,* in these cases, can denote the idea that ideology is something that somehow exists apart from disciplinary ways of knowing or acting (a position sometimes forwarded in the sciences), or it can refer to the position that a particular discipline or field can remain agnostic to ideological commitments in its exploration of them (a position sometimes maintained in the humanities and social sciences). Such positions have received increasing scrutiny as of late, but the link between ideology and college composition seems to be a special case in that few have ever denied its existence, and most have underscored its importance. As LeCourt (2004) puts it, "A key question remains, then: Can students access the power academic discourse provides through its positions as speaking subjects *without* the discourse becoming an inextricable part of their identity? The literacy autobiographies suggest that they cannot . . . In particular, the texts comment on how academic discourse has encroached upon and

DOI: 10.7330/9781607329992.c012

defined their thinking and writing in ways they were unable to prevent" (65). In other words, the introductions to the discourses of the academy that students encounter and their approximations of these discourses in composition curricula (Bartholomae 2003) contribute to these students' identity formations in seemingly unique, interested, and powerful ways. As such, instructors and scholars of composition have not shied away from direct confrontations, contestations, and outright embracing of ideological valences. This has occurred, by and large, almost solely in small-section American college courses. As college composition takes its first steps in international, scaled education, this relationship becomes even more fraught and necessitates more nuance in how we think about ideology in the college composition "classroom."

This chapter explores Arizona State University's (ASU) recently launched college composition MOOCs (Massive Open Online Courses), English 101x and English 102x, and the incredible complexity that surrounds these courses' imbrications with ideology. In this profile of these two classes, I argue that dislocating college composition from a purely American phenomenon provides a moment of disciplinary *kairos* that troubles performances of ideological neutrality in the composition classroom. In addition to exploring how scale and internationalization disrupt college composition's ideologically forward agendas, I chart the troubled pursuit of ideological neutrality in MOOC course design and execution. I argue that the multivalenced heterogeneity of the composition MOOC calls for a more nuanced stance on ideological commitment, a switch from overtly liberatory pedagogies to a grounded progressivism in the MOOC. I contend that rather than being a centripetal force for institutional and disciplinary mores, college composition can become a vehicle for developing personal purposes and selected literacies rather than literacies of dubious transferability. This conclusion, and the internationalization afforded by composition MOOCs like ASU's, productively troubles composition's institutional ideological identities, pushes practitioners towards more complex approaches to ideological commitments in course/curricular/interface designs rather than assumptions of ideological neutrality, and calls for new research directions in the field.

SCALING COMPOSITION, SCALING IDEOLOGY

I will have much to say below about the actual design and implementation of English 101x and English 102x. Before getting to that, though, it will be useful to discuss how the MOOC modality *a priori* complicates the relationship between composition and ideology in new and unexpected ways.

Remediating college composition in the MOOC modality changes the nature of composition via its institutional purposes. Within American higher education, the purpose of composition and its location within educational institutions has been contentious for decades (or even centuries, depending on how far back one goes). That said, there are a few common characteristics: (1) college composition is a first-year-level (or lower division) course, (2) it is somehow preparatory or prerequisite for other disciplinary writing courses, and (3) successfully completing a set number of college composition courses or testing out of them via placement tests is usually required for graduation. Even these assertions are debatable, and individual instantiations may vary widely not only between institutions but also within an individual writing program. However, these general characteristics are quite common and useful in framing the essential difference in composition qua MOOC: literally thousands of the students enrolled within the composition MOOC are not first-year students (or even enrolled within a higher-education institution), are not be taking the course as preparatory for disciplinary work, and are not taking the course to fulfill a graduation requirement. Their purposes are as diverse as the thousands of students participating in the MOOC.

Insofar as college composition does not really exist outside of the United States, students' purposes in participating in a composition MOOC will be more varied than their counterparts in more conventional college composition courses in American higher education. This fundamental difference raises critical questions about what a composition course *should* do at global scale. In thinking about this quandary, our course team faced two fundamental challenges in course conceptualization. First, we needed to design our courses so that they balanced the rigor and requirements of an American composition course (ENG101x and ENG102x are credit-eligible at ASU) with the diversity of purposes that attend a global, nontraditional audience. Second, we wanted and needed to attend carefully to the threat of ideological colonialism and the very real dangers that an overtly liberatory composition course could pose for some of our students.

College composition courses have a history of being ostensibly liberatory spaces. This may be due, in part, to the composition classroom's unique acculturative valences that Bartholomae (2003) traces in "Inventing the University." As students seek to approximate the discourses of power within the university (and the larger world, by extension), the acculturative agent can become identified with the oppressor. As Freire (2005) notes, "at a certain point in their existential experience the oppressed feel an irresistible attraction towards the oppressors and their way of life. Sharing this way of life becomes an overpowering aspiration. In their alienation, the oppressed want at any cost to resemble the oppressors, to imitate them, to follow them" (62). This fraught power-relation foregrounds, in part, why the composition classroom has often been a site of liberatory praxis. I am not interested in tracking the history of this long relationship too closely here, but I do want to make a broad note: the overtly liberatory composition classroom has been incredibly problematic in some American class-rooms because of assumed, applied, or imagined asymmetries between teachers and oversimplified student-functions. The assumption of ideological asymmetry wherein students' ways of being-in-the-world are oversimplified or naïve is the opposite of liberatory. Perhaps more important, overtly liberatory pedagogies can have dangerous material consequences in a MOOC.

MOOCs do not attract students solely from the same or roughly simi-lar sociocultural milieux. Some students come from and are working in countries with oppressive governments, countries where their par-ticipation in liberatory dialog could—in theory—lead to reprisal. One might counter that it is precisely these students who should be sought out, engaged, and encouraged en route to consciousness raising. In a MOOC, however, this is simply not possible. Course designers, faculty, and other staff do not have the fine-grained access to their students' lives and sociocultural contexts that would permit them to engage in any-thing other than paternalistic, potentially dangerous, colonial talking-to. Additionally, given the open nature of MOOCs, the existence of surveil-ling agents cannot be ruled out.

The above considerations led those involved with the development of ENG101x and ENG102x to be wary of course design that is ideologi-cally driven or framed. This left us with a quandary: if writing—and by extension writing instruction—is always already ideological, how could we create an ideologically neutral composition MOOC?

A VIEW FROM SOMEWHERE

The design and implementation of ENG101x and ENG102x began with the axiom that there is no view from nowhere (Nagel 1986). Any work that we might do in designing and facilitating these courses would be undergirded by various ideological commitments, and any composition course that claims ideological neutrality is asserting its inability to recognize its own ideological commitments and runs the risk of re-inscribing extant hegemony. This does not necessarily mean that an ideologically neutral direction is wrongheaded; rather, it means that how we think about ideological neutrality requires more nuance in the MOOC frame.

In the beginning stages of designing both composition MOOCs, the course team aimed at ideological neutrality while simultaneously understanding that such neutrality was chimerical. This is not as paradoxical as it seems. A good analogy is the difference between theory building and theorizing. *Theory building*, in the sense of creating a totalizing or perfectly consistent theory, is akin to tilting at windmills and has largely been abandoned across various disciplines and areas of inquiry. However, *theorizing*, understood as a recursive, always-incomplete dialog between context, data, confirmation, prediction, and the epistemological scaffolding that undergirds them, is an invaluable activity that leads to new exploration and understanding rather than hastily constructed Procrustean beds. Similarly, ideological neutrality as a *direction* rather than a destination helped us to clarify how we wanted to approach the explicit ideological valences of the courses.

Leaving aside overtly liberatory approaches, we recognized a general progressive strain in the field and took as an ideological starting point the assumption that this strain would underwrite our courses. We asked ourselves, though, how we might clarify and capitalize upon this starting point and how we might approach the various literacies that are imbricated with and constitute college composition. To this end, we decided to use discipline- and institution-specific outcomes to crystallize both our pedagogical and ideological commitments.

THE WPA OUTCOMES AND THE *FRAMEWORK FOR SUCCESS IN POSTSECONDARY WRITING*

As discussed above, ENG101x and ENG102x are potentially credit-bearing courses at ASU and so must mirror the rigor and outcomes of their counterparts in the ASU system. They are also, however, courses that enroll thousands of students from around the world, and these students have myriad reasons for taking the courses. To negotiate this seeming Scylla and Charybdis, we decided to use the *WPA Outcomes Statement for First-Year Composition* (CWPA 2014) and the *Framework for Success in Postsecondary Writing* (CWPA 2011) as our broad course outcomes. These outcomes have the virtues of being disciplinary gold standards and providing the flexibility we needed in our MOOC design. As the *Outcomes Statement* explicitly states:

This Statement identifies outcomes for first-year composition programs in US postsecondary education. It describes the writing knowledge, practices, and attitudes that undergraduate students develop in first-year composition, which at most schools is a required general education course or sequence of courses. This Statement therefore attempts to both represent and regularize writing programs' priorities for first-year composition, which often takes the form of one or more required general education courses. To this end it is not merely a compilation or summary of what currently takes place. Rather, this Statement articulates what composition teachers nationwide have learned from practice, research, and theory. It intentionally defines only "outcomes," or types of results, and not "standards," or precise levels of achievement. The setting of standards to measure students' achievement of these Outcomes has deliberately been left to local writing programs and their institutions. (CWPA 2014)

While Abbott (chapter 11 in this collection) argues that that the WPA *Outcomes Statement* is "static, rigid, and generalizable" (187), we believed that it explicitly leaves the specification of particular outcomes (their standards or levels of achievement) up to local programs and contexts. These outcomes and their flexibility gave us a means and a target to bridge our heterogeneous student groups while still working towards rigorous student deliverables. Just as the WPA *Outcomes Statement* gave us a terminal target, the *Framework for Success* gave us a flexible processural framework.

The *Framework for Success* (CWPA 2011) describes skills and habits related to writing that are deemed essential for college success. As the document states:

Students' abilities to enroll in credit-bearing, college-level courses are increasingly associated with the idea of "college readiness." This document, written and reviewed by two- and four-year college and high school writing teachers nationwide, describes habits of mind and experiences with writing, reading, and critical analysis that serve as foundations for writing in college-level, credit-bearing courses. Students who come to college writing with these habits of mind and these experiences will be well positioned to meet the writing challenges in the full spectrum of academic courses and later in their careers. (2)

This "college readiness" and academic positioning is pegged to the United States, as the document acknowledges ("written and reviewed by two- and four-year college and high school writing teachers nationwide"); however, the "Habits of Mind" that the *Framework* (2011) describes are ones that the team believes align with a broad educational progressivism:

Curiosity—the desire to know more about the world.

Openness—the willingness to consider new ways of being and thinking in the world.

Engagement—a sense of investment and involvement in learning.

Creativity—the ability to use novel approaches for generating, investigating, and representing ideas.

Persistence—the ability to sustain interest in and attention to short- and long-term projects.

Flexibility—the ability to adapt to situations, expectations, or demands.

Metacognition—the ability to reflect on one's own thinking as well as on the individual and cultural processes and systems used to structure knowledge. (4–5)

The *Framework* provides more detailed guidance on how to approach these habits through writing education, and this guidance has significant overlap with the *Outcomes Statement*, contrary to Abbott's assertion (chapter 11, this volume) that the "*Framework*, and especially the Habits of Mind, seek to replace the *Outcomes Statement*" (187). While there were similarities in some of the specific guidances and the details of the course structure, the important thing to highlight is that the *Framework* and the *Outcomes* gave us a disciplinary starting point rather than an overtly ideological one. In other words, we did not start with a precise ideological agenda and then move to disciplinary theories or technologies to undergird it. We wanted our students to become better writers and thinkers so that they could, in some way, be more agentive in their own lives.

Our starting point of agency and locality is critically different from a number of other pedagogical and ideological approaches, not just to composition but to education in general. Unlike a number of traditions in higher education, we did not assume ignorance, a need for enculturation, or a need for liberation from epistemological or material asymmetries. Again, this is not to say that we approached composition instruction from a positivist, Platonic, and imaginary ideology-free vector; instead, we were looking for a richer way to localize composition instruction so that students could learn more about their own contexts and better their lives through their own writing actions *in ways that matter to them.*

ENG101X AND LOCAL THEORIZING

The design and first run of ENG101x preceded ENG102x. Both courses were designed by a team of ASU faculty: Duane Roen, Michelle Stuckey, Mark Haunschild, and myself (Adam Pacton). In the initial course design for ENG101x, we aimed at a curricular arc that would honor our international students' diversity of purposes, literacies, and ideological orientations.

In ENG101x students begin by working through an autoethno-graphic sequence of assignments and then moving to an ethnographic assignment sequence. After completing these arcs and their cumulative projects, students then construct a "theory of writing." In this project, students draw upon their work in the previous assignment sequences to take a stand on what they believe the act of writing to be. The final project consists of a curated, rhetorically designed ePortfolio of the given student's work from the course. The broad arc of the course, then, aims at inviting students to parse their contexts from a personal perspective (autoethnography), to explore those same contexts through the lens of a participant-observer (ethnography), and then to abstract from those projects (and the other, shorter writing projects in the course) to a theo-rization of what the act of writing is for the student.

The above arc is certainly underwritten by a number of ideological vectors. There is clearly a formative influence of the WPA *Outcomes* and the *Framework*, and there are also liberatory and social-epistemic inflec-tions (in centering the students' experiences). That said, the larger assignment arc tracks a very abstract ideological curve, and we believe that it is aiming towards an acceptable, workable ideological neutral-ity. Of course, in the initial course design we were not unaware of the ideological dimensions of the learning management system (LMS) and the other technological articulations of the course and how these might complicate an ideologically neutral approach.

TECHNOLOGICAL MEDIATION IN THE MOOCS

All LMSs and, more generally, human-machine interfaces are shot through with various ideological commitments, especially in the ways that these systems construct and center representative users. Tracking precisely how our LMS (edX) does this is not possible in the space provided. However, I can say that the design team worked against these constructions by assuming a rock-bottom minimal level of digital literacy. Our starting point was this: assume the student could enroll and log into the course (we would have no contact with them otherwise), but assume no other digital literacy on the student's part. What this translated to was the creation of scaffolded tutorials (via screencaptures and documenta-tion) that led students through every technological process in the LMS, including navigation, discussion-forum participation, assignment submis-sion, and more. This scaffolding carried over to the ePortfolio as well.

In the initial design of ENG101x, audit-track students (those who enroll in the course for free) were slated to submit URLs rather than assignments. There were a number of technological and pedagogical reasons for this move away from the submission of conventional alpha-numeric essays (more on this below), but these reasons are largely out-side the scope of this project. Both ID-verified students (students who enroll for a small fee and may take the course for credit) and audit-track students hosted ePortfolios on LMS-external sites, but audit-track students used Weebly (a free, public, user-friendly website builder), while ID-verified students used a variant of Digication (a private, institutional website). After the first course run, we switched all users to Weebly to better facilitate peer-review across the course and because of a number of salient interface benefits for students. Building a website is no simple thing, but the literacies required to do so are becoming increasingly more valuable (if not outright necessary), and so the technological mediations combined with our pedagogical and theoretical commit-ments led us to require this modality for doing composition. While our students would learn the rhetorical tools necessary to compose these sites, our digital literacy assumptions about the LMS extended to the construction of these student sites. As a result, we built a number of ePortfolio template sites.

Our ePortfolio template sites contain templates to help students orga-nize and construct the ePortfolio to best meet assignment and course requirements, but they also contain screencapture videos that lead users through almost any process they might need to build these sites. Such videos include how to set up a basic page, how to copy the correct URL for project submission, how to include multimodal elements, and more. We push students up a steep learning curve, but we provide the sup-port to crest the top of that curve. The result is that students are able to compose (potentially) richer texts, curate them in a public forum, share them easily, and display and own a set of valuable digital literacies.

Without a doubt, requiring students to compose their texts in publi-cally accessible multimodal websites is not ideologically neutral. As I have indicated, though, we are always already mediated in our choices (e.g., our LMS's constraints), and composing a variety of texts in digital environments is almost certainly more valuable for students and more agentive than requiring students to produce alphanumeric essays *ad nauseum.* That said, some might voice concern over the required public exposure of these texts and students. This concern is perhaps mitigated by the fact that these sites are not Google-indexed (unless students pay for them to be), and students are not required to include direct identify-ing information in the form of their names or pictures of who they are. For the purposes of grading and feedback, the LMS associates the URL with the username (and students can even remain anonymous by choosing a disidentifying username). I'll have more to say about ePortfolio use and ideological neutrality below, but prior to that it will be helpful to step back and describe ENG102x more directly.

ENG102X AND ALL-IN ACCESS

When our course team initially met to discuss ENG102x, we faced the following fact head on: a generic introduction to research-writing courses would be useless for the majority of our students. The second section of college composition often introduces students to "the academic essay," a 10-ish-page research project that demonstrates a passing acquaintance with some form of argumentation and collation/analysis/deployment of peer-reviewed academic research. Much of the body of such courses is given over to teaching students the technologies (considered broadly) of academic research. Many of our MOOC students would likely not be interested in such research, and many of them would not have access to academic sources, given paywalls, differential access to common search tools like Google, and a number of other technological limitations. In considering this divergence, we again framed our situation as kairotic and asked "what could ENG102x do for our diverse students?"

We looked again to important deliverables for inspiration. To work towards transfer and consistency, we again made use of the WPA *Outcomes* and the *Framework*. Additionally, we turned to a set of our institution's outcomes: "ASU's Eight Design Aspirations." These aspirations are meant to help guide ASU's work as an innovative, engaged university. They are as follows:

1. Leverage Our Place: ASU embraces its cultural, socioeconomic and physical setting.
2. Transform Society: ASU catalyzes social change by being connected to social needs.
3. Value Entrepreneurship: ASU uses its knowledge and encourages innovation.
4. Conduct Use-Inspired Research: ASU research has purpose and impact.
5. Enable Student Success: ASU is committed to the success of each unique student.
6. Fuse Intellectual Disciplines: ASU creates knowledge by transcending academic disciplines.
7. Be Socially Embedded: ASU connects with communities through mutually beneficial partnerships.

8. Engage Globally: ASU engages with people and issues locally, nationally and internationally. (Arizona State University "Design Aspirations")

These outcomes resonated with our desire to aim at a broadly progressive curriculum while still vesting students with authority and purpose,
but they pushed us to consider material transformation as well.

Out of our considerations of differential technological access,
disciplinary outcomes, and the design aspirations of our own institution, we decided to create a research-writing course that—like
ENG101x—centered our students' own experiences. We moved even
further, though, and pushed our sense of which conventional "academic" literacies our students needed to learn. What emerged was a curricular arc that aimed at a course-long project. Students would propose
a research agenda (write a project proposal), gather research materials
(and create an annotated bibliography), craft a persuasive research project, and curate their work in a public ePortfolio. Some primary requirements were that (1) the work must have clear exigency, (2) the work
must address a problem in the student's local context, and (3) the work
must be aiming at leading to some form of material transformation.
These requirements pushed students to engage in real, local problems
and eschew genred "academic" composition projects. Of course, given
the extreme heterogeneity of the student population, this meant that
projects could vary radically. To a degree, this was the point.

Just as our curriculum pushed our students to engage with their communities in new and potentially transformative ways, it also pushed us to
engage with composition in new and unexpected ways. The great variety
of directions that our students could (and subsequently did) take meant
that our instruction had to take place at a level of abstraction that would
allow for application across diverse domains. To meet this challenge, we
focused on rhetorical education, especially the ways in which material
conditions and audience expectations shape and construct the texts we
might produce. We faced an additional challenge, though, in how we
taught our students about "sources."

Given that many—indeed most—of our students would not be writing
conventional academic essays, we needed to take an approach to sources
that significantly departed from approaches we were comfortable with.
In short, we framed every aspect of source use, incorporation, and
acquisition as explicitly driven by the rhetorical situation. In this way, a
student could use only religious sources if, say, she was convincing village elders to participate in water-treatment programs and she had identified those sources as most effective, given her audience and purpose.

In many "academic" contexts, the use of only religious sources would be dismissed out of hand. However, in a case like the one alluded to above, such sources might be the most rhetorically effective for both writer and audience. In any event, we did not have a "library" day where we quickly learned that peer-reviewed sources were sources that "counted" and where we learned how to efficiently find them. Instead, we spent a large proportion of the course learning about primary sources, secondary sources, how to parse those sources, and how to judge whether given sources are appropriate given one's rhetorical situation.

We were delighted by the approach described above and the resultant projects, but how ideologically neutral is such an approach? Clearly ENG102x is framed by a number of sets of outcomes that inflect the work that occurs there, and there are both ideological and material consequences and concerns. Is it colonial to assume that a student's town, city, or village needs improvement? That there must be some problem or issue that needs solving or at least attention? Perhaps, but I would argue that this merely resembles a broad progressivism. What problems might exist, how they might be addressed, who the audience should be, what "counts" as appropriate evidence: all of this is left to the student. Nowhere in English 102x—or English 101x—is the student constructed as needing intellectual or material liberation. They might, in fact, need such liberation, but we leave it to them to decide. We simply give them a set of tools. What they do with them is up to them.

FUTURE DIRECTIONS

Besides being a hackneyed formulation, the closing sentence of the previous section is obviously false. Discursive tools bear the mark of their creators, and there are no ideologically neutral tools. An ideologically neutral rhetoric? This is pretty much an oxymoron. This is all to say that I and the initial course designers are aware that these courses are not—cannot be—ideologically neutral. In pushing the locus of authority and *telos* to the student, however, I do think that we are approaching a kind of ideological equilibrium: we are not actively pushing students towards this or that way of being-in-the-world, but we are inviting them to pursue their own ends with a discursive toolkit that is flexible enough to accommodate their differential rhetorical situations.

So what's next?

This profile of ASU's English 101x and English 102x is necessarily short, and elides many important details in these courses (and the fact that these courses are continually iterating). Rather than being a complete picture, however, I hope that it is an intriguing conversation starter. In particular, I hope others will think about how scale affected these courses, how rather than pushing us to ossify and codify, our students' diversity allowed us to open ourselves and the discipline to new types of epistemological, disciplinary, and ideological abeyance. Thinking about and discussing this opening up and its attendant movement towards ideological neutrality (without ever hoping to achieve it) may spark new discussions about smaller scales and push us to ask: what might become possible when we see our small-section composition courses just as open, indeterminate, and fecund as a composition MOOC?

REFERENCES

Arizona State University. "Design Aspirations." https://newamericanuniversity.asu.edu/about/design-aspirations.

Bartholomae, David. 2003. "Inventing the University." In *Cross-Talk in Comp Theory: A Reader, 2nd ed.*, ed. Victor Villanueva, 623–653. Urbana, IL: National Council of Teachers of English.

Council of Writing Program Administrators. 2014. *WPA Outcomes Statement for First Year Composition*, v3.0. http://wpacouncil.org/positions/outcomes.html.

Council of Writing Program Administrators, National Council of Teachers of English, and National Writing Project. 2011. *Framework for Success in Postsecondary Writing*. CWPA/NCTE/NWP. http://wpacouncil.org/positions/outcomes.html.

Freire, Paulo. 2005. *Pedagogy of the Oppressed*. New York: Continuum.

LeCourt, Donna. 2004. *Identity Matters: Schooling the Student Body in Academic Discourse*. New York: State University of New York Press.

Nagel, Thomas. 1986. *The View from Nowhere*. Oxford: Oxford University Press.

SECTION III

Performativity

13

ENCOUNTERS WITH FRICTION
Engaging Resistance through Strategic Neutrality

Romeo García and Yndalecio Isaac Hinojosa

In this chapter, we, the authors, work to unravel the term *resistance* in our discussions of neutrality, but before this conversation begins, we want to contextualize our subject positions. This context matters because when we enter the classroom, we *all* enter that space a little differently. As practitioners, we teach who we are (see Palmer 1998) in that our bodies remain implicated in the political affective, and in that as practitioners we occupy—consciously or unconsciously—a politics of location. Thus, our bodies are visibly marked and seen as "preeminent material" upon which our culture is inscribed and its particular discourses embedded, regulating "the ways we think and live" (Shapiro 1999, 77). So, when we walk into our classroom, who are we then?

We each self-identify based on our lived experiences: a Mexican American from the Lower Rio Grande Valley (García) and a Chicano from south Texas (Hinojosa). We were born and raised along the US-Mexico borderland, where "the cultural production of the docile manual laborer has long taken precedence over the production of educated Americanized citizens" (Ullman 2005, 249). Coming from the borderlands, we faced hardships, such as racism, discrimination, linguistic terrorism, and poverty. Yet, despite any hardship (and there were many), we persevered, breaking from that cultural precedence in the borderlands by obtaining our PhDs and teaching positions. Our lived experiences and education have informed us that our narratives are embodied; our bodies are rhetorically linked to specific places/realities and set alongside narrative backdrops of salvation and progress. We are raced, gendered, and classed in various ways, and we have learned that what we say and how we say it, particularly within a classroom context, can cause resistance. So, we listen carefully to what we may say to our students and in response to the forms of resistance we encounter.

DOI: 10.7330/9781607329992.c013

Our grandmothers, con sus cuentos y testimonios,[1] played a central role, developing our capacity to listen to others and our capacity to understand and respond to situations. A crucial part of listening is to recognize and acknowledge differences as they emerge, undoubtedly. This skill leads us to find nuances in what we hear (and see) as resistance. As a term, *resistance* is problematic because practitioners refer to resistance often as a way to cast students as the problem; students who disrupt class or defy teacher authority in ways that bring instruction to a halt. Under this lens, student resistance "defies educational goals and the functioning of schools" (McFarland 2001, 613). Thus, we define *resistance* as conscious efforts in subjects to engage and enact opposition. While we do not deny that resistance occurs from time to time, as in incommensurability between peoples or ideas, we would like to add a layer based on our personal student-to-student and student-to-teacher interactions or exchanges. Our experiences lead us to recognize and acknowledge *friction* as a nuance from resistance. To shift away from resistance and from student-as-problem rationales that generally frame any conflict as a negative interruption, we adopt friction, which is a more productive and generative way to work toward disengaging resistance. As a metaphor, friction breaks from resistance. Friction gives credence to the idea that the potential for movement is possible when two or more objects come together. The objects here are subjects, and the movement is the result of interactions and exchanges that hold the potentiality to co-produce knowledges (Tsing 2004). Thus, friction permits us to recognize the organic nature of experiencing something new when we come into contact with others; to shift our understanding from antagonistic dispositions; and to work with students as they struggle to exercise some agency in responding to forms of oppression.

So, in what is to follow, we each present a scene from our experience in a composition classroom. Each scene is from a different institution of higher learning. We do so to call attention to how we acknowledged friction as we encountered resistance. Our scenes illustrate predicaments we each faced as faculty of color that situated us to perform neutrality, but strategic neutrality. *Strategic neutrality* refers to epistemic and performative pedagogical practices (rather than civil disobedience), which can be drawn from and grounded in epistemic violence (see Mignolo 2009). These practices manifest from a view that neutrality is not an option (see de Certeau 2013; Horton and Freire 1990) and involve a cultural-rhetoric to interrupt the flow of hegemonic stories, specters, and traditions. We perform strategic neutrality aimed to acknowledge friction as a means to engage any forms of resistance. To do so effectively, however, requires that we, as faculty of color, need to adopt a subject position that calls on us "to give up our assumptions, admit our inadequacies, acknowledge our biases, and relate to others with more vulnerability" (Toshalis 2016, 308). As Erika Johnson and Tawny LeBouef Tullia suggest in chapter 14 in this collection, our "identities and our experiences based on those identities compel us to turn resistances into engagement" (225). Only then can we perform strategic neutrality, enabling us to "develop and enact innovative pedagogies that will better negotiate students' resistance, precisely so they may more productively engage with difference" in our classrooms (Kopelson 2003, 121).

TIME TO RE-THINK AND RE-EVALUATE
WHAT WE MEAN BY RESISTANCE

A classroom can elicit change in that this site is a "living space, capable of sparking a revolution or reproducing the very inequalities we claim to oppose" (Thompson 2017, 5), and as faculty of color, our rhetorical pedagogies situate what may be at stake for us in being entangled and/or complicit with inequities and inequalities. Rhetoric and composition, as a discipline, offers us a unique position to engage in social action, not only in the fact that we do human work, but that we require ourselves and our students to participate in action–related kinds of work. Throughout the classroom scenes that follow, we hope to illuminate the possibility of re-thinking and re-evaluating what we mean by resistance in ways that offer friction as a more useful rhetorical position, especially for faculty of color. The scenes underscore our goals to focus on accountability for our actions and to "teach for diversity" as our conscientious effort (Caughie 1999, 133). These goals are well grounded in our subjectivity as marginalized subjects and work in our favor toward ensuring that students realize a sense of responsibility in asserting agency.

García's Classroom

I have had the opportunity to work and learn in three states, and in each I have realized that there is an intricate relationship between the discourses about place and the rhetorical performance of place. For many of my students, such a relationship is consubstantial to their foundations of subjectivity, literacy practices, rhetorical dexterity, and knowledge production. Working in predominantly conservative White locales, as I enter the classroom, I am cognizant to the fact that I may very well be their first professor of color (POC). So, more often than not, my students struggle in different ways, I find, because I enter a class-room with specific and particular stories and histories that inform my pedagogical practice and the rhetorical education I intend to provide. As a result, my students will encounter friction. Friction can be seen as a form of *techne*, and the *techne* of friction, I believe, is central for articulating strategic neutrality. Friction not only has the potential to wear down established foundations but also has the possibility to transform energy that resists (materially and symbolically) as those foundations erode. Essentially, what is at stake for me in a classroom is my ability to develop faculties that effectively *move* the body and mind of a student to a protean state. What is my individual responsibility, then, toward friction and the work I engage in?

Conversations I had with my Grandma heavily inspire part of my students' rhetorical education. She manifested her sense of urgency to communicate with me in the following words: "¿Me estás escuchando?" | "Abre tus oídos" | "¡Ay que prender!" | "Te digo esto para que sepas y aprendas" | "¿Entiendes?" and "¡Entiendes!" Her urgency to communicate with me revolved around my potential complacency with one truth/reality and complicity with accepting "así son las cosas."

I admit that as a result, I apply much of the same sense of urgency toward my students. Over the years, however, I have found that students struggle with my sense of urgency to communicate responsible and justly actions with them. As a POC, my goal is to create a classroom environment that calls on *all* students to accept some accountability and responsibility for their actions, and that invites *all* of them to re-think what responsibility and justice mean as they re-evaluate their role as agents of change. This goal provides a rhetorical education moment that breaks from ideas of fixity and instead works from an intermediary disposition informed by concepts such as *techne*-bearing bodies and *kairos*, an opportune moment. I admit that I misinterpreted my students' struggle as resistance, initially, but I reminded myself about my interactions with my Grandma. Every exchange with me provided *kairos* for her to narrate a life lesson. (The readability of her lessons, ironically, still keep their secret.) As I transitioned from así *son* las cosas to así *no son* las cosas (*techne*-bearing), I realized Grandma was teaching me how to use resistance productively as forms of friction instead: through community listening, relationships, and opportunities for redress. Stories and the practice of storytelling offered me a way to do Grandma's *work* while presumably assuming a position of neutrality—strategic neutrality—with students.

Stories matter. We are all woven and entangled by a universe of stories: "the set of stories we tell ourselves, the stories that tell us, [and] the stories others tell about us" (Rohrer 2016, 189). In Utah, where I teach, Pioneer Day commemorates Brigham Young and the first group of Mormon pioneers to enter the Salt Lake Valley in 1847. Every year the state of Utah celebrates this historical *event* as a public holiday. In addition, "This is the Place" Heritage Park and the Salt Lake Temple confirms the story of land promised, salvation brought, and progress and development inaugurated. These stories aid in constructing claims of localism, and that is where I saw similarities between Utah and my home state of Texas. Like in Texas, the danger of localism resides in the impulse to forget past atrocities and/or the desire to claim that those atrocities no longer take place. I came to realize this parallel in my first-year composition course at the University of Utah. "That doesn't happen here," a phrase I heard quite often throughout the course of a semester, especially after I brought my students' attention to racist flyers posted around campus. When students said "that," they meant racism, discrimination, and inequality: "Though racism has always been tied to language, it has always had to be sold rhetorically," according to Victor Villanueva (2006, 10). So, I wondered, how had such espoused rhetoric in "That doesn't happen here" been sold to my students? How was this rhetoric part of the discourse of place and performativity of place? I was reminded of Ashraf Rushdy (2012), who demonstrated a Western "desire" to claim some "event" as the "last" of something. I contemplated, often, how were my students entangled or complicit in such desires?

The language of the *event*, whether it is colonization, settler colonialism, or the Jim/Juan Crow Eras, implies that the residuals of those designs or logics are no longer *presencing* in the normative.[2] Settler colonial studies, like de-coloniality, recognizes not only the event (settlers came), but the structure of logics implemented (settlers stayed). I charged students that semester to consider their set of stories (land promised, salvation brought, and progress and development inaugurated) and how those stories told today remain indebted to a politics of memory that justifies the de-territorialization and re-territorialization of land. However, this *work* of holding them responsible had to be done strategically because after assessing (e.g., conducting surveys, holding forums, inviting guest speakers), I realized that so much of what was at stake for students was their very foundation of subjectivity and knowledge. Stories, however, provided the opportunity to think about inheritance, a debt to said inheritance, a politics of memory. I wanted students to know, as Charles Mills (1997) discusses, that while they were not signatories, they benefited from a system of institutions that allowed them to claim, "That doesn't happen here." The question remained, how do I make visible the designs or logics that traffic in the present? I turned to Jan Blommaert and April Huang, who approach "history" as a category of analysis. They recommend pinpointing "concepts" that connect "between the past and the present in terms of social activities" (Blommaert and Huang 2009, 271). My students bore witness to those social activities daily: their inheritance, debt, and politics of memory told "stories of/about us," and such stories were everywhere, from the monuments to the Temple to yearly celebrations.

Students were not exhibiting problematic resistance, but rather a type of resistance that is a byproduct of friction. It is quite natural to resist when a body such as mine (with specific stories and histories) puts into circulation and flow a different kind of energy that creates some friction to wear down claims to localism. Friction establishes a relationship and an opportunity for interaction or exchange. I learned from my Grandma then, and today from the students I teach, that it is vital to view relationships and opportunities as *co-workers* engaged in *co-working* opportunities. (This is partially where the possibility of new stories resides). It is important, too, to establish co-worker relations and co-working opportunities, particularly in the context of breaking from the language of "events" and rhetoric of "that doesn't happen here," which continues to efface others (e.g., minoritized and racialized peoples, the Utes, Shoshone, and other American Indian tribes). I thought once again of those conversations I had with my Grandma. She was developing in me the capacity to create presence from absence and sound from silence: how to reconcile the past, present, and future. Stories and storytelling provided the opportunity to work with a sense of urgency, to communicate while assuming a position of neutrality. I did this by introducing students to stories of Texas and pushing them toward community listening (e.g., creating presence and sound).

"Settlers *came* to Texas, but they also *stayed*," I reminded students. "Two stories emerge," I continued: "The first story is that there exist a people, but they, the 'other,' are external to 'reason' and closer to 'nature.'" Scholars within the project of de-coloniality, including myself, recognize and acknowledge that the *telos* of Western epistemology is a *topos* of intelligibility, rationale, and totality. Texas, for instance, can serve as evidence of this. As a class, we spent weeks studying and analyzing the rhetoric of settler colonialists like Stephen F. Austin, who in a letter to his cousin wrote about his philanthropy: "my object has always been to fill up Texas with a North American population," and, he asserted that the Mexican people are a "strange people" who "must be studied to be

managed" (quoted in Barker 1910, 271–273). We did this work to gain
a more in-depth perspective of how Western rhetoric of modernity and
its narratives of salvation, progress, and development cloak logics in
order, as Austin might say, to manage and control land, populations, and
resources. "The second story," I said, "is that there now exists a people
'stuck' in a precivilized space and time; the inhabiting bodies 'vanish'
or 'evaporate' and only an 'empty' landscape is observed." The way settler colonial rhetorics and narratives can and do work is by presenting
the idea that prior to the arrival of settler colonialists both the people
and land are wild, savage, and/or dead. As a class, we focused for weeks
studying and analyzing settler colonial rhetorics and narratives that I
found within a local archival box in Harlingen, Texas, from the Special
Collections and Archives at the University of Texas Rio Grande Valley.
We engaged this material both to understand the sophistication of settler colonialism that relies upon rhetorics and narratives of modernity
and to recognize how Western institutions of thought such as archives
and historical discourse justify violence against the "other" in the name
of modernity.

In addition to learning how to read and listen carefully and critically, I called attention to the politics of memory that resided within
my very own Mexican and Mexican American community in the Lower
Rio Grande Valley. I told my students that I encountered friction when
I learned in a class about the humanity that settler colonialists and the
Texas Rangers brought to Texas, which was different from all that I
knew from community history, oral stories, and corridos. This humanity
came at the expense of Mexican and Mexican American people, who
were displaced, both physically and psychologically, from their land and
who experienced further structural oppression imposed upon them.
I needed students to know that despite Western efforts to efface such
a people and exorcize the possibility of their return as specters, there
indeed was a haunting that proves the limits of Western totality (see
Derrida 1994). "We remember the atrocities caused by settlers and the
Texas Rangers through stories, corridos, and celebrations," I told them.
"This is my inheritance," I claimed, "and my debt is to find opportunities
for the past to be remembered differently . . . Therein lies my politics
of memory." In my story, I modeled for students both the importance
of interpreting an inheritance and undertaking a call to responsibility
and justice. What I sought to create was a foundation of *techne* and kairotic moments through stories and storytelling. That is, every moment
students entered my class, I called and pushed them to relate, interrupt,
intervene, and to re-tell new stories.

Place, without a doubt, is a "meaningful component in human life" (Cresswell 2014, 55). But like place, students are not "pre-formed," but rather are subjects in the process of becoming (Pennycook 2010; Pred 1981). For some, teaching first-year composition may be like fighting in the trenches, especially if practitioners perceive student defiance as resistance rather than friction. I see first-year composition as the first point-of-contact I have with many students, and I use that classroom space to set the tone for a new profound sense of ethos and politics, which I attempt to develop in my students by adopting strategic neutrality. In acknowledging this condition, I seek out to establish "co-worker" relations and "co-working" opportunities with my students. I invite students to relate, interrupt, and intervene during their close readings of documents and when they listen to stories. When I shifted in my classroom from stories of Texas to stories of Utah, I posed the following questions: Does history matter? How does history remind us of an inheritance? What is our responsibility? And, how must we re-think concepts such as responsibility and justice? Also, I asked students to do several things throughout the semester: (1) re-search origins stories of Utah, (2) sit down with a family member and record their "story of/ about us," (3) record a series of personal stories "of/about us," and (4) return to that individual mid-semester and introduce another story to them, a story informed by principles of interruption and intervention rooted in a foundation of *techne* and kairotic moments. My pedagogical goals here were to generate friction in-between stories and to use that friction as a way to produce potentially transformative energy: a movement of the mind and a movement towards the possibilities of new stories.

From my lived experiences, agency can and may be generated by relationships and opportunities, providing the possibility of *co-workers* to participate in the production of new knowledge and meanings. Rather than be complacent with resistance as problematic or complicit with inequity, I performed strategic neutrality in seizing the opportunity to draw pedagogy from my own rhetorical education and to articulate a place of neutrality from the parallel in our histories. On a final note, part of my strategic neutrality is entangled in this idea of transparency. That is, when I demonstrated to students my entanglements and complicities as an educator, I acknowledged, first, that I am not immune to such things, and, second, that such things created opportunities for me to adopt a position of neutrality. This task is important. Because if trust is to be established, and furthered into mentorship, then there must be a foundation to do so. Strategic neutrality is my foundation.

Hinojosa's Classroom

Prior to my employment with Texas A&M University–Corpus Christi, I worked at a community college in San Antonio for ten years. It was there, on this diverse campus, where I developed an assignment sequence built around seven terms: *power, freedom, rebel* (or *rebellion*), *liberty, racism, slavery, genocide.* Students select terms from this list to develop three argumentative essays that require them to define, evaluate, and inform based on their term selections. Once, under this assignment sequence, I was fortunate to have an older Iranian woman as a student. She was eager to take my course. She had heard wonderful things about my class. She attended my class every day, always prepared to work. Near the end of the semester, students would read parts from *The Stoning of Soraya M.: A Story of Injustice* by French-Iranian journalist Freidoune Sahebjam (1994) and watch in its entirety the title film directed by Cyrus Nowrasteh (2010). I asked my Iranian student if she was familiar with the text, but she could not recall. A few days later, she spoke to me after class to declare how appalled she was that I would use such things in class, given the current US and Afghanistan, Iraq, and Iranian context. I met this friction with strategic neutrality. I recognized her point of view, and I surrendered to her before she came to resist me. I said that I would like to learn more from her, and I thanked her for the perspectives and point of view she could offer the class. I asked that she join me, have patience, and trust the course direction with her help. I indicated that it would be at that time where I would value her voice even more as we go over this material in class.

She chose to work on *freedom* and *power* throughout the semester. She told me later that she did not miss a single day of class, because she was always excited to see what I would say and to learn not just from her own writing but from what other students were writing based on the assignment guidelines. She would confess to me how fascinated she was to learn how American students defined these terms. She was delighted to see how these students struggled, became frustrated, and resisted learning more about the terms they chose for the second assignment due to the opposing point of view parameter. As someone who worked once as an interpreter for the United States military at Guantanamo Bay, my Iranian student expressed her contentment to see how her peers were learning more about injustices or inequalities as they gained rhetorical competencies in argumentative writing. For instance, at her table sat an African American female student, struggling and resisting writing on what she learned about the United States government. This student voiced how she loved the first assignment because she used her brother, a Marine, to speak about freedom and to define what freedom meant. For her, freedom involved making that autonomous decision to join and to serve a country that had once denied freedom and restricted civil liberties to African Americans. She was proud that he was a Marine serving the United States military. However, for her second assignment, she chose to work with genocide and decided to learn more about the United States government and its reluctance to get involved in the Darfurian conflict. Through writing, students encounter friction when they discovered how such dark things, like the justification of inaction in Darfur, were possible when previously students spent time defining acts of genocide as inhumane atrocities countered with action.

Listening exercises lead students into their last essay. We read and watch *The Stoning of Soraya M.* However, before we watch the film, I ask my students to listen first to an interview with the director, Cyrus Nowrasteh. In the interview, the director indicates what he wants people to "take away" from the film. He hopes that "they have been through an incredible movie experience, an enriching dramatic story. That they've been taken on a journey." To establish strategic neutrality, he declares that he is "not a politician," "not a diplomat," nor "a social scientist." All he wants is for "people to be moved by this story," and that the "irrelevance of what it's about is just there for anyone to take with them." He maintains that he does not "even have to hit that point [the stoning or human rights issue] very far" (*Spinnio* 2010). After the interview, we watch the film, and I ask students to listen closely to the film. I point out that a central character will say, "Voices of women do not matter in here. I want you to take my voice with you." I also indicate that this film depicts a gruesome, violent scene, and if anyone needs to leave the room, then they are more than welcome to do so without any repercussion. For this class, no one left, but sometimes, a student or two will make that conscious decision to resist what is on the screen and step out of the class.

The film runs over two days, and during this time frame, we do not discuss it at all. I hold this silence so as not to crowd the classroom space with voices; I want only voices from the film to fill that space for a time. Also, this quiet time allows us to absorb what the film portrays. Also, over the weekend, I ask students to reflect in writing; this reflection is the first step to process and to analyze the film. After the initial impact—the violent depiction of stoning Soraya M.—has settled, I ask my students to discuss the film with one another. I open the classroom space by stating how we are here to learn from one another, and that we should remain neutral as we listen to one another. Only then, do I invite friction into the classroom by asking students to voice their thoughts and concerns about either the film or text or both. Some say they loved it: a heart–wrenching story. Others are quick to hate it: too violent of a story. Some say they want to join the fight for human rights, women's rights in particular. Others are quick to condemn not the actions of one man or a small group of individuals but an entire people on the other side of the world—realizing the fear my Iranian student articulated early in the semester.

There is no doubt that the film elicits strong emotions in viewers due to the violence depicted. However, I move to remind my students that emotions are, to use Laura R. Micciche's (2007) words, "experienced between people within a particular context (and resides both in people and in culture) and that emotion is an expression, experience, and perception mediated by language, body, and culture" (1). With that position, we begin to contextualize such emotional responses as we begin to problematize the text or film through our Western gaze, a concept previously discussed in class. We learn how the text falls under a male gaze. Clearly, the voices of women did not matter in that a male journalist tells the story. We also learn about Michel Foucault's systems of power, which are depicted not only throughout the film with images of Ayatollah Khomeini but also throughout the director's goal and vision to craft and modify the film for a Western audience. Elements of the story become problematic. My Iranian student was quick to point out how men in that culture would never seek permission to divorce from their wives, and if they wanted to marry another woman, then they had the freedom to do so. Monogamy is a social practice valued in Western cultures, and divorce is a social action performed in Western cultures.

At the end of the semester, student presentations become another valuable listening exercise to help students hear how other students defined terms, to learn how other students justified opposing points of view, and to listen to realities other students concluded at the end about their terms. At first, my Iranian student said she did not want to complete her presentation. She felt that students would resist anything she had to say. Why? Because the majority of my students were young American citizens. Also, she felt students would be put off by her accent. However, I reminded her that her voice, and her voice alone, would matter. I encouraged her to speak, and if she wanted, to speak in her native tongue. This idea, she loved. She started her presentation in Farsi. As she spoke, I took notes only, as I did for all students presenting. Also, I chose not to recognize any of the discomfort taking place in the room, the student expressions of concern while she was speaking. My students found this sound unsettling, probably not so much that they didn't understand but the actual sound itself. They did not understand what was taking place in this space or why I had not interrupted her. I chose to engage this resistance that had emerged by strategically remaining neutral. I tried not to express any concerns at all. A neutral face. No smile or expression of interest or that of concern. A neutral position, without any body language that would be unlike what I would typically maintain. When my Iranian student transitioned into English, she acknowledged the emotional tension in the class and told the class that she wanted her peers to feel—just for a moment—like a foreigner and to feel the same friction she had felt throughout the entire course when she heard us all speaking English.

CONCLUSION: THOUGHTS FOR YOUR CONSIDERATION

Our classroom scenes highlighted how students attempted to "negotiate their circumstances in which they are expected to learn" (Toshalis 2016, 301), and in that process, we performed strategic neutrality to carry out the work we found necessary to do. This performance of neutrality mitigated resistance, we feel, and provided the necessary means to re-think and re-evaluate forms of resistance as friction. For your consideration, we offer thoughts on what we have learned from our experiences in the classroom as well as academia based on our encounters with friction/resistance. We believe the current political climate, where alt-right radical conservatives speak out against people of color, emboldened by President Donald J. Trump's racist rhetoric, places us and our pedagogical practices in danger. There is much at stake, especially for non-tenured faculty of color members. On the path toward tenure, we must consider, year after year, whether or not the classroom can truly be the site to engage resistance that may manifest in our encounters with friction. Sometimes, we consider how strategic neutrality may jeopardize our job security, but our local histories and historical bodies coalesced with our sense of *ethos* and ethics, all drive us to enact strategic neutrality and to be resistant of/to inequities and inequalities. However, this drive and resistance to such ideals can also very well be our downfall. We may be one bad evaluation from being marked as non-compliant or from being labeled too "radical" by department chairs or administrators (De La Torre 2018). Our classrooms can never effectively become the locus of resistance because neoliberal policies undermine (and absorb) forms of resistance and safeguard students from having to be held genuinely accountable. While indeed these conditions depend on institutional settings and programmatic designs, as faculty of color, we find ourselves too many times having to rely on and re-enact strategic neutrality.

Finally, we conclude by acknowledging that classroom encounters naturally present a state of friction between student and teacher, especially when educators engage student resistance, but friction, as previously stated, provides an opportunity to recognize these encounters as the organic nature in experiencing something new. So, we would like to offer a few suggestions on how to cultivate friction in a manner that may generate new energies: (1) align composition and rhetorical pedagogy with care and compassion (see Sandoval 2000); (2) establish a foundation of community listening to move students toward learning how to listen in-between cultures, times, and spaces; and (3) work with students to learn how to create presence from absence and sound from silence so as to see and hear from specters (specters haunted, specters that haunt). These are just a few ways practitioners can cultivate friction, but the key in making friction a productive engagement of differences may lie in mentorship because rhetorical education works best when we mentor one another in productive ways. To make epistemic and political realities visible for students, we must be willing to connect with our students. The stories in our classroom scene narratives tried to illuminate such mentorship, and within those stories, we and our students ventured to imagine the possibilities of creating new stories.

NOTES

1. We choose not to italicize the Spanish language. By so abstaining, we employ what Eugenia Casielles–Suárez calls a "radical hybridism" strategy, whereby Spanish becomes part of English. Our decision to not italicize Spanish is a more common discursive strategy among many Latinx writers. Personally, this strategy normalizes our language in this chapter as speakers of both languages so as not to alienate one from the other.
2. I use the term *presencing* alongside community listening; both as a way of listening between times, cultures, and places and a way of thinking about the rhetorical effect/affect of the non-living in the present.

REFERENCES

Barker, Eugene Campbell. 1910. "Stephen F. Austin and the Independence of Texas." *The Quarterly of the Texas State Historical Association* 13: 257–284.

Blommaert, Jan, and April Huang. 2009. "Historical Bodies and Historical Space." *Journal of Applied Linguistics* 6 (3): 267–282.

Casielles-Suárez, E. 2013. Radical Code-Switching in the Brief Wondrous Life of Oscar Wao. *Bulletin of Hispanic Studies* 90 (4), 475–487.

Caughie, Pamela. 1999. *Passing and Pedagogy: The Dynamics of Responsibility.* Chicago, IL: University of Illinois Press.

Cresswell, Tim. 2014. *Place: An Introduction*, 2nd ed. Malden, MA: Wiley Blackwell.

de Certeau, Michel. 2013. *The Practice of Everyday Life*. Los Angeles, CA: University of California Press.

De La Torre, Miguel A. "Academic Racism: The Repression of Marginalized Voices in Academia." *The Activist History Review*. August 28, 2018. https://activisthistory.com/2018/08/29/academic-racism-the-repression-of-marginalized-voices-in-academia/. Accessed October 04, 2018.

Derrida, Jacques. 1994. *Specters of Marx: The State of the Debt, the Work of Mourning, and the New International*. New York: Routledge.

Horton, Myles and Paulo Freire. 1990. *We Make the Road by Walking: Conversations on Education and Social Change*, ed. Brenda Bell, John Gaventa, and John Peters. Philadelphia, PA: Temple University Press.

Kopelson, Karen. 2003. "Rhetoric on the Edge of Cunning; Or, the Performance of Neutrality (Re)Considered as a Composition Pedagogy for Student Resistance." *College Composition and Communication* 55 (1): 115–146.

McFarland, Daniel A. 2001. "Student Resistance: How the Formal and Informal Organization of Classrooms Facilitate Everyday Forms of Student Defiance." *American Journal of Sociology* 107 (3): 612–678.

Micciche, Laura R. 2007. *Doing Emotion: Rhetoric, Writing, and Teaching*. Portsmouth, NH: Boynton/Cook Publishers.

Mignolo, Walter. 2009. "Epistemic Disobedience, Independent Thought and De-Colonial Freedom." *Theory, Culture and Society* 26 (7–8): 1–23.

Mills, Charles. 1997. *The Racial Contract*. Ithaca, NY: Cornell University Press.

Nowrasteh, Cyrus, dir. 2010. *The Stoning of Soraya M*. DVC. United States of America: Lions Gate.

Palmer, Parker J. 1998. *The Courage to Teach: Exploring the Inner Landscape of a Teacher's Life*. San Francisco, CA: Jossey-Bass Inc.

Pennycook, Alastair. 2010. *Language as a Local Practice*. London: Routledge.

Pred, Allen. 1981. "Social Reproduction and the Time-Geography of Everyday Life." *Human Geography* 63 (1): 5–22.

Rohrer, Judy. 2016. *Staking Claim: Settler Colonialism and Racialization in Hawai'i*. Tucson, AZ: University of Arizona Press.

Rushdy, Ashraf. 2012. *The End of American Lynching*. New Brunswick, NJ: Rutgers University Press.

Sahebjam, Freidoune. 1994. *The Stoning of Soraya M.: A Story of Injustice in Iran*. Trans. Richard Seaver. New York: Arcade.

Sandoval, Chela. 2000. *Methodology of the Oppressed*. Minneapolis, MN: University of Minnesota Press.

Shapiro, Sherry B. 1999. *Pedagogy and The Politics of the Body: A Critical Praxis*. New York: Garland Publishing, Inc.

Spinnio Interview with Cyrus Nowrasteh, Director of The Stoning of Soraya M, Part 1. 2010. YouTube. Spinnio. https://www.youtube.com/watch?v=UdLkCy3Voh0.

Thompson, Becky. 2017. *Teaching with Tenderness: Toward an Embodied Practice*. Urbana, IL: University of Illinois Press.

Toshalis, Eric. 2016. *Make Me! Understanding and Engaging Student Resistance in School*. Cambridge, MA: Harvard Education Press.

Tsing, Anna Lowenhaupt. 2004. *Friction: An Ethnography of Global Connection*. Princeton, NJ: Princeton University Press.

Ullman, Char. 2005. "Globalization on the Border: Reimagining Economies, Identities, and Schooling in El Paso." In *Language, Literacy, and Power in Schooling*, ed. Teresa L. McCarty, 241–262. Mahwah, NJ: Lawrence Erlbaum.

Villanueva, Victor. 2006. "Blind: Talking about the new racism." *The Writing Center Journal* 26 (1): 3–19.

14

TURNING RESISTANCES INTO ENGAGEMENT

Erika Johnson and Tawny LeBouef Tullia

Much of Western European history conditions us to see human dif-
ference in simplistic opposition to each other: dominant/subordinate,
good/bad, up/down, superior/inferior.

—Audre Lorde

Writing is identity-forming, identity-retrieving, identity-awakening, and identity-clarifying work. These are formative and important ideas in our fields—composition, communication, literacy, and rhetoric. The praxis and pedagogical considerations of creating opportunities and spaces in which our students can write from their identities and the epistemic and ontological benefits[1] of such work are continual and ever evolving. What we, as teaching professionals, offer of our own identities and how we choose to perform or withhold our identities, though, is controversial and ought to be considered as the complex consideration that it is. In what follows here we honor that complexity. Initially, we are unsettled with Kopelson's call for "cunning neutrality." Like many others in this collection, we grappled with Kopelson's call to perform a "self-conscious masquerade" (2003, 123). Ours is a choice to avoid a stance of neutrality. We are thoughtful that we will never attain neutrality, bodily, and therefore, pedagogically. Moreover, we believe and understand our predecessors when they write memoirs of exhaustion after having tried (Anzaldúa 1990; hooks 1994; Lorde 1984; Ahmed 2017). Beyond this self-reflective stance, our impetus for this addition to the collection is anchored in the benefits we have all too often witnessed in our students when we choose and practice a pedagogy that engages with difference openly. This does not mean that we arrive in front of our classrooms with, as John Trimbur describes in chapter 5 of this collection, a politically messaged t-shirt. For now, we will leave our Rosa Parks "Nah" shirts

DOI: 10.7330/9781607329992.c014

as after-class wear. But what it does mean for us is that we will lead our composition classrooms authentically inhabiting our identities. Doing so has repeatedly proven to open more conversation than it closes, especially for our students who identify in ways other than the socially constructed White, hetero-normative, mythical norm. We thoughtfully, and sometimes willfully, center difference.

WE ARE NOT NEUTRAL-BODIED

We face a reality that performing neutrality is a privilege we can ill-afford in composition classrooms. What is more, neutrality is a fiction for women and people of color. Thus, its performance resembles not only antithesis to authentic composing processes, but also to who we are as composition-ists and rhetoricians. We are averse to a performance of neutrality. While we do feel a responsibility to negotiate student resistance, student expec-tations should not be a lightning bearer for praxis. Kopelson describes the composition classroom as most of us experience it, as the required writing coursework most of our students are just ready to complete. She suggests that students are expecting "objectivity" in their university educations. Citing the work of Johanna Atwood, Kopelson notes that stu-dents "come to us believing that academia is the quintessential realm of objectivity, that anything overtly political or opinionated is 'biased,' and that 'bias' is most certainly 'something to be avoided by authors, teach-ers, and other authorities'" (2003, 117). We, too, have experienced what Kopelson notes is the backlash of an "anti-PC movement" (117). It seems a requirement of our profession that we be aware of the current iteration of the "anti-PC movement" backlash focused, as it is, on organizing and training prospective students. In these current professional conditions, avoiding the precarious as best we can becomes a balancing act. The conditions we invoke here are those in which we who teach are being "watched." The organization Turning Point USA continues to suss out "endless waves of leftist propaganda" ("About Us" 2018) for inclusion on their ever-growing *Professor Watchlist.* News outlets, pundits, and bloggers surf university webpages and announcements in order to seek the "too radical" among us. Furthermore, we acknowledge the further precarity of choosing to enact radical pedagogies for untenured and contingent faculty. These are not marginal considerations. They weigh heavily, espe-cially for two educators, who although not new to educating, are new to the institution of full-time faculty.

However, based upon our experiences with students, we feel that we must anchor our role in a composition classroom in a performance of our authentic selves in order to facilitate the construction of vibrant classrooms in which critical thinking is analyzed, interrogated, and embodied by students. We strive to offer students spaces in which they can form processes that reflect identity-forming, identity-retrieving, identity-awakening, and identity-clarifying writing, information and research literate processes, and extensive questioning of modalities. We find a performance of neutrality counterproductive to these goals. A performance of neutrality, in our minds, robs our students of crucial and difficult conversations. And although this may at times be work that requires a great deal of energy and an acceptance of a certain level of precarity for ourselves as professionals, offering our subjective and authentic selves and guiding students through difficult conversations is an integral element of their overall educations, especially in a course in which they are being asked to hone skills reflecting the recursive and interpellative act of the discoursal self.

As we begin our chapter, we explicate two important facets of this essay: we identify who "we" are and we define neutrality. We identify as women, who are early in our professional careers. We are Erika Johnson, assistant professor of English at a public university in the southwest, and Tawny LeBouef Tullia, assistant professor at a private university in the south. We earned our doctoral degrees at Texas Woman's University. Erika and Tawny were both born in the United States. Erika is a Black woman whose family origin is not the United States and is a proud Texan. Tawny is a White, bisexual, cisgendered woman whose family origin is south Louisiana. We are both single. Erika is not a parent. Tawny is. We are among less than 2 percent of the United States population who hold doctoral degrees and among the less than 1 percent of women who hold doctoral degrees (National Science Foundation 2017). We are, in our identities, "marginalized teacher-subject[s]" (Kopelson 2003, 118). We are both visibly and invisibly marked in how we identify. Many of those visible markers are read as possessive of inherent bias, as such, we do not deny our biases; we do not choose "cunning;" we do not choose neutrality because such action limits how we enact engagement in our composition classrooms. Kopelson (2003) offers a nuanced engagement with neutrality, to be certain. But, we are transfixed with what cunning neutrality means for students who may read this neutrality as just that: neutrality. While cunning neutrality may prevent resistances from entering or impeding the writing classroom for some students, it may alienate or, even worse, fail to offer students who finally see themselves in us an opportunity to engage with their own identities. In part, it is because of our direct experiences with students who felt they could in turn be their own authentic selves that we engage, here, with the concepts of the performance of neutrality in our classrooms.

Considering how we choose to perform our identities in our classrooms and why, we thought a return to our fields a proper first step. The following is the standing resolution ratified by the members of the National Council of Teachers of English (NCTE) in February of 2017: "Teachers and students should engage in conversations beyond narrow discourse communities. The classroom should be a space where all voices are recognized, where difficult conversations can be explored, and where communication in all its forms—written, digital, oral, visual—is used as a tool to help people enact their ideas and interact with each other. Pedagogy that aims for equity can facilitate these communications. Respectful disagreements develop not only empathy but also engaged, responsible citizens." These leading voices in our field suggests that an invaluable resource of ideas can be and "should be" a classroom space in which "all voices are recognized." Specific to the freedom of discourse within the classrooms, offices, and hallways of our spaces of higher education, the National Women's Studies Association (2016) defends the following: "A robust defense of academic freedom is about creating a climate in our classrooms, the public corridors of our campuses, and within our professional organizations so that we may all speak and debate free of intimidation and harassment. This is fundamental to scholarly inquiry." Here, we invoke these principles of our common workplaces to remind us that as scholars and practitioners of composition, *we* are also practitioners of multicultural and feminist pedagogy. Using the pronoun *we*, our meaning is the more pluralistic *we the scholars and practitioners of the teaching of composition.* For how could *we* not be? Our classrooms are multicultural in identity before we arrive on the first day because our students are multicultural. As compositionists, we request our students to further develop their critical awareness of themselves, their ideas, and their thoughts, turning these into writing through a multitude of methods. We ask of students through writing that they further what Roz Ivani terms "the discoursal self" (1998, 24). Thus, in this chapter, we argue a performance of neutrality can and, often, does work counter to pedagogies that offer students opportunities to learn to appreciate and engage from difference. Furthermore, we argue that there are underlying but considerable benefits for students when a composition classroom offers them an opportunity to present their discoursal and relational selves openly. We offer arguments for praxis—for a methodology of engagement—and most important, we advocate for critical consciousness in our classrooms.

As admission departments seek to invite and enroll a greater diversity of students, realizing the benefits of diversity in classrooms, do we not owe our students a pedagogy that allows them to explore and develop their own multitudinous selves? Addressing the ethical responsibilities of institutions of education, Toni Morrison argues, "it becomes incumbent upon us as citizens/scholars in the university to accept the consequences of our own value-redolent roles" (2008, 196). Morrison states, "like it or not, we are paradigms of our own values, advertisements of our own ethics" (196). She adds that this is "especially noticeable when we presume to foster ethics-free, value-lite education" (196). Now, there is some difference between "value-redolent roles" and what James Berlin argues, that rhetoric is *itself* ideological (Berlin 1988). To that point, Morrison further argues that "acknowledgement is preferable to the mask of disinterest" (2008, 196). It is our assertion that to appear neutral while we are asking students to grapple with their academic identities feels inauthentic, too close to Morrison's point of a "mask of disinterest." And to be sure, we want to be transparent that we do closely consider the precarity of using pedagogies like bell hooks' (1994) engaged pedagogy, AnaLouise Keating's (2012) pedagogies of invitation, or the invitational rhetoric described by Sonja K. Foss and Cindy L. Griffin (1995) because such invitations leave our identities open for interrogation. We are also considerate of other possibilities, like Romeo García and Yndalecio Isaac Hinojosa's "strategic neutrality" (see chapter 13 of this volume).

DEFINITIONS: AUTHENTICITY, RELATIONALITY, AND INTERSECTIONALITY

Though we have no intention of engaging in marginalization Olympics in writing about our identities, we offer our identities to explicate visible and invisible markers because we may encounter various resistances simply founded in preconceived bias based solely on those visible markers. Our identities and our experiences based on those identities compel us to turn resistances into engagement because we possess neither the privilege nor the professional capacity to engage in performances of neutrality. Paulo Freire notes the problem with neutrality when he says, "washing one's hands of the conflict between the powerful and the powerless means to side with the powerful, not to be neutral" (1985, 122). We take Freire's condemnation of neutral to mean that neutrality is an illusion, and its usefulness lies in denouncing or further subjugating the powerless, which exists in direct contrast to our goals here. Freire (2000) argues here, and in much of his body of work, that neutrality in education is

impossible. Most sincerely, neutrality is impossible for critical consciousness that compels interrogation of resistance, of oppressive power dynamics, and of the illumination of its multifaceted components. To be sure,
Freire is referring to power dynamics in Brazil, his home country, but
power is a universal construct of which education is not foreign.

We now turn to the implicit oppressive nature of our roles. As instructors, no matter how hard we try to remain facilitators and attempt to
avoid the role of course community authoritarian, we still choose texts
for readings; we determine assignments for grading; and we guide
classroom conversations. And, while we are advocating for and explicating how to turn known and unknown resistances into engagement, we
acknowledge here, as we would do in our classrooms, that we are not
neutral. We do not "wash our hands of the conflict;" we engage with the
conflict because in our classrooms we are both the powerful and the
powerless. We are powerful in our roles, but we are powerless in how
students come to us with preconceived notions of who we are or who we
are presumed to be. Thus, we choose to be open and transparent. Our
choices are not neutral, and we should acknowledge them with transparency and hope to mitigate ambiguity because our roles in classrooms
demand authenticity when we ask for engagement.[2]

We are careful in an expanded definition of *authenticity* to argue
that using *relationality*, because it highlights intersectionality, replaces
our wont to use the term *authenticity*. Intersectionality foregrounds our
argument here because we are asking students to interrogate biases in
origins and practices. We comprise our biases. We want to be clear here;
being biased and enacting biases are not identical—one is existence,
the other is action. We are concerned with action, the selves we *enact* in
the classroom and throughout the choices we make in designing course
content, even in the comments we offer in response to student writing.
Our actions should not replicate a lack of intersectionality in pedagogical performance. Such performance that does not compel discourses
about intersectionality invariably facilitate the erasure of identities we
cannot and do not suppress. In a later response to her original essay,
Kopelson (2006) acknowledges the problematic nature of performing
neutrality in its erasure of identity. Even if these identities are read as
contrary or compatible to preconceived notions of who our students
presume us to be, we seek to neither fulfill identity preconceptions nor
deny them. We seek to unpack them.

One of Patricia Hill Collins and Sirma Bilge's "core ideas of intersectionality," *relationality*, is defined as "thinking that rejects *either/or*
binary thinking, for example, opposing theory to practice, scholarship

to activism, or blacks to whites" (2016, 27). Working in converse to this *either/or*, binary thinking, relationality is a practice of *both/and* framing (27). In 1980, Audre Lorde offered the following in a speech given at Amherst College: "Certainly there are very real differences between us of race, age, and sex. But it is not those differences between us that are separating us. It is rather our refusal to recognize those differences, and to examine the distortions which result from our misnaming them and their effects upon human behavior and expectation" (2009, 115). Lorde also moves us away from *either/or* binary thinking. It is our fear that keeps us from these critical engagements. That fear is stealing opportunity for engagement and valuable moments of learning from our students and from ourselves. And when we choose silence, we are reifying the institutions of racism, sexism, heterosexism, and so on. When we choose a practice using *relationality*, we build bridges across these differences. But, first we ought to understand—truly understand—our differences, our discoursal differences. In an intersectional practice, rather than dismissing differences, students and instructors negotiate "differences that exist within discrete scholarly and political traditions of race, class, gender, sexuality, ability, nationality, ethnicity, colonialism, religion, and immigration" (Collins and Bilge 2016, 168). Modeling this *both/and* praxis takes attention and a good deal of energy until we become accustomed to it, until it becomes a part of both our epistemology and ontology.

Audre Lorde validates this process as a difficult one and notes the importance of overcoming these difficulties: "it is within our differences that we are both most powerful and most vulnerable, and some of the most difficult tasks of our lives are the claiming of differences and learning to use those differences as bridges rather than as barriers between us" (2009, 201). By overcoming these difficulties and threading these practices into our composition praxis, we offer a modeling of methods to our students. These methods, for Lorde, are a way forward that "can teach us about the future we must all share" (202). Similarly, Gloria E. Anzaldúa (2009) has the following to offer on pedagogy, difference, and critical consciousness: "educators need to create fertile ground for the coming generations of women and men of color and 'white' students; otherwise we relegate all to an impoverished education" (240).

Activities and assignments that offer students opportunities to critically engage with one another and to practice *both/and* frames offer that fertile ground. Anzaldúa offers an echo of bell hooks's suggestion to critical engagement. "Transformation," Anzaldúa argues, "does not happen unless we explore what threatens us as teachers and students; what we sweep under our desks; what brings us into open conflict and disagreement; and what cultural prescriptions and cultural teachings we're rebelling against" (2009, 241). These practices seem, to us, to be antithetical to a practice of neutrality, in any form. As we move from a problematic label of authentic and toward the bridging concept of relationality and the ability of the concept of intersectionality to hold our multiplicities, we address privilege; a concept we feel ought not be ignored in any conversation about multiplicities, identity, and performativity.

PRIVILEGE IN THE COMPOSITION CLASSROOM

Privilege is a loaded word, and we do not use it lightly. We do possess a certain advantage in composition classrooms because of our educations. We use *privilege* here to unpack meaning and problematize its inevitable presence in composition classrooms.

Privilege, as M. Jacqui Alexander notes, has habits and often seems a living, breathing entity. Though, we espouse comprehension of colleges as places for learning, we know that students come to us with a variety of knowledges that will impact their learning and what they might learn both from and with us. While we possess a certain privilege in our abilities to verbalize said privileges and our biases, some of our students may not yet possess the capacities to similarly verbalize their privileges and biases. They will resist not only our efforts to assist in such verbalization, but also what and how we define privilege. We offer Alexander's connotation of privilege as grounding for our explication of and experiences with resistances: "One of the habits of privilege is that it spawns superiority, beckoning it owners to don a veil of false protection so that they never see themselves, the devastation they wreak or their accountability to it. Privilege and superiority blunt the loss that issues from enforced alienation and segregations of different kinds" (2002, 2). However, such privilege is neither protection from nor negation of our responsibilities in composition classrooms. We are unmasking our privilege to facilitate difficult conversations. Though we are in academic bubbles in composition classrooms, we all exist outside of our classrooms and outside of higher education and those existences do inform who we are and what we believe.

Beyond considering our own privilege in our own classrooms, we should consider spectrums of privilege and forms of privilege among our students. It is of utmost importance that we not expect students from historically oppressed identities to carry the burden of presenting their perspectives as if they speak for their multitude of communities.

They speak for themselves alone.[3] Furthermore, we must openly address our privileges within an intersectional classroom and openly engage with the idea that the onus for engagement is not a burden that falls upon a select few. Doing so further models practices of engagement, like practices of invitational rhetoric and pedagogies of invitation as outlined by Sonja K. Foss and Cindy L. Griffin (1995), Cheryl Glenn (2004), and AnaLouise Keating (2012).

Compositions classrooms are likely places where a multiplicity of diverse voices converge. Conflict is inevitable, so we should be ready not to *defend* in response to an attack, but to *engage* with the resulting conflict. Composition classrooms are spaces to invite personal inquiry because precisely what we do is challenging—we invite, we probe, and we interrogate biases that are similar and dissimilar to our own in order to facilitate and encourage discourse. We do not do this because we enjoy discord. We do this to comprehend the veracity of biases of which we are all, students and teachers alike, often indifferent and/or ignorant.[4] We are not naïve to ponder that discourses challenging perception and/or biases are not fraught with resistance. We know conversations that delve into biases are indeed ripe for rejection and negation. While topics of invariable discussion such as abortion, gun control, and issues of race, usually bounced around in composition classrooms, more specifically first-year composition, ostensibly invite exposing biases, topics such as wages and healthcare can also quickly illuminate unknown biases. We take unavoidable conflict that comes from unpacking biases and not performing neutrality and make it—the inevitable conflicts— the discourse (Jarratt 2003). To be clear, we are not referencing a type of conflict that devolves into a clash of wills where one side must retreat. Rather, we are referencing a divergence that is the inevitable difference of opinions, difference in perceptions, and differences that make us all unique and yet prone to dissection.

Because we persist as a society that finds comfort in labels and labeling as we have done here in proclaiming our multiple identities, we open ourselves for critique and for judgment; this is necessary action. In announcing our identities here, we replicate what we do in our classrooms: we embrace our identities and subsequent biases. We are making concerted decisions not to engage in a performance of neutrality because such action privileges or rather creates hierarchies of marginalization that cannot be or rather should not be sustained in composition classrooms. We are making often-benign pedagogical performances more visible. We are nurturing critical thinking by building relationships based on the mutual recognition that nothing of what we do in composition classrooms is without purpose. Our composition classrooms are spaces of well-being. We choose not to quell voices of dissent. Rather, we are committed to processes of self-actualization that empower students to comprehend not just our/their biases, but also multiplicities in their own.

CRITICAL ENGAGEMENT (CRITICAL EDUCATION TO CRITICAL CONSCIOUSNESS)

In our composition classrooms, we are blending critical education with critical consciousness because we are our biases. Embracing the existence of our biases should not be a disclaimer for free speech; it is for everyone or it is for no one. We enact a free-speech or rather an open-door policy that quashes no line of inquiry. In light of the increasing influence of *Professor Watchlist*, which proclaims free speech but denounces professors who use that right both inside and outside classrooms, we need discourse that neither quells nor amplifies engagement with topics and the people who espouse them. Furthermore, we need increased conversations about biases. We can ill afford to ignore their existence. As composition faculty, we possess specific knowledges because of our increased levels of education, but our knowledge is not the only knowledge in our classrooms. Because of the nature of our existence as faculty, we strive, as foci of knowledge, to welcome all knowledges, regardless of our discomfort.

Paradoxically, this means composition teachers are both centered and de-centered. By placing who we are "in the line of fire," we acknowledge we are advocating dangerous work. But, our academic existences are already in danger of suffocation. We are facing real dangers in the academy, which is why we should engage in Peter Elbow's (1973) "dialectic of propositions" and couple it with Anne Doneday's (2002) experiences and suggestions. Elbow's supposition is an argument of realization and balance. Because conceptions and misconceptions are not apparitions, a balanced approach to assist students in realizing how they come to their opinions and positions is delicate work. Thus, we employ Doneday's suggestions, which are essential in composition classrooms when using a radical multicultural pedagogy. Doneday finds that the praxis of creating "safe space" within the classroom tends to silence students from marginalized groups, usually and emphatically creating an effect opposite to that we are seeking (2002, 87). Thus, in these practices, we do not avoid confrontation; we require working together to unpack origins and practices in and of biases. In our classroom, this might simply play out as a response to a student's using the pronoun "they." We may engage the student further by asking the student to clearly define the "they" to which she/he/they refer. In our experience, as we engage students, their biases become clear to them.

Collins and Bilge remind us that a "critical education's emphasis on dialogical pedagogy and intersectionality's focus on relationality speak to a similar theme, namely, navigating consciousness for both individuals and for forms of knowledge" (2016, 168). Susan Jarratt writes that her hopes for engaging with conflict and working through conflict in pedagogically sound ways can be found in "courses that lead students to see how differences emerging from their texts and discussions have more to do with those contexts than they do with an essential and unarguable individuality" (2003, 277). Collins and Bilge echo Jarratt in asserting that "dialogical education takes on the hard work of developing critical consciousness by talking and listening to people who have different points of view" (2016, 168). This is the hard work we suggest has a home and an integral purpose in a composition classroom. In addition to Jarratt, and Collins and Bilge, we find education scholar Sonia Nieto's argument especially important in this consideration. Nieto observes that "the most powerful learning results when students work and struggle with one another, even if it is sometimes difficult and challenging" (2010, 257). A pedagogy that embraces critical engagement and productive forms of conflict should also embrace that we, students and instructors, arrive with knowledges. These knowledges should be embraced, validated, and engaged. Thusly, a pedagogy seated in the praxis of intersectionality and relationality requires that we, as instructors, engage. This engagement is not fully possible from a positionality of neutrality.

INVITING AND ENGAGING PRODUCTIVE CONFLICT

We take Elbow's (2008) "The Believing Game" and Doneday's (2002) suggestions and apply them here as a toolkit for engagement. Before initiating such engagement, an agreement should be made that discourse is not necessarily valid, but nonetheless requires us to listen. However, as faculty we must resist the urge to identify with or protect the resisting students. Our situatedness as faculty requires that we not *use* our privilege. Furthermore, in our classes, as a community, we agree to define and then refuse to engage in language that is demeaning. Since our goal is to turn resistances into engagement, we acknowledge and unmask biases that initiate resistance.

Towards those ends, we make the following suggestions taken from Elbow's "The Believing Game" and Doneday's praxis "to make the interaction part of the discussion of the classroom" (Doneday 2002, 94).

We envision the following as a framework for conversation that might be planned for a class session or is a framework that can be turned to when a class discussion may benefit. When planned, we use this framework as structure to help students consider an assigned reading, an example for digital rhetoric, and/or a situated utterance of rhetoric. Students begin this framework in small groups of three or four and prepare written thoughts beforehand. Students receive instructions to write, not to refute. Write about what we believe in arguments. Write in the positive.

Read. Read, not to refute. Read for comprehension. Read to believe. Read arguments that do not agree with prior education, or prior learning. Disagreement with arguments is natural, but what is written must be in the affirmative.

Anticipate. Anticipate resistance. Resistance is natural and expected because we are a society of doubt. Doubt is an inevitable component of this exercise because "it allows us to discover hidden contradictions;" "it is a tool to scrutinize and test" (Elbow 2008, 5). An essential component of our legal system is "beyond a reasonable doubt," as it too is part of scrutiny and testing. Students converse in the round anticipating resistance.

Listen. We realize this will be difficult, but listen. Listen, not to refute. Listen to be welcoming. Listen to believe. Listen to arguments that likely contradict every ounce of being.

Explain. We realize this may be as difficult as listening, but groups should be allowed to explain what they believe. Whether beliefs are erroneous or valid is not yet the point. Groups should be allowed to explain how they have come to such beliefs. The idea is not that small groups will arrive at consensus, but rather will learn to find some comfort in ambiguity and disagreement.

At this point, the class will return to the larger class group for discussion.

Discuss. Again, we realize this may be as difficult as listening, but discussion must occur. Discussion is an essential component of this exercise. Arguments against certain people in society or arguments negative in nature should still be written in the positive. If the positive is insidious, then ask for basic tenets. Basic tenets: Do people exist? How do people exist? What makes them exist? Build from basic tenets to foster contemplation. Reduce arguments to rudimentary levels to encourage critical thinking. All voices, even those of dissent, should be heard or no voices will be heard. We are likely to both believe and doubt when we have support. When support wanes, we may be less likely to believe.

While we hope this activity will compel critical thinking about biases that impact the everyday existences of people, we are not so naïve as to believe that this activity will overturn years of reinforced biases. In such an activity, our goal is to turn resistances of listening, resistances of discussion, and resistances of engagement to fostering listening, fostering discussion, and fostering engagement. In this activity, we strive to comprehend how biases are constructed, sustained, and disseminated. We acknowledge that some students will refuse participation; we acknowledge that there will be tension. We should be willing, then, to encourage students to participate as soon as irreconcilable tensions develop (Doneday 2002). This type of participation better prepares students for engagements outside of the classroom, regardless of their lived experiences or ideologies. And, we are clear here, and this bears repeating: there will be tension. But, if we do not acknowledge and engage in difficult topics, we are complicit in their proliferation both inside and outside our classrooms.

CONCLUSION

What we propose is a mode of humanizing, humanizing differences, creating bridges, and, dare we echo Lorde, celebrating difference. In closing, we offer some thoughts on the power of critical pedagogies—like a praxis of intersectionality using relationality. Collins and Bilge believe that "when done well" a practice of "examining the heterogeneity of social identities and helping students deal with them humanizes the schooling process for all students" (2016, 183). After all, is this not one of the tenets of our discipline? The answer is reflected in the NCTE's recently ratified "Resolution on Contemporary Discourse and the English Language Arts Classroom," in which we state that we strive, as a discipline, to foster spaces where all voices are recognized, spaces where the difficult conversations are explored, and spaces where the tools of communication we teach act as tools for our students to use beyond our courses to interact with ideas and with each other (2017). Pedagogy founded on the principles of relationality and intersectionality offer us a manner through which to engage in these goals.

NOTES

1. Anzaldúa (1987); Juzwik and Cushman (2014).
2. We also note that the term *authenticity* is problematic. Many activist communities and/or academics use the term *authenticity* as an often-exclusionary tool for

measuring identities. We recognize its problematic history and therefore offer a methodical transition from the authentic to the relational. We consider authenticity to be less a rhetorical representation of *truth* or *honesty* than it is a practice of critical and crucial engagement, and not necessarily one of politic. These seem to us to be flattened versions of authenticity. Authenticity in the classroom and in pedagogy ought not *require* or *necessitate* responses from our students. Furthermore, we find authenticity helps students to observe ways of being their own full and authentic selves, even in the classroom. And we are often struck with just what that means to our students.

3.   Case and Cole (2013) explore the practice of ensuring that students feel that they are being asked to contribute their own perspectives rather than carrying the burden of speaking for entire communities.

4.   We turn to Susan Jarratt's (2003) foundational pedagogical work, "Feminism and Composition: The Case for Conflict," and to Collins and Bilge's (2016) *Intersectionality* for support in this assertion about open conflict and pedagogy.

REFERENCES

"About US." 2018. Turning Point USA. https://www.tpusa.com/aboutus/.

Ahmed, Sara. 2017. *Living a Feminist Life.* Durham, NC: Duke University Press.

Alexander, M. Jacqui. 2002. *Pedagogies of Crossing: Meditations on Feminism, Sexual Politics, Memory, and the Sacred.* Durham, NC: Duke University Press.

Anzaldúa, Gloria E. 1987. *Borderlands/La Frontera: The New Mestiza.* San Francisco: Aunt Lute Books.

Anzaldúa, Gloria E. 1990. "Haciendo Caras: una entrada." In *Making Face, Making Soul/ Haciendo Caras: Creative and Critical Perspectives by Feminists of Color.* San Francisco, CA: Aunt Lute Books.

Anzaldúa, Gloria E. 2009. "Transforming American Studies: 2001 Bode-Pearson Prize Acceptance Speech." In *The Gloria Anzaldúa Reader,* ed. AnaLouise Keating, 239–241. Durham, NC: Duke University Press.

Berlin, James. 1988. "Rhetoric and Ideology in the Writing Class." *College English* 50 (5): 477–494.

Case, Kim A., and Elizabeth R. Cole. 2013. "Deconstructing Privilege When Students Resist: The Journey Back into the Community of Engaged Learners." In *Deconstructing Privilege: Teaching and Learning as Allies in the Classroom* ed. by Kim A. Case, 34–48. New York: Routledge.

Collins, Patricia Hill, and Sirma Bilge. 2016. *Intersectionality.* Malden, MA: Polity Press.

Doneday, Anne. 2002. "Negotiating Tensions: Teaching about Race Issues in Graduate Feminist Classrooms." In *Feminist Pedagogy: Looking Back to Move Forward, NWSA Journal,* 14 (1): 82–102.

Elbow, Peter. 1973. *Writing Without Teachers.* New York: Oxford University Press.

Elbow, Peter. 2008. "The Believing Game—Methodological Believing." *English Department Faculty Publication Series.* Paper 5. Amherst, MA: University of Massachusetts, Amherst. https://www.southern.edu/academics/academic-sites/southernscholars/docs/The-Believing-Game-Methodological-Believing.pdf.

Foss, Sonja K. and Cindy L. Griffin. 1995. "Beyond Persuasion: A Proposal for An Invitational Rhetoric." *Communication Monographs* 62: 2–18.

Freire, Paulo. 1985. *The Politics of Education: Culture, Power, and Liberation.* Westport, CT: Bergin and Garvey.

Freire, Paulo. 2000. *Pedagogy of the Oppressed.* New York: Bloomsbury Academic.

Glenn, Cheryl. *Unspoken: A Rhetoric of Silence.* Carbondale: Southern Illinois University Press.

hooks, bell. 1994. *Teaching to Transgress: Education as the Practice of Freedom.* New York: Routledge.

Ivanič, Roz. 1998. *Writing and Identity: The Discoursal Construction of Identity in Academic Writing.* Philadelphia, PA: John Benjamins North America.

Jarratt, Susan C. 2003. "Feminism and Composition: The Case for Conflict." In *Feminism and Composition: A Critical Sourcebook*, ed. Gesa E. Kirsch et al., 263–280. Boston, MA: Bedford/St. Martin's.

Juzwik, Mary M., and Ellen Cushman. 2014. "Teacher Epistemology and Ontology: Emerging Perspectives on Writing Instruction and Classroom Discourse." *Research in the Teaching of English* 49 (2): 89–94.

Keating, AnaLouise. 2012. *Transformation Now!: Toward a Post-Oppositional Politics of Change.* Urbana, IL: University of Illinois Press.

Kopelson, Karen. 2003. "Rhetoric on the Edge of Cunning; Or, The Performance of Neutrality (Re)Considered as a Composition Pedagogy for Student Resistance." *College Composition and Communication* 55 (1): 115–146.

Kopelson, Karen. 2006. "Of Ambiguity and Erasure: The Perils of Performative Pedagogy." In *Relations, Locations, Positions: Composition Theory for Writing Teachers 2006*, ed. Peter Vandenberg, Sue Hum, and Jennifer Clary-Lemon, 563–570. Urbana, IL: National Council of Teachers of English.

Lorde, Audre. 1984. "Age, Race, Class, and Sex: Women Redefining Difference." In *Sister Outsider*, 114–123. New York: Crossing Press, 2007.

Lorde, Audre. 2009. "Difference and Survival: An Address at Hunter College." In *I Am Your Sister: Collected and Unpublished Writings of Audre Lorde*, ed. Rudolph P. Byrd, Johnetta Betsch Cole, and Beverly Guy-Sheftall, 201–204. Oxford: Oxford University Press.

Morrison, Toni. 2008. "How Can Values Be Taught in the University." In *What Moves at the Margins: Selected Nonfiction*, 191–197. Jackson, MS: University Press of Mississippi.

National Council of Teachers of English. 2017. "Resolution on Contemporary Discourse and the English Language Arts Classroom." Last modified February 28, 2017. http://www2.ncte.org/statement/contemporary-discourse/.

National Science Foundation. 2017. "Doctorate Recipients from US Universities 2016." Last modified December 2017. https://www.nsf.gov/statistics/2018/nsf18304/static/report/nsf18304-report.pdf.

National Women's Studies Association. 2016. "EC Letter in Support of Academic Freedom." Last modified December 22, 2016. https://www.nwsa.org/statements.

Nieto, Sonia. 2010. *Language, Culture, and Teaching: Critical Perspectives.* New York: Routledge.

15

WHO IS AFRAID OF NEUTRALITY?
Performativity, Resignification, and the
Jena Six in the Composition Classroom

David P. Stubblefield and Chad Chisholm

In Beckett, nothing dies.

—Gilles Deleuze

There is probably no single idea inside of composition studies that is considered more politically naïve than the idea of teacher neutrality. In fact, it is difficult to imagine anyone leaving a graduate program in the last thirty years without first being thoroughly convinced of the impossibility of claiming a neutral position of authority. Today everyone knows that to claim that a certain position is neutral is to assert a position outside of power, language, and history, and since no such position exists, claims of neutrality inevitably mask the exercise of power by dominant groups against the marginalized. Hence, this belief functions as the unspoken and taken-for-granted assumption of virtually any contemporary discussion of teacher authority in the classroom.

With this contemporary context in mind, this chapter takes a different approach. That is, unlike most of the contributions in this collection that argue against the notion of neutrality (Brewer, chapter 1; Evans, chapter 2; Pacton, chapter 12), this paper questions the very "for" or "against" logic of such critiques and asks whether or not it might be possible to affirm a particular, rhetorical understanding of teacher neutrality, and whether doing so may be more consistent with some of the very theoretical positions that have often been invoked to dismiss neutrality. In short, it takes the position that if the proposition "there is a neutral position" is not neutral, then—inside of the propositional logic of dialectical reasoning—neither is the proposition "there is no position of neutrality." Moreover, from the rhetorical position of practical argument, it suggests that neutrality is an indispensable concept for

DOI: 10.7330/9781607329992.c015

academic institutions, one that we abandon only at our own peril, and one that when used strategically, can produce unpredictable and desirable pedagogical effects.

To accomplish this task, we begin by discussing the liberal humanist critique of the authority exercised in the current traditional classroom, then proceed to discuss the critique of this critique as put forward by cultural-studies approaches. Despite the apparent differences in these positions, we argue that both positions operate on the assumption that classroom authority and democratic classroom relations are mutually exclusive and static oppositions subject to the principle of non-contradiction that underpins dialectical reasoning.

After questioning and noting the limitations of this paradigm, we find alternatives ways of approaching the problem of teacher authority in the work of Richard Boyd, Stanley Fish, and Karen Kopelson. In one way or another, these theorists depart from an approach to concepts based the static, dialectical logic of contradiction, negation, and exclusion, and instead treat them as contextual and rhetorical performances subject to a "logic of performativity." Such a logic, we argue, holds the key to rethinking an affirmative notion of teacher neutrality. Finally, we offer an example from the classroom where a performance of teacher neutrality not only became the means for invention and discovery, but disrupted some of the existing power relations on campus.

THE DEMOCRATIC CLASSROOM: LIBERAL HUMANIST STYLE

After general social the upheaval of the 1960s, the idea of a more democratic classroom emerged on the charge that dominant versions of pedagogy-based, current-traditional rhetoric produced undemocratic, authoritarian classrooms. In these classrooms, teachers functioned as the sole authority, in charge of transmitting the dominant society's norms to passive students whose ideas and voices were effectively silenced.

In order to remedy this situation, composition theorists, from an array of theoretical perspectives, including the critical-pedagogy perspective of James Sledd, Richard Ohmann, Ira Shor, and Richard Boyd, and the expressivist pedagogy perspectives of Donald Murray and Peter Elbow, eagerly began working on developing a more democratic classroom based on a radical, reworking of classroom authority (Boyd 1999, 590). Composition instructors, they insisted, must give up a significant portion of their authority, share power with students, and cultivate the kind of individual autonomy in students necessary to resist repressive institutions.

Despite the utopian character of this project, a belief emerged that "the democratic classroom" was not only possible, but destined to become a reality. Boyd explains that he and his fellow theorists "held tight to the notion that the Composition classroom would indeed be a site of resistance, but with the crucial change that now had teacher and student united in resistance, struggling against authoritarianism in all of its manifestations and mutually committed to the search for genuine empowerment" (590).

However, the liberal-democratic classroom never actually happened (Boyd 1990, 590). In what could only seem like a cruel irony, rather than join professors in the struggle against authority, students resisted the very "authorities" that attempted to install the anti-authoritarian classroom (Rosenthal 1995, 150). It was as if the one unquestionable assumption that provided the theoretical foundation of the liberal, humanist classroom—the democratic potential of their students—had been proven to be faulty. This unanticipated event sent theorists of the democratic classroom back to the drawing board.

SOMETHING DEEPLY WRONG WITH OUR STUDENTS

Inside of this drawing board, any alternative had to provide an answer as to why students did not want to unite with instructors and resist authority in the democratic classroom. For many, the most compelling answer involved the idea that students were somehow deeply flawed as a result of their immersion in popular culture, a culture that, while experienced as a realm of individuality and free choice, inculcated the attitudes and values of the powerful. Popular culture seizes on the political unconscious of students, reproducing in them the values of the dominant culture, and neutralizing the traditional strategies of liberal humanism. This critical diagnosis explained why a laissez-faire approach to teacher authority did not produce the anticipated resistance to authority, but instead resulted in a cry for more of it. Liberal theorists, according to the authors of this new "cultural studies" approach, misunderstood power, locating it exclusively in institutions, laws, and rights and neglecting the power of popular culture to shape student identities (George and Trimbur 2001, 71–81).

Indeed in such an environment, adopting the neutral stance of the liberal humanist becomes a way of being complicit with existing cultural production. If the initial versions of the democratic classroom showed anything, it was that a more aggressive use of teacher authority was necessary to combat authoritarian subjectivities. Democratic sensibilities are not present in students, waiting to burst forth once authority is lifted; instead, they must be inculcated in students.

In his summary review in a 1995 collection of essays titled *Leftist Margins: Cultural Studies and Composition Pedagogy,* Richard Ohmann notes this shift in approach and the pejorative diagnosis of students that provided its rationale:

> What strikes me about the essays [in this volume] as a whole, when I compare them to similar efforts of the late sixties, is how peripheral now, how qualified, is the ideal of the democratic classroom. Then, many assumed that canceling the normal, dominative relations of pedagogy would release authentic motives for learning along with liberatory politics. Rarely do I see that assumption at work in the present volume. Rather, many of its contributors assume or argue that there is something deeply wrong with our students that disables them as subjects of democracy. (1995, 328)

Ohmann goes on to note that many of the authors express a certain disdain for "the liberal platitudes" such as "everyone has a right to his or her own opinion" and that "tolerance might be welcome in my classroom." For these authors, teacher neutrality "hides real conflict, and prevents students from grasping their relation to the dominant ideology" (328).

THE CALL FOR A BENEVOLENT *HERRSCHAFT*:
WE NEED MORE MUSCLE

As Ohmann was writing his review, other theorists, such as Adam Katz (1995), were doubling down on the lack of democratic potential in students:

> This [the dominant culture's power to construct student subjectivity] means . . . students cannot be regarded as possessing a "good" democratic kernel which needs to be released from external restraints and permitted to flourish, nor as free rational subjects who can simply choose from a variety of options . . . rather they must be understood as contradictory sites constituted by the enormous investment of the dominant culture in producing authoritarian individuals, that is by their resistance to democracy in the sense of any social and material force which would advance democracy in a consistent way. (211)

Comments such as these insist that if the democratic classroom was going to come into being, it would not come from the students, but from the teachers who have to bring democracy to the classroom.

To this end, Colleen M. Tremonte (1995) recommends "aggressive work that leads [students] to unexpected and potentially taboo discoveries, much as the physical act of opening or excavating a burial plot," work which she refers to as "grave digging" which aims to excavate "cultural myths" and, therefore, "gives the reader or writer permission to assault the text" (54). She emphasizes the violence of this struggle as "hostile" teachers "force" students to embark upon "provocative and troublesome search and seizures, those which bore into the very marrow of a first-year student's identity, into her personal values and concrete experiences, . . . [and] assault the myths of family and gender" (59). Likewise, Ohmann (1995) lists one of the goals of cultural studies peda-gogies as performing an "assault on the text of our daily lives," adding that this new approach wants to "dynamite the bedrock of 'my opinion'" by tracing all student opinion back to the contradictions of an unjust society (328). In the same way, Richard Rorty (2000) explains to the hypothetical parents that instructors are "going to go right on trying to discredit you in the eyes of your children, trying to strip your fundamen-talist religious community of dignity, trying to make your views seem silly rather than discussable" (22). At this point, we are a long away from an anti-authoritarian, liberal humanist ethos.

While liberal humanism deplored this kind of use of teacher author-ity, cultural studies advocated an oppositional pedagogy that affirmed the use of force as part of a "benevolent domination." For example, Rorty proclaims that he does not "see anything *herrschaftsfrei* [domina-tion free] about my handling of my fundamentalist students. Rather, I think those students are lucky to find themselves under the benevolent *Herrschaft* [domination] of people like me, and to have escaped the grip of their frightening, vicious, dangerous parents" (2000, 22). Certainly, it would be difficult to imagine a stronger, more unapologetic endorse-ment of the unrestrained use of teacher authority.

For this kind of oppositional pedagogy, the primary task of the demo-cratic teacher instructor is to reverse the values of the dominant culture. For instance, Katz explains, "democratic politics in this case involves attempting to support the subordinate side in these various antago-nisms, thereby undermining domination: presumably, enough reversals of this kind will add to a democratic, or at least more democratic society" (1995, 209). However, it is far from clear that such reversals amount to a new kind of politics. In fact, inside of an increasingly sociological approach to the classroom, what was to be reversed was not domina-tion, violence, or authoritarianism, but who exercises this kind of power against whom.

Despite the differences between this approach to the classroom and the liberal humanist approach, both positions are united in their affirmation of a particular paradigm. That is, both can be understood as operating under a particular understanding of what Gerald Graff

(1995) has called "the pedagogical double bind" (325). This double bind consists the fact that teachers are charged with using their authority to transmit a particular set of norms, but because they are part of a democratic institution, they must also accommodate a diverse student population. We can think of the liberal humanist classroom affirming one side of this logical dilemma and siding with democratic relations and abandoning teacher authority. Likewise, we can think of cultural-studies approaches as siding with teacher authority and abandoning democratic relations.

Hence, both positions understand the use of teacher authority inside of a paradigm based a dialectical opposition between authority and democratic forms of relation, leaving us with no choice but to be "for" one and "against" the other.

PERFORMING THE DOUBLE BIND

One attempt to negotiate the double bind of authority and classroom relation can be found Richard Boyd's (1999) landmark essay, "Reading Student Resistance: The Case of the Missing Other." In this well-known essay, Boyd claims "composition instructors, by their very position within the particular institutional setting that is American higher education and by their very real institutional authority to bestow grades, continue to possess a power that inevitably must be resisted by some (perhaps even all?) students in one form or another" (591). In light of this situation, Boyd affirms his position as an institutional authority, and decides to work inside of this double bind instead of simply choosing the authoritative classroom or the resisting classroom. In doing so, he invokes a notion of instructor mastery, a concept that from the perspective of dialectical logic would appear to be at odds with his goal of a democratic classroom aimed at liberation.

However, the concept of mastery that Boyd invokes is not a one-sided, non-relational, monologue of authority to defenseless students tasked with submitting to it. When discussing a case of a resisting student, Boyd admits to his need "to convince [a resisting] student of my authority and expertise so that she might play the role of disciple to my performance of mastery, and thus allow me to continue to construct my identity as teacher around student admiration and respect" (596). Hence, this performance of mastery is inherently relational, as it requires winning the other's admiration and respect in order to function. In fact, the notion of consent, which amounts to a mutual recognition of each party involved, changes the entire dynamics of a pedagogical double bind in that it no longer seems possible to choose either democracy or authority because the identities of the parties involved, teachers and students, are inevitably tied up to each other.

Cultural studies pedagogies did not know that the authority of a master needs the consent of the resisting students, and liberal-humanist pedagogies did not know that resisting students need the consent of a master. One can say "there is no authority" in the classroom, but the instant one says this, there is an authority in the classroom, since this position has to fight against and keep out all that would not count as democracy. Likewise, one can say "there is a positive democratic authority in the classroom," but the instant one says this, this authority requires the consent of those who would be subjected to this authority. Hence, the double bind remains, but this is not a double bind made up of two static ideas that contradict each other; this is a double bind in which this contradiction has entered time and become subject to an ongoing historical drama between concrete actors.

However, in Boyd's understanding of mastery, there is a sense in which this opposition is both maintained and abolished. Because the instructor's mastery must be recognized by her students, the students become the masters who must bestow their consent on the master for her to exist as a master, and the master becomes the servant who must win the approval of students or have her authority vanquished. The instructor and student remain opposed, but since the master has passed through this moment of servitude, her mastery has, in typical Hegelian fashion, become more universal, and more self-conscious of its activity.

However, and this is the key point, this mastery remains mastery, even if the initial opposition between itself and its other has now been sublated into a higher-level of generality. In other words, this position does not escape either/or logic. Its logic mandates that mastery will always be the choice; it simply must pass through a detour of servitude. The logic of the situation is guaranteed from the start: a moment of contradiction is always "taken in" by mastery and only exists to enlarge mastery. This master, whose mastery always returns to itself, never really had anything to lose. Hence, there never was any real issue of negotiating the pedagogical bind.

IMPOSSIBLE, SO ABANDON AS IMPOSSIBLE, SO AFFIRM AS RHETORICAL

If Boyd thought that the recognition that the concept of mastery contained its dialectical opposite inside of it—that the mastery needed the consent of the servitude in order to function—launched a historical dialectic of recognition. Stanley Fish (2016) appears to argue that if a concept cannot keep its other outside of itself, then this concept should be abandoned because it does not exist.

As a simple look at titles such "Liberalism Does Not Exist," or "Free Speech Does Not Exist and It Is a Good Thing" makes clear, Fish has been adamant about asserting these kind of non-existences. Thus, when discussing free speech, Fish (2016) argues that because the speech/ action distinction does not hold up to scrutiny, "the category of speech as a form of non-action unproductive of harm has no members" (140). Likewise, he asserts that the concept of the ahistorical liberal subject, or a subject stripped of all empirical predicates such as ethnicity, gender, or family background, is a legal "fiction" (136). In both cases, he seems to argue from the impossibility of an untainted or pure concept to the conclusion that what such a concept claims to denote does not, nor could it ever, exist.

However, this is only part of the story. That is, for Fish, the "non-existence" of these concepts does not mean that they should be, or even could be, abandoned, Instead, even if a pure form of these concepts is impossible, they are necessary "fictions" that enable a particular discourse to function. Thus, he explains that "[the liberal subject] is a fiction . . . but it is a fiction required by the law's resolution to be impartial; for to be impartial is to treat all equally, whether they are or not, and therefore to set aside—not take into consideration as a basis for judgment—whatever differences may actually exist" (137). Likewise, when discussing free speech, he explains, "In the area of First Amendment law, the enabling fiction is the distinction between speech and action in the absence of which there would be no First Amendment" (137). He goes on to insist that "the fact of legal fictions, like the distinction between speech and action, is not an embarrassment to the law but a key to the way the law necessarily works" (137).

Fish's point is that, in order to work, any normative discourse must employ certain conceptual oppositions, even if an absolute distinction between them cannot be maintained. In other words, "all legal arguments unfold against a background of some authorized institutional fiction that marks out the territory and serves both to constrain and enable lines of legitimate inquiry" (137). However, it is precisely this fictional character or the conceptual impossibility of an absolute distinction between certain binaries that makes rhetorical arguments possible. For instance, because this distinction between speech and action is inherently unstable, one can argue that sleeping in the park sends an expressive message (hence, it ought to be protected as speech), that protesting with signs at a merchant's house becomes an incitement to violence (hence, it ought not to be protected), that flag burning is speech (hence, it ought to be protected), or that it is an inaudible grunt (hence, it ought not to be protected) (140–142). Thus, the instability of these terms proves the very thing that opens the space of argument.

> The fact that these judicial determinations go back and forth, and the transformation of speech into action and vice versa sometimes takes and sometimes doesn't, is evidence of the malleability of the speech/action distinction. Given a friendly court and sufficiently ingenious attorneys almost any form of speech could be characterized as action if it could be linked to the production of violence, and almost any form of action could be characterized as speech if it can be shown to have "expressive elements" (a term of art in the discussions). (140–141).

Hence, from a practical perspective, the fictional character of the speech/action distinction does not mean that one term "does not exist," but that "almost any form of action could be characterized as speech," as the meaning of these terms must continually be renegotiated through what will inevitably be different performances in different contexts.

Hence, the idea that Fish argues that free speech—or any other concept for that matter—does not exist and therefore should be abandoned, is incredibly misleading. The conceptual impossibility of a particular term is important, but it is only important insofar as this impossibility makes argument possible by making these terms endlessly available for rhetorical and performative re-inscription. Thus, if anything, Fish urges us to adopt a different orientation towards language, one that moves us from understanding these terms as strict philosophical concepts based on a dialectical logic to one that understands them as rhetorical terms inside a logic of performativity. Inside of this orientation, he does not deliver bad news about notions like the liberal subject, free speech, or neutrality, or ask us to abandon these ideas. He tells us that we cannot live without them. Without the "necessary fiction" of a neutral educational authority, it would not be possible to make an argument about the legitimacy (neutrality) of our work anymore than it would be possible to make an argument for legitimate (neutral) science or legitimate news reports. With these considerations in mind, the challenge may not be how to abandon or critique neutrality, but how to find a better way to approach the concept.

PERFORMING NEUTRALITY AS A MEANS OF RESIGNIFICATION

Like Boyd's important text, Karen Kopelson's 2003 article "Rhetoric on the Edge of Cunning; Or, The Performance of Neutrality (Re)Considered as a Composition Pedagogy for Student Resistance" also attempts to find an alternative way of responding to student resistance that avoids opposing authority and democratic relations. However, in her case, the object of affirmation is not teacher mastery, but teacher neutrality. The exigence of the affirmation lies in what she sees as the shortcomings of what she calls "pedagogies of difference."

This pedagogy, with which Kopelson confesses to sharing similar goals, has, in her opinion, become a decontextualized pedagogy that ignores the reality of today's hostile student audiences (2003, 120). This audience demands neutrality, objectivity, professional authority, and mastery from instructors, shunning those who break away from these expectations, seeing them as personalizing the course, pushing their own agenda, and failing to teach their subject matter. Ignoring this context, pedagogies of difference insist that instructors adopt and perform alternative or oppositional subject positions, despite their pragmatic ineffectiveness. The result has been damaging for minority instructors, as the demand to "make difference visible" has undermined their authority.

Citing Indira Karamcheti, Kopelson argues that instructors who signify difference are put in a difficult position, and that pedagogies of difference serve to further limit their classroom authority and their pedagogical effectiveness:

> [Instructors who signify difference] are read/cast, in other words, as teaching the personal but usually unspoken story of ourselves in the world . . . In fact, I would argue that in today's suspicious and resistant classrooms, it is often this very conscientiousness, the concerted effort with which we do "teach for diversity," that itself delimits pedagogical effects and effectiveness, especially if we are marked or read as "different" in such a way that students may ascribe political agendas to us the minute we walk into the classroom. (Kopelson 2003, 120)

To counteract this situation, Kopelson suggests that we revisit the notion of teacher neutrality and begin to develop a non-dialectical, rhetorical version of the concept.

Kopelson is aware that prima facie her appeal to neutrality goes against many of the conventional canons of progressive and feminist pedagogy: everything is political, there is no position of neutrality, and Audre Lorde's celebrated feminist credo that "you cannot dismantle the master's house with the master's tools." Indeed, Kopelson confesses sympathy with these positions and hesitates to affirm a concept that has historically been thought to occupy a position in the master's house. Like Boyd and Fish, she approaches the concept of neutrality with a performative logic; however, she goes beyond Boyd in her analysis of how the performative use of concepts can produce multiple effects and she goes beyond Fish in her belief that this performative logic does not simply allow existing discourses to function, but can create effects that re-work their underlying logic.

One of these effects of particular interest is what she calls *resignification*. In order to explicate this process, she cites Karamcheti, for whom the ability to seize an authoritative, impartial, or neutral role is not an assimilatory move, but "a co-opting" one. One way this "co-opting" proceeds is by what she calls *delegitimation*, which she defines as "the destabilization, of students' identity-based presumptions" (Kopelson 2003, 123). When marginalized instructors perform traditional forms of authority, they potentially reconfigure students' perception of authority, often revealing that marginality "is not an inborn, natural category" but something constructed and "something learned" (144).

She compares this performance to a "Brechtian performance," which results in Brecht's famous alienation effect on the audience. Such an experience of de-familiarization, according to Karamcheti (1995), "alienates the viewer from the spectacle, discomforts rather than fulfills audience expectations" (145). Through this performance, Karamcheti claims, the minority teacher can "seize control of the machinery of representation" and use this machinery to play de-legitimizing "visual and epistemological games" (143). The result is that while traditional authority is affirmed, the performance of this form of authority signifies in different and unpredictable ways. Hence, rather than thinking of concepts in terms of dialectical opposition, the door is open to think of them as *performative names*.

To this end, Kopelson also cites the work of Judith Butler, who argues that by working inside of the system, Sophocles's Antigone utilizes "a politics not of oppositional purity but of the scandalously impure" (Butler 2000, 5). In her resistance to the state, Butler claims, Antigone uses "the very language of the state against which she rebels" and "the language of entitlement" from which she is purportedly excluded, so that she may "produce a new public sphere for a woman's voice" (5, 82). The language of entitlement becomes useful once we think of this language as consisting an impure set of "performative names." Deborah Youdell (2004) discusses how these impure performative names function in Butler's work:

> Understanding these performative names as bearing equivocal meanings offers both possibilities and limitations. As Butler has argued, it means that they are open to strategic reinscription, they can take on

non-ordinary meanings and they can function in contexts where they have not belonged. This suggests that a given identity is not either wounded or privileged, inert or capable of resistance. Rather, the possibility of both injury and resistance is intrinsic to performative constitutions (485).

Hence, a given term, in and of itself, is neither privileged nor marginal, and it becomes difficult to simply be "for" or "against" a term. In our current situation, Kopelson suggests that the performative re-inscription of neutrality better accomplishes the pedagogical goals of a politics of difference. Kopelson, Butler, and Karamcheti show how the strategic performance of such a "privileged term" can resignify this term and produce differential effects.

A politics of difference, then, is indeed at work in Kopelson, but it is a politics of *internal* difference and not a politics of external difference (or dialectical difference) between two opposing self-identical concepts. The task of such a politics involves affirming a term by repeating or using it "differentially," rather than "getting outside" of the term. In short, it allows us to work inside of bodies, discourses, institutions, and identities rather than transcending, replacing, or moving beyond them. Change becomes more a matter of how things are done, that is, ethical engagements and strategic performances.

While we often associate difference with the external, visible differences of race, class, and gender, this not what deconstructive notions of difference are about. In fact, external difference is precisely what deconstruction responds to and tries to change. G. Douglas Atkins and Michael L. Johnson (1985) make just this point in their introduction to an anthology they edited entitled *Writing and Reading Differently: Deconstruction and the Teaching of Composition and Literature*. Contrasting Derrida's difference with Saussure's notion of difference, Atkins and Johnson claim that "Derrida has shown how meaning derives not so much from differences between terms as from differences within each term" (2). When describing how to interpret the effects of deconstruction on the binary logic of dialectics, they quote Barbara Johnson's introduction to Derrida's *Dissemination* where she explains that concepts "are no longer opposed, nor are they equivalent. Indeed, they are no longer equivalent to themselves. They are their own difference from itself" (3).

Said differently, concepts are now performative names. And thinking of neutrality as a performative name means thinking of it as something other than the dialectical opposite of that which is political, but as something "different from itself" and, therefore, continually performing different functions in different situations. Within the deconstructive logic, nothing dies; nothing is negated. Instead, terms are retained but in a manner that disrupts the whole system of oppositions that has tradition-ally governed them. As Derrida (1988) explains, "deconstruction does not consist in moving from one concept to another, but in reversing and displacing a conceptual order as well as the nonconceptual order with which it is articulated" (21). While it is certainly worthwhile to point out that the distinction between a neutral and a political authority does not hold, the point was never to stop here. That is, the end game of deconstruction was never to get rid of neutrality or a new concept, but to performatively re-inscribe or "graft" this term in a manner that disrupts the general economy that governs concepts.

NEUTRALITY IN THE CLASSROOM

Sometimes a performance of neutrality requires an advocacy in and of itself, which was the position that I (Chad) found myself in the fall of 2007. I taught then at a small historically Black college, and some of my colleagues favored complete Afrocentric designs in their classrooms. Because the college had so many Academic Enrichment Placement activi-ties that emphasized racial heritage and ethnic awareness, I kept the gen-eral arc of my courses the same, though I added readings from African American authors such as Langston Hughes and Zora Neale Hurston.

However, some circumstances were atypical and demanded a dif-ferent treatment than I often take in my teaching today. One instance occurred when I entered my English composition classroom on that late September morning: I saw that all of my first-years, with no exceptions that I can recall, were dressed entirely in black.

I took roll and then asked, "Did I miss that memo?" There were a few forced smiles, but it was disconcerting how serious the students were. I was accustomed to their laughing, joking, and preparing before our classes, each according to their personalities and preferences. When I did ask why everyone was in black, there was silence—perhaps because they were baffled at how I could have missed news of the large rally (supposedly student led) that was going to take place on campus that afternoon, or they thought as a professor and European-American that I could not understand.

Finally, a female student said, "We're showing solidarity with the Jena Six in Louisiana." As an English professor, I can sometimes be absorbed in earlier centuries than my own, but I knew enough to be concerned and felt a need to challenge the outrage that they (or the political forces outside my classroom) were using to shield themselves from using criti-cal evaluation to measure their assumptions.

I placed them in groups and gave them twenty minutes to consider a couple of questions I gave them. The question that got the most response was, "What could have been done differently in order to avoid the tension over the events in Jena, Louisiana?" I received answers such as, "They should have expelled the White kids who told the Black kids they couldn't sit under their tree; the police should have arrested those White kids who put nooses in the tree; if the Bush administration wants to show they are serious about fighting discrimination, they would not allow racist opinions to exist."

While all of the answers, even if they were sometimes extreme, were understandable, the students were not questioning their assumptions, which were that (1) the injustice suffered by the "Scottsboro 9" in the 1930s was a parallelism of the arrest of the six Jena youths for assault and attempted murder, (2) a group assault on one individual was an equal or reciprocal response for racial insults, and (3) this cause was worth the interruption of their schedules, which were filled with rigorous academic, personal, and religious commitments. I added another question for discussion, which was, "In what way does the Jena 6 situation embody the historical Civil Rights Movement of the 1950s and 1960s?" This, after all, was the claim of those organizing the rally. For whatever reason, the students were unwilling to confront the question.

At this point, I had a choice. I had listened for nearly thirty minutes to their arguments and justifications, and while my emotions might have been swayed a little, my logic and evaluation of the situation was unchanged. Furthermore, I was becoming convinced that the students, because of their assumptions and the pressure to conform that was coming from outside, were not going to reach positions of compromise if someone did not somehow challenge them.

I chose to submit them to a cross-examination not from my own beliefs or opinions about Jena Six, but from the very values and history they claimed to cherish. I asked how many of them were Christians; this was a Methodist-affiliated school, and many raised their hands. I asked them to remember what Jesus told people to do when someone insulted them. There was silence, perhaps because they felt themselves cornered. To make them more at ease, I smiled and added, "Did he say to beat some sense into them?" This made them laugh a little.

I also talked to them about Martin Luther King Jr. I reminded them (because so many African American teenagers have not been taught this) that many White Americans across the United States—Democrats, Republicans, and independents—supported King and became involved with the 1960s Civil Rights Movement because of his message. I asked them why, and one student said, "Because he preached nonviolence and working together?"

After this cross-examination from their own values, most would expect the students to be silent, either ashamed or resentful. However, none of this happened because by then I had built a trust between me and my class, so I quickly added another question which was less nuanced than before: "Because of the actions of the six Jena youths, is this cause worthy of its high publicity? Is this incident really reminiscent of the bygone days of the Civil Rights Era?"

At this point, something remarkable began to happen. After my mock cross-examination, I noticed that the earlier conformity of the class—serious and dressed in black—seemed to evaporate and there was an explosion of opinions in every direction. There were some students who said despite their feelings, the teachings of Jesus were too important to forsake. Another female student said, "I love Jesus, but I don't agree with turning the other cheek. I think justice is more important." Some students chose to disagree, warning her as Hamlet warns Polonius, "Use every man after his desert, and who should 'scape whipping?" Others modified their opinions by admitting the six youths were not in the same league as the Scottsboro men, but that the Jena authorities had also mishandled the situation.

Most stunning of all, others chose to debate the ideas of King, which is an amazing development because, while King is something of a revered icon for eighteen-year-old African Americans, his teachings and ministry are not often viewed as ideas to be analyzed, contemplated, or applied in everyday life. Students began to discuss if King's ideas were still relevant today, some asking if he were not an idealistic dreamer, while others expressed their bewilderment that some of their feelings did not coincide with what King taught.

Throughout most of my teaching career, I have found it hard to judge changes or improvements: often these happen at such a slow, painstaking pace that I'm given to wandering if they are really happening at all. However, this "Jena Six" discussion was one of the few instances where I could visually observe a reaction. Rather than being part of a human wall, my students were again part of a community with different opinions all converging on a central issue.

In this way, my performance of neutrality did not stifle politics, difference, or diversity, but facilitated the emergence of these things by encouraging the exchange of ideas, functioning as a mode of invention and discovery, and reconfiguring some of the existing power relations on campus.

REFERENCES

Atkins, G. Douglas, and Michael L. Johnson. 1985. "Introduction." In *Writing and Reading Differently: Deconstruction and the Teaching of Composition and Literature*, eds. G. Douglas Atkins and Michael L. Johnson. Lawrence, KS: University Press of Kansas.

Boyd, Richard. 1999. "Reading Student Resistance: The Case of the Missing Other." *JAC* 19 (4): 589–605.

Butler, Judith. 2000. *Antigone's Claim: Kinship between Life and Death*. New York: Columbia University Press.

Derrida, Jacques. 1988. "Signature, Event, Context." In *Limited Inc*, 1–21. Evanston, IL: Northwestern University Press.

Fish, Stanley. 2016. *Winning Arguments: What Works and Doesn't Work in Politics, the Bedroom, the Courtroom and the Classroom*. New York: HarperCollins.

George, Diana, and John Trimbur. 2001. "Cultural Studies and Composition." *A Guide to Composition Pedagogy*, ed. Gary Tate, Amy Rupiper, and Kurt Schick, 71–91. New York: Oxford University Press.

Graff, Gerald. 1995. "The Dilemma of Oppositional Pedagogy: A Response." In *Left Margins: Cultural Studies and Composition Pedagogy*, ed. Karen Fitts and Alan W. France, 325–329. Albany, NY: State University of New York Press.

Karamcheti, Indira. 1996. "Caliban in the Classroom." In *Teaching What You're Not: Identity Politics in Higher Education*, ed. Katherine J. Mayberry, 215–227. New York: NYU Press.

Katz, Adam. 1995. "Pedagogy, Resistance, and Critique in the Composition Classroom." In *Left Margins: Cultural Studies and Composition Pedagogy*, ed. Karen Fitts and Alan W. France, 209–218. Albany, NY: State University of New York Press.

Kopelson, Karen. 2003. "Rhetoric on the Edge of Cunning; Or, the Performance of Neutrality (Re)Considered as a Composition Pedagogy for Student Resistance." *College Composition and Communication* 55 (1): 115–146.

Ohmann, Richard. 1955. "Afterword." In *Left Margins: Cultural Studies and Composition Pedagogy*, ed. Karen Fitts and Alan W. France, 325–331. Albany, NY: State University of New York Press.

Rorty, Richard. 2000. "Universality and Truth." In *Rorty and His Critics*, ed. Robert B. Brandom, 1–30. Oxford: Blackwell.

Rosenthal, Rae. 1995. "Feminists in Action: How to Practice What We Teach." *Left Margins: Cultural Studies and Composition Pedagogy*, ed. Karen Fitts and Alan W. France, 139–155. Albany, NY: State University of New York Press.

Tremonte, Colleen M. 1995. "Gravedigging: Excavating Cultural Myths." In *Left Margins: Cultural Studies and Composition Pedagogy*, ed. Karen Fitts and Alan W. France, 53–67. Albany, NY: State University of New York Press.

Youdell, Deborah. 2004. "Wounds and Reinscriptions: Schools, Sexualities and Performative Subjects." *Discourse: Studies in the Cultural Politics of Education* 25 (4): 477–493.

16

MOVING FROM TRANSPARENT TO TRANSLUCENT PEDAGOGY

Jennifer Thomas and Allison L. Rowland

Courses that focus on gender, race, and sexual identity are politically "charged" regardless of the instructor's performance of neutrality in the classroom. Consider the syllabus, or even just the title, of our team-taught first year course: "Queer Performances On and Off the Stage." Before we even enter the classroom, this course is marked as politically and ideologically charged. While this perceived political charge appeals to some students, it elicits negative responses from other students (or their parents, as we have recently discovered). As a way to productively manage this political charge, this chapter explores the role of *teacher transparency* as a corollary concept to *teacher neutrality*. Like teacher neutrality, teacher transparency is a both fraught performance and emerging imperative in contemporary higher education.

Neutrality is an impossibility in identity politics courses such as Queer Performances. It is imperative that our classroom encourage students to move beyond naïve engagements and resistant behaviors regarding gender, race, and sexuality to more complex and justice-oriented understandings. As such, our classrooms cannot be neutral. We teach about deeply personal and political concepts, and in so doing we are firmly invested in what Bob Lingard and Amanda Keddie call "productive" (as opposed to indifferent) pedagogies (2013). We offer *translucent pedagogy* as an example of productive pedagogy that offers a way to manage resistance in the classroom. Our essay uses transparency as a point of departure for the following question: What is the best way to address student resistance to conversations centered on gender, race, and sexuality in the current political climate of the neoliberal university?

As applied to higher education, *transparency* is a tricky, Janus-faced term that requires parsing. We offer the following working definitions in an effort to understand the distinctions of, and to move beyond, transparency and toward a translucent pedagogy. On one hand, *transparency*

DOI: 10.7330/9781607329992.c016

can refer to "explicit (transparent) conversation about beneficial learning and teaching practices" between teachers and students (Winkelmes 2013, 6). This type of transparency, which we identify as *learning-centered transparency*, assists students in understanding, for example, the learning goals or grading criteria for a particular assignment. On principle, we have little objection to learning-centered transparency, a process-based teaching strategy conducive to liberal-arts values and potentially focused on social justice (on the latter, see Winkelmes et al. 2015 and Winkelmes 2015). By comparison, we identify *consumer-centered transparency* as a product-based, often compulsory movement that departs from liberal-arts values and strives to maintain the status quo. The political right has appropriated rhetorics of transparency in an attempt to promote conservative principles and foster distrust in institutions of higher education (see GOP 2016; Texas Legislature 2009). This consumer-centered transparency can be particularly sly, because it comes packaged in the pro-student rhetoric of learning-centered transparency. While our critique of consumer-centered transparency is damning, it is not the focus of this chapter. Instead, we hope to highlight the conflation of competing transparency rhetorics in higher education in the United States, offer a set of criteria in which to tell them apart, and suggest ways of adopting learning-centered transparency to the contemporary neoliberal moment.

Towards that end, this essay offers a set of criteria that assists in navigating the different learning- and consumer-centered practices of transparencies in higher education. First, we contextualize the emerging imperative of transparency, and continue to develop our distinction between learning-centered and consumer-centered approaches to transparency. Second, we develop the concept of translucent pedagogy as a strategy for managing the "charged" classroom as well as a supplement to learning-centered practices of transparency. What we call *translucent pedagogies* strategically withhold learning goals for a classroom activity or course in order to preempt potential defensive responses to classroom content around social difference and prime students for more intentional engagement with course material on difference and power (Rowland and Thomas, forthcoming). Finally, a pedagogical reflection involving our first-year program course illustrates our discussion of translucent pedagogy.

CONTEXTUALIZING TRANSPARENCY IN HIGHER EDUCATION

A diverse array of voices in higher education appeal to transparency. This demand for transparency in higher education is not new. In fact, the rhetoric of transparency has been used "in the context of institutional reform following public criticisms in the 1980s calling for more accountability of colleges and universities" (Anderson 2013, 39). At first blush, it appears that all reasonable people ought to be on the side of transparency—who would not want transparency, and by association, accountability, visibility, and honesty? However, as Marilyn Strathern noted in 2000, the "tyranny" of transparency in higher education often results in the erosion of trust, rather than an increase in trust.

In this section we introduce the distinction between trust-eroding transparency (consumer-centered) and trust building transparency (learning-centered). By offering this distinction between two types of transparencies, our intention is not to promote a false binary, or to suggest that these categories are clean-cut. Rather, we provide consumer-centered and learning-centered transparency as useful heuristics for educators who necessarily operate within the matrix of political exigencies—including teacher neutrality—that comprise contemporary higher education.

Consumer-Centered Transparency

Consumer-centered transparency has reframed education as a commodity, as something to be bought, repackaged, and sold. In the neoliberal age, as universities are increasingly managed as businesses, the principles of business management displace those of academic quality and freedom (Giroux 2014). In line with these neoliberal contractions, consumer-centered transparency tends to invest in maintaining the status quo by focusing on higher education as product-based, compulsory, and politically neutral. Joanna Williams states that "higher education is essential for employability and is therefore a prerequisite for social mobility and social justice. Such social and economic goals mean that education is far less likely nowadays to be linked to a moral or intellectual vision of truth, enlightenment, knowledge or understanding. Given the paucity of intellectual purpose, students are perhaps left with few models with which to identify other than that of the consumer" (2013, 15). Williams's critique of higher education's move toward an individualistic model and away from the public good draws a sharp comparison to the calls from proponents of consumer-centered transparency. As a consumer the student is placed in a position of power and examines institutions of higher education, courses, professors, and academic practices in terms of business.

With the rising costs of higher education rapidly outpacing the inflation rate, students and families are encouraged to run the numbers on their institutions (discount rates, graduation outcomes, student loan loads, wage potential, etc.). A leader in this consumer-oriented effort is Jay Schalin, director of policy analysis at the John William Pope Center for Higher Education Policy. His 2008 report titled "Opening Up the Classroom: Greater Transparency through Better, More Accessible Course Information" demands a more consumer-based relationship between families and higher education. Schalin states, "greater transparency and accountability are coming to higher education, one way or the other. Students, their parents, and government officials want to know whether their money is purchasing a quality education or merely financing an expensive system of meaningless paper credentials." In fact, such legislation passed the US House of Representatives with the bipartisan support and an endorsement from the National Education Association in July 2016. The "Strengthening Transparency in Higher Education Act" (HR 3178) calls for a College Dashboard and net price calculator, which would allow students and families a much simpler and easier overview of each college's cost. While we are sensitive to the cost of higher education, this brand of consumer-centered transparency pledges to be working for taxpayers and student families with a keen focus on perceived value. Consumer-based transparency moves higher education from a transformative education experience toward a myopic focus on value, job acquisition, and graduate earning potential.

Meanwhile, just beyond the student-centered focus is a very clear play for conservative political agenda-making. Consumer-centered transparency levies compulsory demands on syllabus structure, course content, and assessment outcomes against educators. Professors are bound by state legislation, institutional demands, and departmental expectations to provide transparency in multiple arenas of their career. One such example is Texas HB 2504, which was passed in June 2009. In short, all institutions of higher education in Texas are now legally required to post syllabus content, professor education and background interests, and funding sources for the department prior to student enrollment. These policies allow politicians, educational institutions, families, students, and other publics to ferret out the potential political alignments of the course, faculty member, and department prior to enrollment. These requisites are examples of how consumer-centered transparency have infiltrated the higher education, legislation, and political economies as well as highlight growing support of consumer-centered transparency. The Texas legislation is a single example of how consumer-centered transparency seeks to maintain the status quo while allowing and advocating for students to avoid that which creates discomfort.

Finally, consumer-centered transparency often promotes legislation that allows students to avoid learning experiences that are different or uncomfortable. Goaded by conservative ideologies, students may dismiss instructional efforts as "political correctness," or assume that they are being taught to avoid offending anyone. In fact, the 2016 Republican platform states, "we call on state officials to preserve our public colleges, universities, and trade schools as places of learning and the exchange of ideas, not zones of intellectual intolerance or 'safe zones,' as if college students need protection from the free exchange of ideas" (GOP 2016, 35). Additionally, the platform advocates dismantling Title IX: the Democratic Party "agenda has nothing to do with individual rights; it has everything to do with power. They are determined to reshape our schools—and our entire society—to fit the mold of an ideology alien to America's history and traditions" (GOP 2016, 35). Instead of promoting the values of the liberal arts, students may perceive our positions as biased rather than reasoned, and dismiss us as radical or liberal members of the professoriate.

Consumer-centered transparent teaching assumes that we teach in a sanitized and ideologically neutral classroom, somehow devoid of difference. And yet our students enter the classroom every day as individuals with personal stories and both visible and invisible identity markers. As Karen Kopelson argues, "many of our students view the increasing pedagogical focus on 'difference' as an intrusion of sorts, resenting and often actively rebelling against what they may experience as the 'imposition' of race, class, gender, sexuality, or (more generally) cultural issues on to their 'neutral' course of study" (2003, 117). Resistance arises when students are asked to see the world from a secondary position that requires them to confront and identify their own privileges.

At its core, consumer-centered transparency denies the student transformative educational experiences by treating higher education as a means to a job (rather than a career) by creating compulsory and surveillant demands on professors, courses, and research (Ball 2012) and by creating a space that allows students and faculty to remain ideologically unchallenged in the classroom. While not all consumer-centered transparency is wholly negative, the language is largely co-opted by conservative ideologues.

Learning-Centered Transparency

We define learning-centered transparency as explicit conversation about beneficial learning and teaching practices between teachers and students. As such, learning-centered transparency is process-based, conducive to liberal-arts values and social justice. At its best, learning-centered transparency engages students to think about *how* they are learning, rather than just focusing on the content of a course (Head and Hostetler 2015). Participation in learning-centered transparency is voluntary for instructors, offered as a beneficial tool to be employed at their discretion and judgment. Learning-centered transparency realizes the liberal-arts mission of assisting students in becoming lifelong learners by enlisting them to start thinking about their learning process from the beginning. Finally, learning-centered transparency dovetails with many social-justice goals. For example, recent research suggests that this kind of transparency provides specific benefits to groups traditionally underrepresented in higher education, because it teaches them *how* to learn (Winkelmes et al. 2015).

The most publicly visible example of the trend towards learning-centered transparency is the Transparency in Teaching and Learning in Higher Education Project, based at the University of Nevada at Las Vegas and headed by Mary-Ann Winkelmes. This project champions transparency in education as a form of making the hidden curriculum less hidden. Specifically, Winkelmes and her colleagues (2015) recommend communicating with students regarding the *task, purpose,* and *criteria* of a particular assignment. Since its inception, the project headed by Winkelmes has returned remarkable results for institutions, including increased retention and completion rates. Furthermore, students see increased short- and long-term learning benefits and an increased awareness of critical-thinking skills. There are even promising suggestions that transparent teaching practices can better serve underrepresented and marginalized university students (Winkelmes et al. 2015). The rationale behind these results is that it is precisely those students who come from families with minimal university experience that benefit the most from coaching about *how* to learn. The often-unspoken element underlying learning-centered transparent teaching is that there is more buy-in from students, or deeper engagement with the material, if they understand the *how* and *why* of their learning.

At its core, learning-centered transparency builds trust between teachers and students. P. Sven Arvidson and Therese Huston locate trust and honesty at the center of transparent teaching, which they define as "honesty and courage in the classroom . . . designed and executed to increase the openness between instructor and student" (2008, 4). The mode of learning-centered transparency favored by Arvidson and Huston is predicated on the idea that the best teachers are simply those who connect with students. They advocate for transparent practices such as sharing lecture notes with students and collaborating with students on assignment design. By contrast, the trust-eroding compulsory demands of consumer-oriented transparency offer no opportunities to build a learning community based on mutual trust.

Despite the patent benefits of learning-centered transparency for students listed here, we want to offer a few words of caution. If we are not vigilant, learning-centered transparency can too easily shade into consumer-centered transparency. Even something as simple as clear learning objectives for assessment could be warped into a disciplinary tool in the hands of even well-meaning administrators. For this reason, we are wary of any institutionally imposed requirements for transparent teaching; if the transparency is not instructor-driven, then it is not student-centered.

Evidence of the benefits of learning-centered transparency have resulted in its being championed by the Association of American Colleges and Universities and extolled in books such as *Becoming a Student-Ready College* (McNair et al. 2016). This has resulted in transparency's integration into programs across numerous universities. We support the tenets of learning-centered transparency in almost all contexts. However, there are certain situations in which learning-centered transparency may not work. Specifically, learning-centered transparent teaching practices may be less effective or even counter-effective when teaching about race, gender, and sexuality from a critical perspective. In other words, course content that asks students to identify privilege or the social construction of identity, or course content that may engender feelings of defensiveness, warrants strategic rhetorical framing designed to mitigate defensive responses.

TRANSPARENCY AND PRIVILEGE IN HIGHER EDUCATION

We take no issue with the goals of transparent teaching, especially as it forms a central platform of learner-centered paradigms. There is no question, for example, that grading criteria should be explicitly and clearly communicated to students prior to the completion of an assignment. What we do take issue with, however, is that not all course material is neatly exportable to a transparent model. Specifically, the delivery of course content that asks students to do the difficult and personal work of confronting the intersection of their social privileges and disprivileges may benefit from less transparent learning goals at the outset.

As educators we agree with Sara L. Crawley and her co-authors (2008) when they write, "I believe as effective teachers our goal is to attempt full contact with students—to capture their attention and engage them even when they themselves are reluctant to be engaged . . . I think it is disingenuous to argue that we hope for anything less than full intellectual contact with our students" (2008, 13). Asking students to interrogate their privilege can create discomfort, but it is exactly the kind of full-contact pedagogy Crawley advocates. Students are reluctant to identify their privilege and instead deny their privileges while simultaneously drawing attention to an area of their life where they may perceive a lack of privilege. Crawley goes on: "our goal as teachers is to incite students to claim their own educations—to engage them so fully in the given discipline we are teaching that they can claim it as a scholar would" (13). Instead of reifying our students' identities as stable, we should be challenging our students to understand that "identity is a persistent and provocative question, but never a certainty" (Kopelson 2002, 32). The cultural contingency of identity surely will challenge even the most socially aware undergraduate. The resistance to identifying one's own privilege is not surprising. García and Hinojosa (chapter 13, this volume) recast resistance with a metaphor more suited for movement: friction. Susanne Bohmer and Joyce Briggs (1991) note, "it has been our experience that students from privileged class and race backgrounds are frequently hostile, or at best neutral, to presentations on race, class, and gender stratification; often they respond with guilt, anger, or resistance" (1991, 154). For example, students often contest the idea that the mere act of sitting in a classroom learning and speaking about privilege is an act of privilege. The classroom is not a neutral space and acknowledging our personal privileges creates space for learning and friction.

Our analysis dovetails with Karen Kopelson's observation that when teachers are *interpreted* by students as "political," it can instantly incite resistance. Kopelson argues for a performance that cunningly appropriates "traditional academic postures such as authority, objectivity, and neutrality" (2003, 118) while still maintaining feminist and queer values. We have witnessed Kopelson's observation at work in our classrooms. As we enter the learning space students quickly and easily identify us as women. As soon as either of us begins talking about feminism or gender-related issues, the students can, and have in certain instances, dismissed our messages merely because of our gender identification. The lesson becomes demoted to little more than a professor who has an "axe to grind" rather than an experience to interrogate and investigate. In her 1993 article "Lesbian Instructor Comes Out: The Personal is Pedagogy," Janet Wright states: "One way of diffusing the potency of those labels is by redefining them, reframing them, so that they lose their negative power. Coming out in the classroom opens the dialogue on sexual orientation and on oppression on the personal level. This can be empowering for the faculty person as well as the lesbian and gay students. But it can also model an authenticity and acceptance which challenges, empowers, and honors all the classroom participants who, regardless of sexual orientation or preference, are unique and diverse individuals" (31). Likewise, some students will draw the link between our gender identity and the gender-studies course title and make assumptions about our political commitments. Although it is not identical to outing a sexual orientation, outing ourselves as feminists allows our classrooms to engage in the positive and negative historical and rhetorical narratives surrounding that word in a way that harboring that as a secret would not allow. This pedagogy leans more toward the previously identified learning-centered transparency. However, one can delay the feminist identification to later on in the semester in order to maintain the ideals of translucent pedagogy. As discussed earlier, there are some visible identities that aren't able to be delayed, such as our identities as women. We offer a discussion of the debriefing process when identities are withheld. Coupling learning-centered transparency with our idea of translucent pedagogy is key in attempts to sidestep resistance. In the current cultural climate, there are better alternatives to transparency when teaching about divisive, personal, and political issues. The justification for translucent pedagogy when discussing social justice is two-fold. First, the current trend of hypervisibility of racialized and sexualized difference in media and culture promotes the idea that difference is widely accepted in mainstream society. While increased visibility is a step in the right direction, it is also a distraction from the work that needs to continue in order to create a safe and equitable spaces. As stated earlier, and as persuasively argued across a number of chapters in this collection, classroom spaces can never be neutral. Instructors must employ nuanced practices that call power positions into question in the composition classroom and beyond. Second, the move toward transparent teaching asks educators to directly engage students in conversations of privilege and difference. The combination of these two ideas has created a perfect storm in the classroom that sounds something like, "The fight is won. Why do I need to understand anything about 'them'?" Thus, the need for translucent pedagogy.

TOWARDS A TRANSLUCENT PEDAGOGY

What is *translucent pedagogy*? By coining this phrase, we gesture to the possibilities inherent in strategically withholding learning purposes, goals, or other information from students. This withholding of learning goals for a particular classroom activity or lecture should happen only in the initial phases, and the strategic withholding should always be. disclosed in a "debriefing" discussion activity. A translucent pedagogy inherits and continues the principles and ethical commitments of learning-centered transparent pedagogy while shifting its practices slightly.

There are other instructors doing a similar form of translucent pedagogy, even if they have not identified it as such. For example, when Kopelson advocates for a performance of political neutrality in the classroom in order to shore up traditional attributions of authority, her queer pedagogy can be described as translucent. In other words, she is committed to teaching social justice learning goals, but she purposely withholds information that may impede achieving these goals. In order to further illustrate the paradigm of translucent pedagogy, we turn to one particular classroom technique.

In the following pedagogical reflection, we defend the rationale for our purposeful translucence, discuss its benefits, and provide suggestions for how this technique may be exported to other lesson plans regarding difference. This reflection outlines a low-stakes, in-class writing exercise we have successfully implemented in order to introduce first-year students to issues of identity. This exercise demonstrates translucent pedagogy by temporarily withholding learning goals from students in order to prime introspection and engagement with issues of difference.

Reflection One: "I Am . . . / I Am Not . . ." Writing Exercise

A driving goal of our university's first-year program is to help our students develop the intellectual habits of mind, the writing, speaking, and research skills, and the ethical self-reflection that comprise the core of a liberal education. Additionally, the program explains that it "will ask you to consider new perspectives on the world and your place in it and will challenge you to confront many of the hidden assumptions you bring to college with you" (St. Lawrence University 2011). While these learning goals are communicated to students in a multitude of formats (introductory emails, websites, registration packets, and ultimately course syllabi), students are often surprised by the content of the first set of readings in our course, which complicate static notions of identity, problematize the very nature of gender, and highlight how social locations impact our understanding of the world. While the readings are developmentally appropriate and accessible for a first-year audience, they routinely cause students to bristle and resist the foundational identity concepts of our course. The low-stakes writing exercise outlined below is a way to engage students in the first-year program goals as well as our course content.

Some pedagogical strategies for lower-level courses encourage reading guides, comprehension quizzes, or other preparatory materials, offering students a roadmap or way to engage with the course content. However, in order to enact translucent pedagogy with this opening set of readings, we do little in the way of introductory comments to the materials beyond showing students where the readings are located in the online classroom management system and asking students to note statements or ideas they are in complete agreement with as well as ideas that cause questions or resistances to emerge. In the following class period, students often express confusion or resistances in response to the readings. For example, a common pushback we might hear from White students would be, "Why don't we talk about Black privilege?" We ask students to grab a chair and, instead of placing the chairs in a circle, to find a private spot in the room. (We teach in a mobile-feature classroom and, as such, we have flexibility in the classroom setup.) Students are asked to put everything away except for a notebook and a writing device. Maintaining the silence of the classroom and the personal space of each student is important in this exercise as it helps the students focus internally rather than externally.

The initial instruction to the students is simple: write "I am . . ." at the top of the left-hand side of the page. Students are then instructed to fill in the entire left side of their paper with statements that complete the phrase "I am . . ." We frequently offer simple identity-marker examples such as: I am right-handed, I am a professor, I am a Minnesotan, and so on. We do not reveal political affiliations, sexual identities, or other invisible markers as personal examples in order to lessen the impact of our own personal identities on the classroom in this early phase of community building. We remind students to respond to the phrase with as little judgement or editing as possible. This is a good time to remind students that the writing exercise will remain with them in their notebook throughout the semester. It is not a graded exercise and there is not a sharing element to what they are writing. When we see students hit a block in writing, we offer another broad personal identity statement to reinvigorate the writing. Ideally, students should be able to fill the left-hand side of the page with their "I am . . ." statements in less than five minutes.

The next phase in the exercise asks students to write "I am not . . ." on the right-hand side of the page directly across from each "I am . . ." statement on the left side of the page. For example, "I am a student" could be followed by "I am not a teacher." Once again, encourage students not to think too long about the opposition statement, but to write their immediate "gut" response of what they perceive the opposite of their "I am . . ." statements to be. The final step in the exercise is for students to circle the "I am/I am not" statement that holds the dominant position for each of the identity markers they have provided. Using the previous example, a student would most likely circle "I am a teacher" as the dominant position.

Up until this point in the class period, students have not discussed the content of the course readings. We ask students to look at the notes they took while reading and to focus on the ideas they were in complete agreement with as well as the questions and/or resistances they had to the readings for the day. In their personal space we ask the students to examine how their agreements, questions, and/or resistances are reflected by their "I am/I am not" statements. We encourage the students to do a free write that asks the student to critically self-reflect on their social location and the reception of the course readings, but we do it using translucent pedagogy. Instead of directly asking students to identify why they are resistant to certain aspects of identity politics in the readings, students are indirectly making the connections as to how their own identities impact their understanding and willingness to engage with classroom materials.

In this case, translucent pedagogy engages the student privately about their own identity (in order to prime introspection and engagement) rather than publicly or directly interrogating a student's positionality (in a way that might prime resistance or defensiveness). The learning objectives for this activity include the concepts of dominant and subordinate positions, as well as the idea that your social location will impact your responses to the world (and to the course material). By translucently withholding these learning goals, we find that students are more willing to engage with critical self-reflection. While we ask for volunteers to share how their responses to the course content are reflected in their "I am/I am not" statements, this is not an imperative part of the exercise. As previously mentioned, our students are in a living/learning community and have an established set of community norms and agreements. We have found students eager to share, but we do not force the conversation either.

At the end of the class period, we encourage students to return to their "I am/I am not" statements whenever they experience passionate affirmative or negative responses to course materials or conversations. We also clearly disclose our learning goals for this exercise, and explain to students why we introduced them to these concepts of power and social location in a private, introspective way. Teaching the students that our identities are not neutral and cannot be washed away in the classroom (or any other setting) is an important learning process, but perhaps even more important is teaching students how to self-reflect on their responses to understand more fully their own positionality.

CONCLUSION: MANAGING THE CHARGE
WITH TRANSLUCENT PEDAGOGIES

In conclusion, translucent pedagogy represents one strategy for mitigating the defensiveness that may appear in a "charged" classroom. Temporarily withholding the learning goals for specific discussions and exercises allows students the space to interact with the subject matter without immediately taking a defensive or resistant position. Ultimately, translucent pedagogy reveals itself as students discover how their own social locations factor into the ways they receive and interpret challenging classroom content. We have found students in our first-year courses resistant to and uncomfortable with the idea of dismantling widely held social constructions, such as static notions of gender. Deploying translucent pedagogy in writing exercises, classroom discussions, and supplementary cultural activities during a travel component has primed our students to understand social location and power more effectively.

As we reflect on our challenging and rewarding semester of Queer Performances, we also are looking forward to the next incarnation of the course in the future with a new cohort of first year students and parents. This new class will bring in students born in the new millennium, who have always understood the world as a post-9/11 world, and who have always had access to technology and information. These students also will enter higher education during a time of intense scrutiny on the value of college, intense political stratification, and tightly held moral beliefs that extend into the politics of race, gender, religion, and sexuality. As students (and parents) transition to the world of higher education, we must be prepared to engage in difficult conversations with an audience that has had less practice in engaging in these taboo conversations. The recent arguments over the place of higher education in our society isn't a new conversation. As Joanna Williams writes, "Arguments as to whether higher education should be liberal, academic and for the public good, or for individual economic benefit and social mobility, have raged in different forms for well over one hundred years" (2016, 47). What has changed in the recent years is an increasing anxiety over the actual monetary value of higher education and a growing resistance to challenging conversations that interrogate social positions and identities. For those of us who teach in disciplines intrinsically connected to identity politics, the pedagogical challenge remains for us to continue to develop and enhance the ways we engage students in these conversations. We offer translucent pedagogy as a technique suited to this growing challenge in higher education.

REFERENCES

Anderson, Alecia D., Andrea N. Hunt, Rachel E. Powell, and Cindy Brooks Dollar. 2013. "Student Perceptions of Teaching Transparency." *Journal of Effective Teaching* 13 (2): 38–47.

Arvidson, P. Sven, and Therese A. Huston. 2008. "Transparent Teaching." *Currents in Teaching and Learning* 1 (1): 4–16.

Ball, Stephen J. 2012. "Performativity, Commodification and Commitment: An I-Spy Guide to the Neoliberal University." *British Journal of Educational Studies* 60 (1): 17–28.

Bohmer, Susanne, and Joyce L. Briggs. 1991. "Teaching Privileged Students about Gender, Race, and Class Oppression." *Teaching Sociology* 19 (2): 154–163.

Crawley, Sara L., with Heather Curry, Julie Dumois-Sands, Chelsea Tanner, and Cyrana Wyker. 2008. "Full-Contact Pedagogy: Lecturing with Questions and Student-Centered Assignments as Methods for Inciting Self-Reflexivity for Faculty and Students." *Feminist Teacher* 19 (1): 13–30.

Giroux, Henry A. 2014. *Neoliberalism's War on Higher Education*. Chicago, IL: Haymarket Books.

GOP. 2016. "Republican Platform 2016." www.gopconvention2016.com.

Head, Alison, and Kirsten Hostetler. "Mary-Ann Winkelmes: Transparency in Teaching and Learning," email interview. Project Information Literacy, Smart Talk Interview, 25 (2 September 2015). https://www.projectinfolit.org/mary-ann-winkelmes-smart-talk .html.

Kopelson, Karen 2002. "Dis/integrating the Gay/Queer Binary: 'Reconstructed Identity Politics' for a Performative Pedagogy." *College English* 65 (1): 17–35.

Kopelson, Karen 2003. "Rhetoric on the Edge of Cunning; Or, the Performance of Neutrality (Re)Considered as a Composition Pedagogy for Student Resistance." *College Composition and Communication* 55 (1): 115–146.

Lingard, Bob, and Amanda Keddie. 2013. "Redistribution, Recognition and Representation: Working against Pedagogies of Indifference." *Pedagogy, Culture and Society* 21 (3): 427–447.

McNair, Tia Brown, Susan Albertine, Michelle Asha Cooper, Nicole McDonald, and Thomas Major Jr. 2016. *Becoming a Student-Ready College: A New Culture of Leadership for Student Success*. Hoboken, NJ: John Wiley & Sons.

Rowland, Allison L., and Jennifer Thomas, forthcoming. "Slip it in the Back Door: Queering the Transparency Imperative in Higher Education." In *Queer Affective Literacy: Fostering Critical Emotional Sensibilities in the Classroom*, ed. by Justin Jimenez and Nicholas-Brie Guarriello.

Schalin, Jay. 2008. "Opening Up the Classroom: Greater Transparency through Better, More Accessible Course Information." Pope Center Series on Higher Education Policy.

St. Lawrence University. 2011. "Philosophy and Goals Statement." www.stlawu.edu. www .stlawu.edu/fyp/philosophy-and-goals-statement. Accessed October 26, 2017.

Strathern, Marilyn 2000. "The Tyranny of Transparency." *British Educational Research Journal* 26 (3): 309–321.

Texas Legislature. 2009. *House Bill No. 2504.* https://legiscan.com/TX/bill/HB2504/2009.

Williams, Joanna. 2013. *Consuming Higher Education: Why Learning Can't Be Bought.* London: Bloomsbury Press.

Williams, Joanna. 2016. *Academic Freedom in an Age of Conformity: Confronting the Fear of Knowledge.* London: Palgrave Macmillan.

Winkelmes, Mary-Ann. 2013. "Transparency in Learning and Teaching." *NEA Higher Education Advocate.* 6–9.

Winkelmes, Mary-Ann. 2015. "Equity of Access and Equity of Experience in Higher Education." *National Teaching and Learning Forum* 24 (2): 1–4.

Winkelmes, Mary-Ann., David E. Copeland, Ed Jorgensen, Alison Sloat, Anna Smedley, Peter Pizor, Katherine Johnson, and Sharon Jalene. 2015. "Benefits (Some Unexpected) of Transparent Assignment Design." *National Teaching and Learning Forum* 24 (4): 4–6.

Wright, Janet. 1993. "Lesbian Instructor Comes Out: The Personal is Pedagogy." *Feminist Teacher* 7 (2): 26–33.

SECTION IV

Conclusion

17

FULL DISCLOSURE / NOW WHAT?

Daniel P. Richards

FULL DISCLOSURE

Say what you will about teaching evaluations, but I take them very
seriously.

And, if I'm being honest, never *more* seriously than I did when reading
over the student feedback from the Fall 2016 semester. I had just finished teaching an introduction to rhetorical studies course at the third-
year level, which I had themed around presidential rhetoric. The course
was never wanting for conversation as students were processing the
lead-up to the November 8 election through classical and contemporary
rhetoricians. They were asked to write rhetorical criticism of presidential
speeches, from State of the Union addresses, to convention speeches, to
impromptu speeches given from the rubble of domestic terrorist attacks.
We covered campaign rhetoric, religious rhetoric, and invocations of
Cicero on the Senate floor. We would end class early and head over to
the local movie theatre—which was streaming the final three debates for
free to a public audience—to watch the debates leading up to election
day, even noting and analyzing the mild heckling from those in the seats
behind us using our backchannel app. I had articulated early on in the
semester that their final paper would be a rhetorical analysis not of the
presidential *victory* speech but of the *concession* speech, insisting throughout the semester that it would make for a more intriguing analysis and
have them explore an undertheorized genre.

I was right.

But as much as I would (or would not) like to share with you the
impressive twenty essays analyzing Secretary Hillary Clinton's poignant
concession speech, the feedback I was rabid to read was about how I
handled negotiating the various viewpoints held by the students. Within
the class were outspoken supporters of both major candidates as well
as more subdued or even apathetic support for third-party candidates,
ranging from Gary Johnson to deceased gorillas from the Cincinnati

DOI: 10.7330/9781607329992.c017

Zoo. There were—as you might either imagine or have experienced yourself—contentious, impassioned moments near the end of the semester to go along with the detached analytical frames I was trying to craft for all students near the beginning. I wanted to see if I met my goals of treating each student with the same degree of respect, granting each student the same platform, and not revealing my own preference for the electoral outcome. I wanted to be elusive, even playfully performative in attempts to counter student expectations and student readings of me as a person. I was curious to see if students gave positive feedback of this approach or if, considering the unique circumstances of the election, they wanted something different, something more. Did they want more disclosure, as a person, a private citizen[1] who has strong politics? Or were they content and actually pleased with some semblance of the opposite?

As I read through—and now reread through—the written comments of what our institution maddeningly calls "student opinion surveys," I was searching for any specific comments related the student perspective of my "some semblance of the opposite"—whatever that means, if it might be construed as opposed to disclosure, or vain attempts at abstracted neutrality. In response to the standardized question, "What did you like most about the class and your instructor?" I found, among others, the following comments (I have italicized some key words and phrases):

- "Appreciation of *conversation* and student contribution."
- "He was always respectful of others' viewpoints and at one point when some controversy arose, he handled it and *reeled everyone back in.*"
- "He is approachable and welcomes your thoughts and gives you insight on how to think *objectively.*"
- "The *diverse* readings and class discussions."

In response to the standardized question, "What factors about this class contributed the most to your learning? What aspects of this class helped you to learn to think critically?" I found two more:

- "Group discussion helped flush [sic] out ideas and *variety of viewpoints.*"
- "The class discussions were, by far, the most helpful. I really enjoyed *talking* and *listening* to the other students, and the articles we read in addition to our textbook readings helped me apply what we were learning to contemporary contexts."

I can safely assume in the second point to the first question, the reference to the "controversy" that "arose" was during the class on November 9 where emotions were the most evident. At one point there was one student crying, sharing fears; another attending at a distance via WebEx, whose joy was only more pronounced by the cheerful shouting of "Make America Great Again" by the young daughters of the student; and another, in class, jaded, who would share near the end of class that they were tired from having all their professors that day unload their opinions and tell the students "how to think and feel." With the class starting at 7:00 pm, this student had already attended three classes before mine that day.

Of course, it is impossible to know which student wrote that comment, and I don't recall the specific strategies associated with "reeling students back in," but it reads as though I was trying to temper any emotional outbursts and reinforce what comment number three articulates: giving students "insight on how to think objectively." I find it hard to believe that I would say anything like, "Let's calm down for a bit here," but I could imagine myself saying something along the lines of, "I understand. Why do you think President-elect Trump would choose to frame the issue this way?" I do know before class on November 9 I reached out to a mentor over Facebook and posed the following question:

ME: Do you have any advice on how to handle a political rhetoric class tonight? I feel the need to open up a space for emotional inventory and immediate reflection. Any thoughts on this?

MENTOR: You are definitely in a different situation than we are here [in Canada]—to some extent, we can step back in ways that will be hard for you. I'm going to have students write for a few minutes about how we might think about what happened purely in terms of rhetoric and the rhetorical theory we've read this semester. Then go to a discussion from there. Of course, more general discussion is going to come out there. Then I'm going to show the NY Times material about the trends in voting. We also have to pick 5 key rhetorical moments in the election for panel discussions in class. So, I hope all of it will allow us to think about it all in terms of rhetoric. But again, a different context here. I hope that helps in some way.

ME: It does. Very good advice and a strong way to allow for reflection but keep it focused on rhetoric. I needed this because I am fearful that I am not thinking straight this morning.

"Keep it focused on rhetoric"—what an odd thing for me to say. It made sense at the time, while I'm sure it is an easily dismissible statement, as if visceral emotions stemming from a response of a politician's rhetoric are not also "keeping it focused on rhetoric." And my fear of "not thinking straight [that] morning," well, that is messy as well.

Like most good rhetoricians, I stayed up right until the final election results were posted and the postmortem was covered by the surprised and weary faces of the political left. My wife and then eleven-month-old daughter were asleep. For the first time since our daughter was born, I was longing earlier that evening for her to wake up. (She was still doing so three or four times every night, and 2:00 am was the cutoff my wife and I had established: any wakeups from bedtime to 2:00 am were covered by me, anything after 2:00 am, by my wife.) Knowing the final results would be established just before 2:00, I was cherishing the idea of opening the door to pick up my crying daughter, and gently place her over my shoulder, bouncing up and down, and being able to hold her for the first time with the knowledge that a woman was president-elect, thinking of how her first memories in this country to which we immigrated would be of the presidential office occupied by a woman. Having the news on in the background, with images of a female president etched into her malleable memory. Selfishly, my work as a father would be a bit easier, being able to point to President Hillary Clinton as evidence of the endless possibilities of women in America versus having to explain, well, the opposite.

Instead, when entering my daughter's room my eyes were waterier than hers. My spirit broken. Betrayed. I had just, *unlike* most good rhetoricians, posted a Facebook status immediately responding to the evening but also the last eighteen months: At 3:02 am I posted:

> When the Klan is happy and our most vulnerable are fearful and at risk, we will all lose. I came to live here by choice but you've broken my heart and shattered my spirit tonight, America. You are no longer who you say you are.

Choosing to immigrate to the United States. Fathering a young daughter. Sleeping three hours total. This was my fear of "not thinking straight" during class. I, again, genuinely wanted to provide a space for emotional inventory and immediate reflection, as I stated to my mentor, and the final course evaluations seem to indicate that was I generally successful in doing so in what I deemed to be an appropriate manner. I think.

However, when I got home at 10:30 pm after class and was stress-eating in the kitchen, I saw that I had an email from one of the students in the class who underwent a struggle of their own during discussion—trying to put into analytical terms their emotional response, most likely because that was the expectation I set up throughout the semester. It was titled "Parting remarks" (I think referring to remarks after parting that specific class, as this student did stay enrolled and active throughout) and began with a thought on our in-class coverage of Secretary Clinton's concession speech—something they now knew they had to analyze. It began abruptly:

Saying that Clinton seemed relieved to go back to being a grandmother
is a touch sexist.

Also, sorry for rambling [during class discussion]. It was hard to articulate in a way that overcame my level of emotion and refrained from making my own political opinions evident.

Lastly, the tenure [*sic*] of the discourse was at times a trigger for me.
I believe you do try to foster a safe space, but that isn't always the case.

As someone who is naturally drawn to Bill Thelin's (2005) reflections
on "blundering" through teaching, I know very well that every semester, every class, there are areas for improvement. I was disappointed in
myself for allowing a student to not feel as though I had created a safe
space—and also disappointed in my off-the-cuff read of Secretary Clinton's speech. I responded a few minutes after reading:

Dear [student],

Thank you for pointing that out. That was an unfair interpretation of the
speech and you are correct in saying so. Don't apologize for rambling.
Your point [communicated in class] was very well thought out and an
accurate assessment in my estimation of how Trump was able to achieve
his goal. You are open to making your political views apparent if you wish.

On the last point, how can I foster a more safe space going forward as
we will be discussing the results, inevitably, again?

Dr. Richards

The student responded a half hour later:

Dr. Richards,

Thank you for the reply. I apologize that I was so agitated as to not follow
appropriate email etiquette and also for [misspelling] tenor/tenure. I'm
just not in the right head space. Your email was very kind. I'm reasonably
certain I was a mess.

I understand we want to allow for free and open discussion of opposing viewpoints, however as a moderator it isn't enough to just help explore the topic. There was a moment when a student was expressing her
friend's fears and another student began to talk over her. The exchange
became a little elevated. Imagine that the first student was expressing
her own fear, to be seemingly attacked at that point only validates that
sentiment. I think a small interjection there was required to keep anyone
from feeling threatened.

Best,
[Student name]

The "moment" referred to here I am quite sure is the same "moment"
mentioned above where another student claimed I was able to "reel
things in." This student read that transaction differently, and interpreted

my "reeling in" of things as an implicit validation of the perceived attack and a way of handling the situation that ignored the real emotion of the student. My objective reeling to one student was a lack of validation to another, my own personal success a failure to protect an emotionally vulnerable student.

The student's email also, read closely, communicates a nuanced vision of the role of the professor. First, the student adapts the metaphor of "moderator" when referring to the behavior of the professor during class discussions. This certainly is befitting of my own teaching philosophy (most of the time) and I would contend the vision most students have of what a professor ought to be. Second, there are circumstances for this student in which being a moderator "isn't enough," where exploring the topic should not be the only role taken by the professor. The student then recounts her experience as an observer of a Clinton supporter expressing the fears felt by her friend, an immigrant, whom she met at college, but being "talked over" by another student, the Trump supporter with the celebrating children. The concerned student notes that this was a time for "interjection"— one I thought I took in my head but either (a) did not do or (b) did not do in a way appropriate for the situation at hand, a situation the concerned student thought epitomized or validated the fear being expressed by the student.

My follow-up email is one I regret. Still do. Not all of it, mind you—I did think it was important to reply back and thank the student for their honest feedback, and it helped me make sense of the complexity of blunders. But the part where I disclose. Daughter in the other room, and salt on my fingers from my stress-food of choice, I type on my phone the following response about 15 minutes later:

[Student name],

Again, no apologies necessary. Full disclosure, tonight's class was the hardest I've been through, and the last 24 hours the darkest since I moved to the US, so I really value your thoughts.

I spoke with [student expressing friend's fears] afterwards. I will follow up with [her] to ensure. I take pride in being attuned emotionally to students, but I lapsed there. Thank you for pointing that out and for looking out for your fellow classmates.

Thank you, [student name], for the conversation and the initial email.[2] I'm not offended by the original format. Proper addressing in emails is the least of our concerns right now.

Dr. Richards

I regret the email because of the extent to which and nature of how I disclosed my own emotional state. And my pedagogical challenges. And my political inflections. And my teaching philosophy, although to a much lesser extent. I read this email now as an attempt to genuinely forge a personal connection with a student, perhaps as a way to assuage the situation. That is my personality—I avoid conflict. My personality is perhaps why I am sympathetic to Maxine Hairston's (1992) aversion to intentional conflict in the classroom. But I digress.

Disclosing to students—even to only one of them, and even only via email—the emotional difficulties of teaching and the "darkness" of immigration life is certainly not common practice for me, and a part of my life I did not want to make evident during that particular semester. I am sympathetic to Lad Tobin's (2010) thinking on teacher disclosure as not having a set answer but defined by the approach: "It depends." This student was provided insight into my emotional state that the others did not get. While the "why" behind this decision is more appropriate for a book of another kind, and one that should be based in psychological research, I responded to the open and honest feelings of a student with those of my own. Selfishly, perhaps I did this because I wanted sympathy and understanding for not giving an appropriate interjection. Less cynically, perhaps I did this because I was longing for an emotional connection with the students I just spent three months processing politics with and consistently putting my own emotions aside. Or perhaps I did it because it is my natural inclination outside the classroom to be vulnerable interpersonally, especially when first showed vulnerability by another. Frankly I'm not sure, but I am grateful for senior scholars in the field providing reflections on "blundering" to make me feel better about the on-the-ground contradictoriness of my own pedagogical practice.

I disclose this narrative to you, the hopefully generous reader, because I want to paint a picture of some sort that relays the complex facets of non-disclosure and disclosure in the context of teaching rhetoric and writing in a way that helps better approach the maligned and increasingly magnified concept of *teacher neutrality* from the perspective of someone who strives, often haphazardly, towards its dim light, though it leads me to an impossible location.

NOW WHAT?

I do not claim that the above perspective is correct; I'm not even entirely sure myself how and why I have come to believe what I believe about higher education and my place within it.[3] I know in my mind that I try

to make myself gray—or in the case of presidential rhetoric courses, perhaps purple—to direct student attention towards something other than
me, something bigger than the class, something beyond us. I have books
and mentors and inspirations and experiences that have shaped me but
to claim that my approach is the most effective, the most justified, or the
most accurate would be very uncomfortable. And I think that any one of
us who claims to be teaching the *right* way in whatever capacity we operate as political agents in the grand operation of American higher education is on shaky ground. For as this collection reveals, the landscape of
higher education is so kaleidoscopic, our institutions so different, our
politics so divergent, our students so diverse that working towards any
uniform model of political self-disclosure would be pretty short-sighted.

Given the exigence of the collection and the external pressure we feel
from the outside, I'm wondering if our efforts would be better invested
not in grappling with each other but in bringing our students more
directly into this wild ride. I have my own reasons for how I teach the way
I teach. So do you. And that's fine. In fact, it's more than fine—it is perhaps the most beautiful picture of academic freedom there is. But given
the lack of stasis in this treacherous notion of teacher neutrality and the
fact that students might not see the beauty in such a multicolored por-
trait, and that so much of what we do and teach and talk about and grade
is ineluctably political, might explicit conversations or prompts or projects or courses not be a remedy for it? At least in part? I'm not necessary
talking about a first-year writing course where the theme is *The University*
and the readings are populated with various theories and critiques of
American higher education (although, maybe?), but more about fore-
grounding the classes we teach with meta-institutional, meta-curricular,
and meta-performative conversations about why we are or are not choosing to be political in a certain way and what our "rights"[4] are to do so.
Would students resist as much if they knew the role of tenure, historically, in its original design and purpose? If they knew of the existence of
the AAUP and its tenets and our relative alignments with them? If they
knew the difference in social function between K–12 and higher education, and how public K–12 teachers, as spokespeople[5] of the boards for
which they work, cannot really be political in the ways university professors can? Would students resist as much if we ourselves knew more about
current theories of cognitive and moral development from psychology
research? If we were more empathetic and reflective about, for example,
how we as youthful nineteen-year-olds would have responded to a radical libertarian first-year writing teacher implicitly encouraging students
to compose essays about the social injustice of government overreach

on individual liberty after just getting out of twelve years of education where the main presence of anything political was in the border art of the classroom walls? I mean, sure they would—they're students taking a writing course. And if we're being honest, we might even find some of ourselves in the resistive students (I know I do). However you answer these questions, if you humor them at all, I sense it is becoming near-imperative that we enter into these birds-eye-view discussions about higher education and our collective places within it *with* students and guide and co-explore more educationally the language of teaching performance and politics.

So, how to do this? There are myriad ways, and the authors included in this collection provide various levels of guidance on what this work might look like. I myself, in line with how Patricia Roberts-Miller speculates in the foreword, like to think of this work potentially being done through metaphor. As Roberts-Miller writes: "If we stop talking about teacher neutrality, what are more useful models or metaphors?" The word *useful* here rings true here for me, and this is the pragmatic intellectual space in which I'd like to end this book. Scratching and clawing each other to the bone about the possibility of neutrality is not a useful endeavor because teacher neutrality never was and never will be an epistemic or ontological claim. Students know this. They know we're political creatures. The concept of teacher neutrality, even when uttered by those outside the academy, still reads as metaphorical not epistemic. It reads as an operative metaphor for being fair, considerate, self-aware, and critical of all standpoints. It reads as a way of acting, not being. And this really might be where useful metaphorical connections might be made between the embattled parties in this larger conversation about higher education.

I have written before about the "active potential" of metaphor to bring about change in student perceptions towards argument and education in the "ruins"[6] of the posthistorical university (see Richards 2017), and my arguments were supported with five decades' worth of work in rhetoric and composition pointing to the value of metaphor for ourselves and our students to bring about *conceptual* and—if you're a believer, as I am, in Lakoff and Johnson's (1980) social cognitivist approach to metaphor—*behavioral* change. My light critique of the field in that piece rested upon the fact that we don't typically bring students as directly into conversations about metaphor as we perhaps should. And this is a problem because, while metaphors can be playful and productive ways to bring students into a conversation, metaphors also develop out of material experience. So, to have your performance as a teacher inspired by the metaphor of, say, a trickster—as one who playfully stirs the pot with secret knowledge and seems to have ulterior motives but in the end is the hero who establishes a new normative order—is well and good but it might not resonate with students who just had the very real material experience of working with banks and family and the government to scratch by for another semester's tuition. Their financially centric experiences with various institutions might lead them to see you as a job trainer, and college as their ticket out of this mess, and after spending hours on the phone with a bank might not have any energy or sympathy left for trickery.

But rather than paint this picture as cynical, why not as hopeful? Why not as an opportunity to make the classroom space an opportunity to have higher-level discussions of how it has come to this? How it is that the one behind the lectern repudiates the notion of teacher neutrality at every mention of it but ten feet away in a chair there is another who expects such a thing to exist and to be acted upon consistently? What would it look like to theme our courses around the political state in which we all have a stake and a mindset and in which we collectively as institutional bodies find ourselves? What if those willing to email photos of our charming faces to have them pasted on some subversive wanted list for the professoriate are doing so because they've never really had a chance to fully explore and understand the nature of higher education and its histories? And is this our role to do these things? To bring some semblance of stasis? I think, given our expertise in rhetoric and the fact that the loudest wailings and lamentations of our "ruined" campuses can be traced back to English departments, it can be. Maybe it *should* be—I don't know.

What I *do* know is that students are primed to use metaphorical language and have strong feelings about the education they are getting, positive or negative as these feelings may be. For example, the student of focus in the vignette beginning this chapter called my positionality as a teacher "moderator." In the email exchange, the student wrote: "I understand we want to allow for free and open discussion of opposing viewpoints, however as a moderator it isn't enough to just help explore the topic." I did not explicitly state this as an operational metaphor in class; I never shed insight with the students about my own teaching philosophy, particularly the unique one for presidential rhetorics. And yet here was this student, in one mere sentence, shedding insight for me on how they see my role ("moderator"), the purpose of higher education ("free and open discussion of opposing viewpoints"), and the limitations of it all ("as a moderator it isn't enough to just help explore the topic").

We may have shared similar metaphoric structures—something loosely resembling moderation, whatever that might mean—but the details along the contours of this shared metaphor differed. It "wasn't enough" for me just to moderate. No, I needed to "interject" to ensure students did not feel "threatened" by the speech of their peers. For this student, moderation includes more than just rational guidance but about having your finger on the emotional pulse of the room. And then there are still the other students who appreciated my sense of "objectivity" and abilities in "reeling things in" when conversations got too heated, the latter of which offers a different view of the emotional exchange. Metaphorically, these discursive units can be coded under the larger category of "neutrality," not in the perfect, elusive epistemological sense but in the performed sense. There is opportunity here to make clear, transparent[7] connections with students.

In re-reading the email conversation, I was also curious about the statement in the student's initial email: "Also, sorry for rambling [during class discussion]. It was hard to articulate in a way that overcame my level of emotion and refrained from making my own political opinions evident." I was curious as to whether or not my own detached method of teaching communicated or modeled to the rest of the students that, first, emotion is something to be "overcome" and, second, that one should strive to refrain from making one's political view evident. I have no way of knowing, now, but there might have been different outcomes had I had more explicit conversations about the nature of the higher education, our specific contentious course, and our roles within this ecology.

If you are encouraged to pursue such metaphorical musings with your students, I might prompt you to consider the following. First, these conversations might vary by discipline. This book has as its envisioned readership rhetoric and composition, specifically, and the humanities, more broadly, but metaphors will be situated differently depending on the epistemic and methodological considerations of each discipline. Since many students we teach are not English majors, this could be a productive source of conflict and connection. Second, it might be important that we don't overly structure it. Metaphor is steeped in experience but is still creative and generative—a space of what Lakoff and Johnson call "imaginative rationality." Third, metaphor is a strong conceptual space for younger individuals to reside in, since it rests on a form of mental capacity that does not dwell with paradox but with comparison for the sake of highlighting. Fourth, metaphor highlights the characteristics of the thing to which we are drawing comparisons. It highlights what we see and allows for an entry point into higher-level conversations.

And last, it might be less important to work towards consensus of metaphor and more important to merely talk about it. To students: You see education as an orientation for work? You see teachers as mirrors? You see teachers as judges? All great—let's explore why. For while we might all have different backgrounds and experiences and thus experiential metaphors, it is the unacknowledged and underdiscussed set of assumptions behind these beliefs and the utter lack of stasis among them that is fueling a considerable amount of paradigmatic conflict. Can we open up and work together and briefly talk about what the heck we are even doing here? Can we shift this car into drive with everyone on board?

NOTES

1. I'm not a citizen of the United States but of its neighbor to the north. I received my permanent resident card two months before the semester began and still, at the time of writing, am a resident alien. I did find that this form of "detachment," as being able to position oneself as an "outsider," played a significant role in how students read me and my politics.

2. It should be noted that this was not the first email exchange I had with this particular student. This student attends at a distance and, about a month or so earlier, had reached out after the student's spouse overhead one of our discussions in class concerning offshore drilling in the coastal waters of Virginia. I was discussing research I had done on the Deepwater Horizon blowout and for one reason or another we found ourselves talking about the complicated conversations about energy production (so much for "reeling things in"). The student's spouse offered feedback on my thinking, and corrected one of the statements I had made about the nature and scope of the moratorium on offshore drilling along the Atlantic. I felt I had an existing relationship with this student more so than others, given that fruitful exchange.

3. In fact, as I am writing this section I keep having a nagging thought: Why do we even concern ourselves with student resistance, with what students think? I mean, who cares? The English departments on our campuses seem to have produced the most scholarship on this topic but still faces the most resistance from students. Other disciplines and departments seem to care so little about what students think about them and their topics of coverage and get far less flack. Why? I mean, isn't this the purpose of college? To get exposed to ideologies you distrust or despise and just learn to live with the fact that they might exist in places you don't like? Like, get used to it, right? And listen to what we're saying about rhetoric so you can do something about it, right?

4. Insert inexhaustible list of caveats here about the weakening political power of bodies such as the AAUP and the crumbling "pillar" of tenure and the fact that most of us don't have it and never will.

5. Professors are not necessarily extensions of the institutions in the classroom, but they can be in social media and governmental contexts. However, in public K–12 settings, they can be seen as such. The logic, as held by the Supreme Court in *Garcett v. Ceballos* (126 U.S. 1951 [2006]), is that: "When public employees make statements pursuant to their official duties, they don't have First Amendment protection. If teachers are speaking on behalf of the district, they must represent the district's

views. In the context of public education, teachers deliver the curriculum for a school district. Their speech within this curriculum is what they have been hired to do. As such, the district can control speech during the delivery of instruction" (Underwood 2013, 29). This stronger linkage between teacher and institution in K–12 settings provides insight into how courts interpret the agency of publicly paid teachers, which is framed as acting as discursive extensions of the institution. It requires the work of organizations like the AAUP to advocate for a disconnect between the teachers and the institutions, lest the logic of Wisconsin Assembly Bill 299 (see https://docs.legis.wisconsin.gov/2019/proposals/ab299) gets combined with *Garcett v. Ceballos* in some potentially corrosive K–16 amalgam policy.

6.   Borrowing from the language of Bill Readings's (1994) *The University in Ruins.*

7.   See Anderson et al. (2013).

REFERENCES

Anderson, Alecia D., Andrea N. Hunt, Rachel E. Powell, and Cindy Brooks Dollar. 2013. "Student Perceptions of Teaching Transparency." *Journal of Effective Teaching* 13 (2): 38–47.

Hairston, Maxine. 1992. "Diversity, Ideology, and Teaching Writing." *College Composition and Communication* 43 (2): 79–93.

Lakoff, George, and Mark Johnson. 1980. *Metaphors We Live By.* Chicago, IL: University of Chicago Press.

Readings, Bill. 1994. *The University in Ruins.* Cambridge, MA: Harvard University Press.

Richards, Daniel P. 2017. "Dwelling in the Ruins: Recovering Student Use of Metaphor in the Posthistorical University." *Composition Forum* 37. http://compositionforum.com/issue/37/dwelling.php.

Thelin, William H. 2005. "Understanding Problems in Critical Classrooms." *College Composition and Communication* 57 (1): 114–141.

Tobin, Lad. 2010. "Self-Disclosure as a Strategic Teaching Tool: What I Do—and Don't—Tell My Students." *College English* 73 (2): 196–206.

Underwood, Julie. 2013. "Do You Have the Right to Be an Advocate?" *Phi Delta Kappan* 95 (1): 26–31.

ABOUT THE AUTHORS

Tristan Abbott is the writing center director and an assistant professor of English at Morgan State University. His work focuses on the intersection of political and academic discourses. He has previously published scholarly pieces in *Postmodern Culture* and *Composition Studies*. He was the recipient of a 2018 Benjamin Quarles Grant, and is currently working on a project to document how theories of race are manifested within the actually existing practices of writing centers located in historically Black colleges and universities.

Kelly Blewett is an assistant professor of English at Indiana University East, where she teaches writing and pedagogy courses and directs the undergraduate writing program. Her essays, which explore writing pedagogy, editorial practices, and reading, have appeared in *College English, Journal of Teaching Writing, CEA Critic*, and *Peitho*.

Meaghan Brewer is an assistant professor at Pace University, where she teaches courses in rhetoric, composition, and literacy theory and directs the writing across the curriculum program. Her research interests include teacher education for graduate students, literacy theory, and rhetoric and women's science education in nineteenth-century America. She has published articles in *Peitho, Composition Studies, Applied Linguistics Review*, the *Journal of Adolescent and Adult Literacy*, and *Composition Forum*. She is the author of *Conceptions of Literacy: Graduate Instructors and the Teaching of First-Year Composition* (2020).

Christopher Michael Brown is a PhD candidate in rhetoric, composition, and the teaching of English (RCTE) at the University of Arizona. His research considers how writing teachers can draw on students' deeply held beliefs to encourage and facilitate critical thinking. His work has appeared in *Community Literacy Journal* and an edited collection from Clemson University Press. He has served as assistant editor of *Rhetoric Review* and is coeditor of the forthcoming 38th edition of *A Student's Guide to First-Year Writing* from Hayden-McNeil Press.

Chad Chisholm is an English professor at Southern Wesleyan University. He has received awards for teaching such as the Exemplary Teacher Award from the United Methodist Board of Higher Education. Chisholm has publications in journals such as *Mississippi Folklife; The South Carolina Review; Connecticut Review; Mallorn: The Journal of the J.R.R. Tolkien Society; The Mississippi Encyclopedia; Saint Austin Review; Mythlore: A Journal of J.R.R. Tolkien, C. S. Lewis, Charles Williams, and Mythopoeic Literature*; and *Classis: The Quarterly Journal of the Association of Classical and Christian Schools*. Chisholm's collection of essays, Requiems and Reveries, is available through Freedom's Hill Press.

Jessica Clements is an associate professor of English and the Composition Commons director at Whitworth University in Spokane, Washington. She has served as style editor for *Present Tense: A Journal of Rhetoric in Society* since 2012 and will step into the role of co-managing editor in fall 2020. Her scholarship centers on *ethos* and the role of human- and object-oriented actors in contemporary multimodal communication. She is currently collaborating on an interdisciplinary book evaluating the influence of social media networks in shaping binary-bound parenting decisions. She has published in *WLN: A Journal of Writing Center Scholarship* on "The Role of New Media Expertise in Shaping Writing Consultations" and on using game-studies ethnography to raise tutors' intersectional awareness.

Jason C. Evans is professor of developmental writing and English at Prairie State College in Chicago Heights, Illinois. His work has appeared in *BWe* and *Open Words*, and his research examines the relationships between composition, racial identity, and social class in community-college writing programs.

Heather Fester teaches creative writing and composition courses at the University of Colorado at Colorado Springs (UCCS). Before she returned to school to earn her MFA (2017) as the Allen Ginsberg Fellow at Naropa University and began teaching at UCCS, Heather directed the Center for Writing and Scholarship at the California Institute of Integral Studies (CIIS) and coordinated the first-year writing and writing-across-the-curriculum programs at Lincoln University of Missouri. Her current research interests include alternative rhetorics and composing processes, poetic theory, creative and contemplative pedagogies, Ann E. Berthoff's impact on composition studies, and the rhetoric of ideologies.

Romeo García is Assistant Professor of Writing and Rhetoric Studies at the University of Utah. His research on local histories of settler colonialism, settler archives, decolonial critique, and Mexican Americans in South Texas appear in *The Writing Center Journal, Community Literacy Journal, constellations, Rhetoric Society Quarterly,* and *College Composition and Communication.* García is co-editor (with Damián Baca) of *Rhetorics Elsewhere and Otherwise,* winner of the 2020 Conference on College Composition & Communication Outstanding Book Award (Edited Collection). Garcia's current interests include the decolonial research paradigms impact on composition and rhetorical studies; archival research; the cultural imaginary of border(ed)landers of South Texas; and, community building in and outside of academia.

Yndalecio Isaac Hinojosa is assistant professor of English at Texas A&M University, Corpus Christi. He holds a PhD in rhetoric and composition from the University of Texas at San Antonio. His work centers on Chicana feminist theory and writing-studies intersections. He is the coeditor (with Isabel Baca and Susan Wolff Murphy) of *Bordered Writers: Latinx Identities and Literacy Practices at Hispanic-Serving Institutions,* published by SUNY, and the coeditor (with Sue Hum and Kristina Gutierrez) of *Open Words: Access and English Studies,* published with WAC Clearinghouse.

Mara Holt was professor of English at Ohio University, where she taught graduate and undergraduate courses, directed dissertations, and served as director of composition three times. She published *Collaborative Learning as Democratic Practice: A History* (NCTE 2018). Recently retired, she is working with David Johnson, Erica Leigh, and Garrett Cummins on an article titled "Embodying Antiracist Pedagogy: Why Doesn't It Feel Right?" and with David Johnson on an article titled "Rethinking Relevance: Centering Racial Literacy in First Year Writing."

Erika Johnson earned her doctoral degree in rhetoric and her graduate certificate in multicultural women's and gender studies at Texas Woman's University in Denton. She is an assistant professor in literacies and composition at Utah Valley University, where she teaches two levels of basic composition. She has experience teaching British literature and digital rhetoric. Her pedagogy and research focus on the marginalization of basic writing, syllabi, visual rhetoric, digital literacies, and women's studies.

Lauren F. Lichty is an associate professor in the School of Interdisciplinary Arts and Sciences at University of Washington Bothell, teaching courses in community psychology; gender, women, and sexuality studies; and first-year writing and rhetoric. The school's research and pedagogy focus on building more just and inclusive university campuses through power-conscious participatory evaluation and action. Her current projects seek to promote healthy relationships, disrupt the gender binary and rape culture, and nurture sustainable-change work through integrating contemplative practices into higher-education curricula and activism.

Adam Pacton is a lecturer of English at Arizona State University. His research interests include writing program administration, disability studies, user experience, and MOOC design/facilitation. His work has appeared in *Composition Studies, Modern Language Studies, Pedagogy,* and *Writing on the Edge.*

Daniel P. Richards is an associate professor of English at Old Dominion University. His research interests include environmental rhetoric, risk communication, posthuman rhetorics, American pragmatism, and the politics of writing instruction, and his work has appeared in the *Journal of Business and Technical Communication, Technical Communication Quarterly, Communication Design Quarterly, Composition Forum,* and in several edited collections. He is the coeditor of *Posthuman Praxis in Technical Communication* (2018), published through Routledge's Studies in Technical Communication, Rhetoric, and Culture.

Patricia Roberts-Miller is a professor in the Department of Rhetoric and Writing, and director of the University Writing Center at the University of Texas at Austin. She is the author of *Rhetoric and Demagoguery* (2019), *Demagoguery and Democracy* (2017), *Fanatical Schemes: Proslavery Rhetoric and the Tragedy of Consensus* (2009), *Deliberate Conflict: Argument, Political Theory, and Composition Classes* (2004), and *Voices in the Wilderness: Public Discourse and the Paradox of the Puritan Rhetoric* (1999). She is also a scholar and teacher of train wrecks in public deliberation.

Karen Rosenberg directs the Writing and Communication Center at the University of Washington Bothell. Her work focuses on liberatory pedagogies, creating social change to foster healthy relationships, and intersectional feminist writing praxis. Her scholarship has appeared in *Signs: Journal of Culture in Women and Society, Violence against Women,* and the *Canadian Journal for Studies in Discourse and Writing,* among others. She is also the lead author of the Washington State Coalition against Domestic Violence's interactive public education tools *In Her Shoes* and *In Their Shoes.*

Allison L. Rowland is an assistant professor of performance and communication arts at St. Lawrence University, New York, where she also directs the Rhetoric and Communication Program. Her research interests include rhetorical theory, necropolitics, and reproductive politics, and her work has appeared in *Rhetoric Society Quarterly* and *Rhetoric and Public Affairs,* among other venues.

Robert Samuels teaches advanced writing at the University of California, Santa Barbara. He is the author of eleven books, including *The Politics of Writing Studies* (2017), and the former president of UC-AFT, a faculty union representing over five thousand non-tenure-track lecturers in the University of California system.

David P. Stubblefield is an associate professor of English at Southern Wesleyan University. He holds an MA in Philosophy and a PhD in rhetoric and composition from the University of South Carolina. He specializes in rhetorical theory, affect theory, and continental philosophy. He has published multiple articles on affect, performativity, and aesthetics.

Jennifer Thomas is associate professor of performance and communication arts at St. Lawrence University, New York. She teaches courses in theater history, theory, and acting. Working at the intersection of theory and practice, Thomas's scholarship focuses on aging and old age in British theater, higher-education pedagogy, and community-building through theater practices. She is the coauthor of *Inclusive Character Analysis: Putting Theory into Practice for the Twenty-First-Century Theatre Classroom* (2020).

John Trimbur is a professor of writing, literature, and publishing at Emerson College in Massachusetts. He has published widely in composition and writing studies. His latest book is *Grassroots Literacy and the Written Record: A Textual History of Asbestos Activism in South Africa* (Multilingual Matters 2020).

Tawny LeBouef Tullia is an assistant professor of English at Christian Brothers University, Tennessee, where she teaches rhetoric, composition, and literature. She earned her doctoral degree in rhetoric at Texas Woman's University in Denton. She studies sport and rhetoric at the intersections of race and gender. She has taught composition, gender studies, rhetoric, and American literature coursework. She practices pedagogies of invitation (Keating) and engaged pedagogy (hooks). Her pedagogy and research fall within the intersections of rhetoric, critical race theory, and identity studies.

INDEX